POLITICAL THOUGHT
IN EUROPE
1250–1450

ANTONY BLACK

*Reader in the Department of Political Science and Social Policy,
University of Dundee*

CAMBRIDGE
UNIVERSITY PRESS

Published by the Press Syndicate of the University of Cambridge
The Pitt Building, Trumpington Street, Cambridge CB2 1RP
40 West 20th Street, New York, NY 10011–4211, USA
10 Stamford Road, Oakleigh, Melbourne 3166, Australia

First published 1992
Reprinted 1993

Printed in Great Britain at the University Press, Cambridge

A catalogue record for this book is available from the British Library

Library of Congress cataloguing in publication data

Black, Antony.
Political thought in Europe, 1250–1450 / Antony Black.
p.   cm. – (Cambridge medieval textbooks)
Includes bibliographical references.
ISBN 0 521 38451–6. – ISBN 0 521 38609–8 (pbk.)
1. Political science – History. 2. Political science – Europe –
History. I. Series.
JA82.B53 1992
320'.09 – dc20   91–25110 CIP

ISBN 0 521 38451 6 hardback
ISBN 0 521 38609 8 paperback

POLITICAL THOUGHT IN EUROPE, 1250–1450

Why did European civilisation develop as it did? Why was it so different from that of Russia, the Islamic world and elsewhere? In this Cambridge Medieval Textbook Antony Black explores some of the reasons, looking at ideas of the state, law, rulership, representation of the community and the right to self-administration, and how, during a crucial period, these became embedded in people's self-awareness, and articulated and justified by theorists. Dr Black stresses the importance of the distinction between church and state, and the maintenance of an international society in the face of independent state sovereignty.

Political thought in the later Middle Ages was diverse and complex; it developed separate 'languages' out of the Bible, Cicero, Aristotle and Roman law. Theorists arrived at different conclusions about the locus of sovereignty and the best constitution: some were for monarchy, others for 'popular sovereignty'; most espoused the rule of law and regular advice from 'the wise'; some supported representative assemblies such as parliament and church councils while others opposed these. It can be argued that by *c.* 1450 the idea of the modern state was in place.

This is the first concise overview of a period never previously treated satisfactorily as a whole: Dr Black uses the analytical tools of scholars such as Pocock and Skinner to set the work of political theorists in the context of both contemporary politics and the longer-term history of political ideas. Specific thinkers examined include Aquinas, Ptolemy of Lucca, Dante, Marsiglio of Padua, Ockham, Bartolus, Nicole Oresme, Leonardo Bruni, Nicholas of Cusa and many others.

This book provides students of both medieval history and political thought with an accessible and lucid introduction to the early development of certain ideas fundamental to the organisation of the modern world. *Political Thought in Europe, 1250–1450* also contains a full bibliography to assist students wishing to pursue the subject in greater depth.

Cambridge Medieval Textbooks

This is a series of specially commissioned textbooks for teachers and students, designed to complement the monograph series 'Cambridge Studies in Medieval Life and Thought' by providing introductions to a range of topics in medieval history. The series combines both chronological and thematic approaches, and will deal equally with British and European topics. All volumes in the series will be published in hard covers and in paperback.

Already published

Germany in the High Middle Ages *c.* 1050–1200
HORST FUHRMANN
Translated by Timothy Reuter

The Hundred Years War: England and France at War *c.* 1300–1450
CHRISTOPHER ALLMAND

Standards of Living in the Later Middle Ages: Social Change in England, *c.* 1200–1520
CHRISTOPHER DYER

Magic in the Middle Ages
RICHARD KIECKHEFER

The Struggle for Power in Medieval Italy: Structures of Political Rule
GIOVANNI TABACCO
Translated by Rosalind Brown Jensen

The Papacy 1073–1198: Continuity and Innovation
I. S. ROBINSON

Medieval Wales
DAVID WALKER

England in the Reign of Edward III
SCOTT L. WAUGH

Other titles are in preparation

To Aileen

CONTENTS

—————— . ——————

PREFACE

———— · ————

This book has been written in the belief that the period from 1250 to
1450 was seminal for the values and politics of the modern world,
especially but by no means exclusively in Europe; that this has been
strangely neglected or misunderstood; but, above all, that it is fasci-
nating in its own terms. State sovereignty, separation of church and
state, representation, the popular origin of government, property
rights – these are just a few of the ideas formulated, often for the first
time in their modern form, during this period. We must get away
from the idea of the 'Middle Ages' as esoteric. Political thought then
was about as varied and fluid as later.

This book is aimed at students both of history and of political
thought. I have attempted to set the subject matter in the context
both of contemporary politics and of the history of ideas. Nothing
less would have been fair to the subjects treated. It assumes no special
prior knowledge. If I have been motivated by anything other than
the usual reasons for writing books, it has been a desire to set the
record straight and do justice to this epoch and the thinkers in it. This
has become a work of exploration in its own right because, while
other and better scholars have done justice to individual thinkers and
topics, this period has not been satisfactorily treated as a whole.
(Indeed, it has become an adventure playground for prejudice.) And
when one sets a thinker or idea in a wider context, one does not
merely add to the background but sees that thinker or idea itself in a
different way.

I have included the whole of Europe, in the face of a customary division between the 'early Renaissance' in Italy and the 'late Middle Ages' everywhere else, because in politics and ideology the links seem too manifold to permit either to be comprehended alone. The book has been planned according to topics rather than time, mainly for the sake of clarity; but chronological development is observed within topics. I have dealt with major individual thinkers in different places, but most extensively in the context that seemed most appropriate (for example, Marsiglio at pp. 56–71). Chapter 1 discusses the political community or state, and values attaching to it. (I found this the most difficult chapter to write and it may be the most difficult to read.) Chapter 2 discusses the relation between spiritual (ecclesiastical, clerical) and temporal (secular, lay) power – the vertical division of authority; and chapter 3 the relation between universal and local powers – horizontal levels of authority. Chapters 4, 5 and 6 discuss the structure of authority within political societies. (These issues were often connected: the conflict between pope Boniface VIII and king Philip IV of France, for example, involved secular and ecclesiastical jurisdiction, a universal and a local ruler, and theocratic and popular conceptions of power.)

Political communities and our perceptions of them change constantly over time; the history of the twentieth century has ensured that this era is of more than antiquarian interest: we can learn from history because it is still moving and we are still in it. This stage in European political thought may be of special importance at a time when the relationship between politics and religion is again a major issue.

Information on sources used and authors mentioned in the text, together with suggestions for further reading, are in the bibliography. This is designed to be used alongside the text. It is divided into section 1, Original texts and Studies: Selections of original texts in translation; Authors, original texts and studies, Authors: original texts and studies; section 2, Further reading; section 3, Works of reference. Section 2 is sub-divided into General; Historical Background; and the following specific topics: Aristotle; Church and state; City-states and civic government; Florence; International relations and state sovereignty; The jurists; Kingship, law and representation; Liberty and the individual; Natural Law; The political community; The Renaissance; The state. For names of individuals, I have followed what I took to be convention and when in doubt used vernacular forms.

ACKNOWLEDGEMENTS

———— · ————

I would like to thank the British Academy for a grant to cover expenses incurred in the research for this book; and the European Science Foundation (Humanities) for allowing me to participate in the project, *The Origins of the Modern State*: the sub-group on 'The Individual in Theory and Practice', chaired by Dr Janet Coleman, has been a source of immense stimulation. I would like especially to thank the reader for Cambridge University Press whose comments have saved me from more errors than I care to recall, the remaining errors being all my own. I sometimes criticise the views of my former teacher, Walter Ullmann, but I owe to him both a unique inspiration without which this would never have been written, and the lasting affection due to a great man.

ABBREVIATIONS

———— · ————

CC   *De concordantia catholica* (*Catholic Concordance*) by
                Nicholas of Cusa
CHMPT *Cambridge History of Medieval Political Thought*
CIC   *Corpus iuris canonici*
DP   *Defensor pacis* (*The Defender of the Peace*) by Marsiglio of
                Padua
LTK   *Lexikon für Theologie und Kirche*
MPI   Ewart Lewis, *Medieval Political Ideas*
ST   *Summa Theologiae* by Thomas Aquinas

INTRODUCTION

———— · ————

Europe during the high and later Middle Ages and Renaissance experienced a particular kind of diversity and a particular kind of unity. The population had grown significantly; agriculture, commerce and manufacture had expended dramatically. It was a society full of change and innovation. Linguistically people were divided up by the vernacular speech of everyday life and law, and united by the Latin of religion, philosophy, diplomacy and higher adminstration. There were points of separate evolution within a common culture: the Netherlands and Italy, England and France were more distinct in 1450 than they had been in 1250. Political societies and forms of government were in flux. Papacy and Empire stood for unity and the name of Rome; local customs, group allegiances and individual rights varied almost endlessly. Balances of power began to emerge in inter-state relations. France and England were becoming centralised national kingdoms. The Swiss and the Scots were fighting for independence. The German Empire was dissolving into a very loose confederation of feudal-princely territories and, on the other hand, commercial urban communities. While the feudal monarchies of Castile and Aragon reconquered Spain from the Muslims, in the Low Countries, northern Italy and the Rhineland merchants, artisans and day-labourers organised themselves into city-states and guilds. Free cities like Florence, Cologne and Ghent revolved from oligarchy to democracy and back. In England parliament was becoming partner to the Crown.

There was, as we shall see, no less a plurality of intellectual trades and languages. What we know as 'political thought' emerged out of theology, law, Ciceronian rhetoric and Aristotelian philosophy (see below, pp. 7–10). Not least, popular history has exaggerated the uniformity of the Catholic world and the hegemony of the church. Religious thought and practice varied from place to place and class to class; it was a notable strength of this old religion that it could both adapt itself at the intellectual level and incorporate local peasant ('pagan') forms. This, together with the wealth and power of the clergy, was why 'reform' was never off the agenda. 'The authority of the church', while nearly everyone paid lip-service to it, was already a radically contested concept. The church–state conflicts exposed a raw nerve in the Christian republic, and during the fourteenth century became entangled with issues of corruption and reform. 'Heresies' generally took the form of asserting a perceived New Testament ideology against 'corruption' in the contemporary church. By the middle of the fourteenth century the authorities had succeeded in stamping out Manichaeanism with its dualism, rejection of the flesh and more immediately of the clergy whom it replaced with its own 'perfected ones'; but in the 1410s a religious revolution with strong national and social undertones, inspired by Jan Hus, took permanent hold in Bohemia. What the two had in common was anticlericalism.

Theories of knowledge, morals, nature and humanity, society and the state varied enormously depending on whether one approached them via Roman and canon law, Christianised Platonism, Aristotle, or Cicero and the Latin poets. The period 1250 to 1350 was especially innovative in philosophy. Mental life was not merely a repetitive rediscovery of past achievements; new problems of understanding and action were perceived and new conceptions sought. With Aquinas, Scotus and Ockham, ideas about God, human beings, social life and ethics developed anew and were perceived as improvements; the word 'modern' was used to describe the new trends in thought associated with Ockham. This intensity of intellectual enquiry dated back at least two centuries, stimulated, in the political sphere, by the church–state conflict of the late eleventh century. It was facilitated by commerce, technical skills and a bourgeois–civilian society. Christianity differentiated itself from Islam: it could more easily be interpreted as permitting and even encouraging intellectual enquiry.

The spiritual proximity of Virgil, Ovid and Horace had helped to keep some groups in touch with pre-Christian sensitivities and to generate a new world of romance. Cicero and the Roman historians taught models of conduct which enabled merchants, artisans and citizens to see themselves as senate, people and republic. About 1260 the translation of Aristotle into Latin was completed with William of Moerbeke's rendering of the *Politics*; once regarded as a revolutionary moment in the history of political thought, the significance of this has to be carefully assessed. Overall, Aristotle provided a new element in intellectual life; but Plato, whose works became more fully known during the fourteenth and fifteenth centuries, remained an inspiration and an exemplar. The ultimate driving force was the tension and complementarity between the Judaeo-Christian and the Graeco-Roman. This was surely why 'Europe' developed along such different lines, intellectually and in the long run politically, from eastern Christendom and the world of Islam.

In this as in other periods political thought dealt with specific salient issues of the day; at the same time it focussed upon topics raised in traditional texts. Where these coincided we often find the greatest concentration of intellectual effort: on church and state, king and people, ruler and law. On the other hand, some aspects of contemporary experience, which we know about from other sources, evoked little theoretical discussion. The relation of lesser associations to the state was of interest only to jurists; this was no doubt because Cicero and Aristotle had little to say except to assert the complete primacy of the state. Thus while the period was corporatist in practice, there was no theory of corporatism.

Writers on politics in the later Middle Ages and early Renaissance had a distinctive view of the relation between theory and practice, ideal and reality, and of the theoretical importance of facts, historical or contemporary. Many believed that some set of institutions – whatever it might be – was intrinsically right and valid for all time. The problem of political philosophy was (1) to state clearly and authoritatively what these institutions were, with full reasons given, and then (2) to see how contemporary institutions could be made to measure up to them. The point was that social and political reality, experienced here and now or learned second-hand, did not enter very much if at all into the first stage. This was what Machiavelli complained about; whereas Luther changed the criteria for what ought to be. Our thinkers should not be unduly blamed for this: facts played as great a part in the reasoning of Marsiglio and Cusa as they did in Hobbes or Locke. Thinkers of these times are commonly described as 'otherworldly'; but this distinguishes the religious sources of their moral and political values rather than the abstract nature of those values. It would not be easy to find among them a theorist more abstract than Kant or Rawls.

To put this another way, thinkers continued to pursue the question posed by Christian Platonism: what is the perfect or best state? They did not take up the Aristotelian question: what are actual states like? Those concerned principally with, say, England or France may be said to have been answering in effect Aristotle's intermediate questions: what is the best constitution for most existing states, or for a particular state? It was increasingly common to remark that, whatever the ideal, something else was required 'things being as they are now'; the age (*seculum*) was deteriorating. But scholars seemed to lack the incentive to examine the details of their own political environment; these were of no intrinsic interest, had no real meaning. 'Political science' meant finding the best constitution and reforming existing states in the light of it, not examining the works of man as a source of greater enlightenment. Hence the project of Aristotle's *Politics* books IV to VI remained on file.

Yet this outlook was already being subverted. Most medieval as well as Renaissance authors appealed to 'experience, the teacher of all' (*experientia, rerum magistra*). Jurists relied on custom and precedent; the greatest medieval jurist made much of the distinction between *de jure* and *de facto*. Moralists were concerned with individual salvation and therefore with right conduct in every detail of everyday life. Much political thought – in Ockham, for example – was an offshoot of moral theology in the sense that it was designed to discover the right course in any imaginable circumstances; and in this context facts could be supremely important. Christian doctrine was itself based upon the facts recorded in Scripture and, when it came to the church's constitution, upon historical development.

Public records which express political sentiments, and from which one may expect to learn something about political attitudes amongst a wider public, have to be treated with caution. What one learns from official letters, charters, chronicles and so on is the kind of discourse that prevailed and what was acceptable, or calculated to influence people. Such documents were usually written by rhetoricians, lawyers or churchmen; their language was very formal, and they tended to use the criteria and express the values of their author's profession. A textbook on composition (*c.* 1276) recommends for use in communication between one *universitas* (city or community) and another a choice of phrases such as '"to unite" or "to bring together the multitude of the community" or "of the citizens under the blessing of harmony"'; '"unanimously" [or] "communally" [or] "harmoniously" [or] "peacefully to depart from civil discord"'.[1] One may conclude that the appearance of such phrases in public documents cannot be taken as evidence of public opinion. Religious-minded chroniclers and philosophers had their own messages to preach, such as peace, justice and the common good. These values may have been part of the mentality of those on whose behalf they were written or to whom they were addressed; but they may not have been.

Was the period 1100 to 1500, then, one in which communal rather than individualist values predominated? Most people belonged to several groups with overlapping functions – family, guild, village, town, domain, church, realm–giving intersecting or concentric allegiances. But, given the nature of the sources, one may say that communal discourse was the order of the day, but this does not mean that people saw themselves in collectivist as opposed to individualist terms; to begin with, poetry and sculpture, not to mention economic activity, attest the opposite.

The opinions of the uneducated common people are seldom recorded. Extreme statements about liberty and equality in times of revolt probably do not reflect everyday sentiment; on the other hand, the evidence does not suggest that people were particularly subservient. It is quite possible that the consciousness of ordinary folk has changed much less, or more slowly, than the political languages of the articulate.

Differences in political outlook and language existed between town and country, aristocracy and peasantry. There is little evidence of class differences in political ideology within towns. There was some difference in outlook and language between urban and courtly milieux, though successful city-states like Venice and Florence appropriated some courtly language. There was little difference in language (though there was in outlook) between secular and ecclesiastical courts: each employed university men and humanists to fight their corner. Jurists and humanists argued the case of their employer, using whatever arguments they thought would count. Leonardo Bruni, who boasted that Florence's republican liberty was far nobler than Milan's monarchy, passed in and out of papal employment during the conciliar controversy without the slightest intellectual embarrassment.

The most remarkable dividing-line in political thought and lan-

[1] Konrad von Mure, 'De arte prosandi', in L. Rockinger (ed.) *Briefsteller und Formelbücher des 11. bis 14. Jahrhunderts* (Aalan: Scientia Verlag, 1969), pp. 403–82 at p. 450.

guage was the geographical one between the Italian peninsula and the rest of Europe, including Spain. This was due to the early development of communes and cities, and the successful establishment of city-states, in northern and central Italy; and to the adoption of Latin, Ciceronian rhetoric as a mode of discourse from a relatively early time. This, together with a unique national awareness of the Roman-Italian past, republican and imperial, fed into the Renaissance: by the middle of the fourteenth century rhetoric was becoming humanism as a mode of speech deepened into an attitude to life. Civic ideas spread from Italy to the Low Countries, where both civic independence and popular government were advocated on the Italian model.

Similar religious and ecclesiastical issues were common to the whole of Europe but evoked very different responses and solutions in different parts of the continent. The church–state question was still discussed in general terms, but by 1300 it was in practice largely a question of the relation of the papacy to specific lands and rulers. Conciliar theory evoked much enthusiasm in central Europe but was of little concern to Englishmen and heartily disliked by Italians.

Outside Italy, regional and national differences in political thought were less marked. This was largely due to the church, the Latin language, the spread of religious ideas through pulpit and art and the cosmopolitan character, at least until *c.* 1400, of the university system, where the learned élite (*doctores*) were trained. Oresme was the only major theorist who wrote in the vernacular; Aegidius' *The Rule of Princes* (*De regimine principum*) was, untypically, translated into French soon after it was written. Theology and philosophy were the most cosmopolitan disciplines; the revival of Aristotle was a European event. Theologians and philosophers like Aquinas and Marsiglio also commuted comfortably between the intellectual worlds of Italian civic patriotism and the northern monarchies. Canon law was international. Roman civil law was much more widely studied in Italy than elsewhere, and there alone did it become a starting-point for political theory.

The northern and Hispanic monarchies could be perceived as conforming to a constitutional type with certain common features and problems, such as the relation of king to law, to nobility and parliament, hereditary versus elective succession and the right of resistance. Nevertheless many, perhaps most, major authors wrote with a particular kingdom in mind: what 'Bracton', Lupold von Bebenberg, Oresme and Fortescue said was aimed at the specific problems of their own country, and much of it would be incomprehensible if read as a general statement. Writers on the Empire such as Dante and

Cusa were particularly mindful of the misfortunes of, respectively, Italy and Germany.

Nearly all the political treatises and other documentary evidence of political thought in this period were written in Latin. This was a dead language in the sense that no-one learned or spoke it as their first language; it was, however, the language in which religious worship, diplomacy, university discourse and some day-to-day administration in the church were conducted. It is probable that, at most, only a few individuals 'thought in' Latin. The texts and documents which we have are, therefore, the product of a peculiar kind of composition. (Some later theorists wrote their works in both Latin and their native tongue.) Given the links we assume today between thought and language, this ought to create alarming problems of interpretation, which we have not begun to addesss. (Gierke raised the issue when he argued that élites using learned Latinity superimposed Roman absolutist ways of thinking upon the democratic traditions of the Germanic peoples: they translated the contemporary *commune* or *Gemeinde*, for example, as *universitas* (see below, p. 14–15) and then proceeded to treat it as the *universitas* of Roman law.)

Educated people employed several distinct 'languages' in the special sense of separate vocabularies (all written in the same tongue) with their own concepts, prose styles, methods of argument and criteria of judgement, standard texts and authorities: distinct ways of articulating and presenting to their audiences political facts and ideas. To identify these and to be aware of them precisely as 'languages' will avoid needless confusion, and is an indispensable prerequisite to understanding the political thought of the period.

Theological language (1), deriving from the Old and New Testaments of the Bible (including the Wisdom books now commonly known as the Apocrypha) in the Latin 'Vulgate' translation of St Jerome, and from church fathers such as Ambrose and Augustine, was used in most discussions about government and social relationships. It could give rise to ideas about kingship and obedience but no less to ideas about the moral responsibilities of rulers and ruled and the moral equality of human persons before God. The allegorical method was a common way of deriving contemporary political messages from Scripture, as when the church was compared to the beloved lady in the Song of Songs, and when Jesus' reply to Peter's statement that they had two swords ('It is enough') was cited to prove that Christians needed both the ecclesiastical and the secular powers.

Numerous terms stemmed from the native languages and customs of the European peoples, the Franks, Lombards, English, Saxons and so on, and formed an identifiable vocabulary in official documents and in regional, national and civic laws, old and new. Sometimes this was feudal, referring to oaths, allegiance (*fidelitas*), lordship (*dominium*). The use of *dominium* to express political authority indicates a connection with landed property; but it also had religious overtones, suggesting the derivation of all power from Christ the Lord. Sometimes this language was communal, referring to the rights and dues of all members of a given community. Here one spoke not of liberty but of liberties, not of natural law but of particular 'rights' (*iura*) and privileges; of justice and honour. This native language (2) was frequently supplemented by (3), the language of the academic jurists.[2]

This language derived, first, from the laws and jurisprudence of ancient Rome, collected and expounded in the second and third centuries AD and codified under Justinian in the *Digest*, *Codex* and so on, known collectively as 'the civil law' (*ius civile*). Its political concepts were predominantly those required by the Roman principate and Empire, but there were in the *Digest* nuggets of republican sentiment, and Roman-imperial legal thought had been deeply influenced by Stoic ethics and philosophy. Together with certain much more recent imperial legislation, and as interpreted by the standard twelfth-century 'gloss' of Accursius, all this comprised, for Italians especially, 'the laws' (*leges*) *par excellence*, or 'the common law' (*ius commune*) shared by the whole Roman world of Christendom. While it was quite separate from the local or national laws actually administered in England, Saxony and so on, it exercised a pervasive influence upon these through the schools and jurists as a model and authority, a point of reference when there was doubt or reform was needed. Leading teachers of law, especially in Bologna and the other great Italian schools, wrote 'commentaries' based on their 'lectures' which, especially from the later thirteenth century and culminating in Bartolus (1313/14–57), used the original text as a point of departure for discussion of contemporary legal and constitutional problems.

The 'canon law' of the church, effective in church courts all over Europe, comprised another set of authoritative texts, the *Decretum* of Gratian (*c.* 1140) and the ever-expanding books of *Decretals* (*Decretales*) compiled out of more recent papal and conciliar legislation. These were similarly glossed and commented upon in the universities; the Decretists and Decretalists actually anticipated the civilian Commentators in their wide-ranging discussions of contemporary political issues. Church law and jurisprudence combined vocabulary

[2] See bibliography p. 203

and norms derived from the Bible, church fathers and earlier popes and councils with those of the Roman law. While civilians on the whole adhered to the theory of imperial sovereignty and were friendly to the independence of the secular power from the church, the canonists, as their texts required, elevated the authority of the pope and favoured more extensive powers for the church. The works of civil and canon jurists are available in sixteenth-century printed editions but have not been critically edited; their method of citing authorities, and each other, sometimes makes it impossible to be sure who exactly first said certain things.

Ciceronian (4) formed a distinct political language throughout the Middle Ages and the Renaissance;[3] it derived principally from Cicero's *On Duties* (*De officiis*), which was very widely read and its Latin-Stoic account of public and private life and duties taken as a practical ethical companion to the Bible. Some of Cicero's speeches and other works, including parts of his *Republic* (*De republica*), were also current. From the middle of the fourteenth century, after Petrarch, imitation of Cicero's oratorical style was a basic component of the humanism of the literary Renaissance. Cicero was an important source for a catalogue of virtues, for the notion of *humanitas* (it is distinctively human to be humane), and for the view that a sensitive literary education made one gentle and virile. One of Cicero's fundamental points was the ultimately Platonic doctrine, unchallenged till Machiavelli, that virtue and honesty coincide with one's true self-interest (*nihil utile nisi quod honestum*).

Aristotelian political language (5) derived from the *Nicomachaean Ethics* and the *Politics*.[4] It was the richest in constitutional terms and analysis; it provided new conceptual tools for the moral evaluation of many different forms of government: kingship, oligarchy, democracy and so on. Medieval authors and academics did not, however, pursue Aristotle's approach so far as the close, empirical study of how different states were actually governed was concerned; they did not engage in his particular mix of classification, empirical study and subsequent analysis. Rather, they took over as ready-made Aristotle's classifications, arrived at mostly through his study of the different constitutions of Greek city-states, and tried to apply them to their contemporary political world. They used his ethical judgements as tools with which to justify their own preferences. Since Aristotle regarded the *polis* (city-state) as the normative political community, one might have expected his revival to reinforce civic autonomy and

---

[3] See bibliography, p. 206.   [4] See bibliography, pp. 201–2.

republicanism; but this was not what happened. Medieval scholars showed little interest in city-states as a distinct category of political community; rather, they applied the category *polis* (*civitas*) to whatever political units existed. And – partly as a consequence of this – they were much less interested in Aristotle's discussions of oligarchy and democracy in the *polis*. Indeed they often played havoc with Aristotle's original meanings, taking them, deliberately, out of context. This was partly a consequence of their refusing to see their own political world as fundamentally different from that of Greece in the fourth century BC, or (to put the same point another way) of believing in the eternity of the truths expounded by the greatest philosopher of all time. But it was also partly because they were using 'Aristotelianism' as a language and not as a doctrine (see bibliography, p. 201).

Those who used Aristotelian vocabulary have been called 'scholastics' because they came from the 'schools' or universities; but this lumps together too many different types of thinker. Although they all had a university training, they occupied a wide variety of roles in public life, as clergy, members of religious orders (notably Dominicans and Franciscans), university teachers (*doctores*), advisers to governments, pamphleteers. Some wrote for university students, some for the clergy and lay rulers, some for a wider and less expert public. Aristotelian political language gave them a new panoply of conceptual tools with which to classify, investigate (which they did not bother to do) and assess forms of government and particular states. (Bartolus, the greatest medieval jurist, said that jurists would have to learn Aristotelian if they were to advise on political and constitutional matters.)

Usually when people employ the concept of a political (or moral) language in this post-Wittgenstein sense, they have in mind primarily 'the interdependence of the propositional content of an argument and the language ... in which it is made': 'the language determines what can be said in it'.[5] But for our purposes it is equally important to distinguish languages from doctrines or ideologies. (At least one purpose of human languages in the ordinary sense is that people can express different points of view in them; they were designed for dialogue – as Homer put it, 'When two men go together, each one spots different things first'.) This enables us to avoid such false but persistent clichés as that there were intrinsic connections between

---

[5] Anthony Pagden and John Pocock, respectively, in Anthony Pagden (ed.), *The Languages of Political Theory in Early-Modern Europe* (Cambridge: Cambridge University Press, 1987), pp. 1 and 20.

divine authorisation and (absolute) monarchy, between 'feudalism' and authoritarianism (Gierke) or popular government (Ullmann), and so on. As Cusa saw, divine authority could work through the Christian *populus*; it did not take seventeenth-century philosophers to observe that the fact that a king had signed certain agreements with his subjects (such as Magna Carta) could be interpreted in different ways.

It has come to be assumed that Roman and canon law favoured princely, or papal, sovereignty. Often, probably more often than not, they did. But Brian Tierney has demonstrated how canon lawyers also developed — were perhaps the main architects of — a theory of the superior authority of assemblies and general councils. Similarly, the idea of a civic or other community (*universitas*) as a partially or wholly self-governing unit was given its fullest expression by Bartolus, the greatest medieval Roman-law jurist. The reason why non-jurists, like Ockham, adopted juristic language to such an extent was not that they found there a doctrine with which they agreed but that it was the obvious mode and vocabulary in which to discuss rights and so forth.

Still greater confusion has been generated by the assumption that the use of Aristotle in political philosophy led to the formulation of specific new political doctrines; for example, by Walter Ullmann's view[6] that Aristotle's notion of 'man' as 'a political animal' implied, and was understood to imply, that all citizens should have a say in government ('populism'). An examination of medieval authors who used Aristotle soon reveals that his arguments were used to support papal authority, the supremacy of church over state, imperial overlordship, monarchical sovereignty, as well as government in accordance with the laws and rule by the few or the many. Michael Wilks concluded, perhaps understandably, that this was 'an age of confusion'.[7] But the confusion is entirely our own. These people did not take their political convictions from Aristotle; rather they used him, usually, to bolster what they already believed in. If we employ the concept of a political language, the texts of this period become much easier to understand and to explain. This point is further borne out by

---

[6] Walter Ullmann, *Principles of Government and Politics in the Middle Ages*, 4th edn (London: Methuen, 1978; 1st edn 1961); *A History of Political Thought: The Middle Ages*, 3rd edn (Harmondsworth: Penguin, 1975; 1st edn 1965); *The Individual and Society in the Middle Ages* (London: Methuen, 1967).

[7] Michael Wilks, *The Problem of Sovereignty in the Later Middle Ages: The Papal Monarchy with Augustinus Triumphus and the Publicists* (Cambridge: Cambridge University Press, 1963), p. ix.

the way in which the same writers often used different political languages even in the same work, in the course of arguing a case.

It remains true, none the less, that certain cases could be stated more easily in one language than in another. Although civic republicans frequently employed theological and juristic language, Ciceronian was probably the mode that suited them best; while Aristotle made it possible to distinguish more clearly between oligarchy and democracy.

The political thought of this period has been investigated from many different viewpoints. Otto von Gierke opened up the field in his *Das deutsche Genossenschaftsrecht*, volume III (1881), by setting out to prove that Roman absolutist 'lordship' (*Herrschaft*) had gradually ousted Germanic democratic 'fellowship' (*Genossenschaft*). Maitland and others showed how the origins of England's unique constitutionalism lay in her medieval law and parliament. Gierke himself was a Lutheran in religion, a cross between Proudhon and Hegel in political theory and later a conservative nationalist in politics. Corporatists and Guild Socialists looked back nostalgically to a time before the modern state and modern capitalism, and have like Gierke tended to exaggerate its corporatist and communal aspects. Lagarde was a corporatist in the Catholic tradition. In truth there was no abrupt break between medieval 'collectivism' and Renaissance 'individualism'; there was plenty of individual awareness in the Middle Ages, and communal loyalties did not disappear overnight, even amongst humanists; in some aspects, they have lasted till this century. Modern Roman Catholics have been tempted to regard the Middle Ages as normative, while Protestants have found their antecedents in Marsiglio, Wyclif and the Hussites. Many Catholics, again, still look to Thomas Aquinas as an authority in moral and social philosophy. His theory of natural law is regarded by others too as a classic of its kind. The most recent tendency has been to see this period as the time of germination for the theory and practice of the modern state.

Walter Ullmann (himself a traditionalist Catholic) classified all medieval thinkers and movements as either 'descending' and theocratic or 'ascending' and democratic ('populist'), but with the latter prevailing as the Renaissance came on. I hope it will become clear why this view is simplistic. It is amazing that the Middle Ages is still subject to the kind of generalisations that would be laughed at by specialists in other fields. Finally, Quentin Skinner has interpreted the early Renaissance as a story of civic liberty.[8] Here too there is the

---

[8] Quentin Skinner, *The Foundations of Modern Political Thought*, vol. 1: *The Renaissance* (Cambridge: Cambridge University Press, 1978).

danger of a favoured theme playing too great a role in interpretation. Skinner himself has reminded us that these times, like all others, have to be read in their own terms. (They can only be read at all by recognising in them something human, not alien to ourselves.) European political thought from 1250 to 1450 was not essentially feudal, hierocratic or authoritarian, nor was it essentially comradely or civic. It is a copse containing many different species.

I

THE POLITICAL COMMUNITY

How did people understand their political communities? We will look first at *universitas* (literally, all-togetherness); then at body – including the 'organic analogy' between society and the human body; and then at *civitas* (the ancient Roman term for civic community or state) – including both Cicero's and Aristotle's political languages. Second, what were the salient political values? We will look at purposes ascribed to political communities and the concept of 'the common good'; at liberty and the relation of individual to community or state; and at the state in relation to justice and the law.

There existed an enormous diversity of expressions for units of government: a random list would include *regnum, civitas, universitas* or *communitas regni* or *civitatis, dominium, corpus, provincia, ducatus, commune.* Among these diverse expressions, *universitas, communitas, corpus* and *civitas* were generic terms which could be used of any state, and the first three of other groups (cities, monasteries, villages, guilds and so on) as well; *civitas* could also refer either to a city or a city-state. These terms referred, moreover (with the occasional exception of *civitas*) to the political group, *without* implying any specific distribution of power within it (compare 'nation' today), as *regnum* and *commune* usually did. *Universitas*, originally a Roman term for a sub-political corporate body or 'lesser association', had by the high Middle Ages become a *general* term and one very commonly found in political and legal documents of many different provenances. For example, when the English barons expressed their opposition to aspects of royal government under Henry III they called themselves and their supporters *universitas regni*, implying that they summed up the community of the kingdom *as a whole* (as the Latin word *universi* would imply). The Scots used *communitas regni* in the same sense when they defied Edward I; while in England and elsewhere from the thirteenth century *communitas regni* referred to 'that group of the politically significant – king, prelates, barons – which represented the people as a whole'; and as parliaments or Estates developed it came to include the politically active Commons or Third Estate – wealthier burghers and gentry – as well.[1] The mutual defence treaty among the three cantons which later developed into the Swiss Confederation (1291) styled the participants as: 'The men of the valley of Uri and the *universitas* of the valley of Schwyz and the *communitas* of the men of the lower valley of Nidwald.' The term *populus* referred to the whole society with its existing political structure (and not to 'the people' in a modern sense).

Society was, again, commonly called a body (*corpus*). By the thirteenth century *corpus* did not necessarily imply any deliberate comparison of human society to the human body, any more than 'body' does in this context today. The organic analogy was, however, a favourite rhetorical, literary and philosophical device. It signified the relationship between members (*membra*: limbs) as that of parts having separate functions within a single unit, and at the same time suggested that a society was a structure with a common interest, and perhaps a common motive, purpose and will. It did not, however, *necessarily* imply any particular mode of organisation for society or structure of authority within it. It is true that the commonest political use of the organic analogy was to draw attention to the different functions of different parts, and then to insist that the king or ruler, as head, must be obeyed. But it could equally well be used to point out the duties of rulers to other parts and the need for fraternal harmony. The message of the organic analogy was, none the less, most often conservative, whether against a tyrant or a rebellion.

The organic analogy derived emotional and intellectual force both from classical antiquity and from Christian theology. Two of the commonest descriptions of the church were 'association [corporation] of believers' (*universitas fidelium*) and 'the body of Christ', and the latter had by far the deeper theological, liturgical and devotional roots. The church was often called 'the mystical body of Christ', meaning his invisible but ultimately *real* body. A separate kingdom or other political community was no less habitually called a *corpus*.

[1] Jean Dunbabin in *CHMPT*, pp. 482, 512.

This was intended in part to describe and explain the unity in diversity held to be characteristic of all human societies and states: many members in one body. In a political context, it could be used to explain and justify the relationship between clergy and laity and especially, on the part of pro-clerical writers, some subordination of the latter to the former. It could, again, be used in such a way as to remind us that what we call 'church' and 'state' were in many contexts viewed as separate branches of a single whole. John of Salisbury compared the clergy to the soul, the king (*princeps*) to the head, the council (*senatus*) to the heart, officials and soldiers to the hands, agricultural workers to the feet and so on.

Another frequent, indeed practically universal, meaning was that society was naturally divided into ranks; this was so deeply built in as hardly to need explicit statement. Medieval language abounded in words for rank: *status, honor, ordo, gradus, dignitas* and so on. (Since such social boundaries were not entirely hereditary and could be crossed with greater or less ease in different places and circumstances, 'rank' seems here preferable to 'caste' or 'class'.) The organic metaphor stated that it was indeed right that different persons should perform different tasks; it tended to sanctify the division of labour in its existing form; people should be content with their 'station in life'. The opposing vices were pride, greed, ambition and strife, which could include what we would call competition. One point of the organic analogy was to say that the good of each was identical with the good of the whole; therefore it was in everybody's interest, and just, that each should subordinate what they saw as their good to what others saw as the good of the whole. This justified social inequalities, including hereditary ones, and separate privileges for separate professions. This is indeed part of what is meant by 'medieval corporatism'. From a political viewpoint, this ethic culminated in the development of separate 'estates' (*status, Stände*) representing clergy, nobility and commoners or towns (in Sweden later also peasants).

Yet an at least relative openness in organic language can be traced even to its two main sources. The whole argument of Plato's Republic (although known only indirectly until the fifteenth century) centred around the analogy between different parts of the soul and different socio-psychological types constituting the three separate ranks among citizens. Justice consisted in recognising these differences and coordinating them in a harmonious whole; this justified radical inequalities between the abilities and status of different individuals. Some see a connection between Plato's ranks and the medieval division of societies into those who pray, fight and work (*oratores*, *bellatores*, *laboratores*: roughly, again, clergy, nobility, commons). St Paul, on the other hand, in passages much more directly determining medieval religious perceptions (Rom. 12:4–8; 1 Cor. 12:12–14, 18–21; Eph. 4:12, 16; Col. 2:19), insisted both on the legitimacy of a division of labour (between those who teach, heal and so on) and at the same time on the equal incorporation of all into Christ's body and the infusion of the Spirit through all. If the functional differences implied by the organic analogy had been pressed, this might have ruled out social mobility. But in fact the idea that one could legitimately improve one's inherited status was present in many parts of European society. It was justified by certain aspects of Christian teaching which, together with educational institutions and, later, humanism, supported the principle that office and responsibility should go with merit. Religious vocation was a statement of free choice enabling a person to enter a rank (*ordo*). This was echoed not only in lay religious communities, which flourished in the later Middle Ages especially in large towns, but to some extent in the crafts and also in the humanists' notion of their own vocation as orators and authors. *Ordo* was not, therefore, the antithesis of liberty.

But the idea of an organic division of labour was, in pre-modern times, the antithesis of the idea of equality. Only a few revolutionary movements, mostly inspired by an imminent Second Coming of Christ, advocated the abolition of ranks, dispossession of the wealthy or communism. The perspective of articulate society and of most people was that equality, or communism, had been the norm before the Fall or, as the Stoic jurists had it, in the pre-civil state of nature. It was entirely legitimate – more so than in modern society – for certain people with a special religious vocation to live under these conditions; indeed to do so was a mark of high sanctity. And there would certainly be no property, and therefore no economic inequalities, in the eventual Kingdom of God; ranks there would be, but based on wholly different criteria to those of existing society. But in ordinary affairs, apart from these exceptions, the ideal of equality should be used as a moderating influence, inclining us towards gentleness (*mansuetudo*) and humanity (*humanitas*), but not as a blueprint for a radically new kind of society. It is typical, if startling, when Nicholas of Cusa (a great organicist himself) proclaimed the natural liberty and equality of all mortals only to conclude that they had willingly invested the princes of the Empire to act on their behalf (*CC*.III.4). The general view was that divisions between ranks, while not rigid, were indispensable.

Another message of the organic metaphor was social harmony:

society and polity are by nature intrinsically harmonious; strife, rebellion and tyranny are manifestations of sin, pride and greed. All members of society should avoid quarrels and live in friendship with one another. This need was acutely felt in the rapidly developing and relatively unstable cities and city-states, especially in northern and central Italy, where friendship, love (*amor, caritas*) and brotherhood were frequently stated as the proper pattern and motive for civic relations, and as the appropriate moral cure for turbulent unrest among the poor – or new men, including immigrants; for arbitrary acts by the upper classes (the powerful, magnates, *potentes*); for the institution of tyranny or despotism and for political violence and factionalism generally. (In some cities, the guilds were called the *membra* of the city.) Love and friendship were held up as political virtues in feudal monarchies too, but *fraternitas* with its implication of social equality less so.

The use of all such terms, from *universitas* to *caritas*, did not mean that political communities were affective, tied together by strong emotional bonds, nor (as some have believed) that a peculiarly 'Germanic' sense of social and political comradeship (*Genossenschaft*) existed in parts of Europe, nor again, as many (especially sociologists trying to explain the rise of modernity) still believe, that people generally identified themselves with social groups so as to diminish the sense of individuality. It did mean that most ideologists thought society *ought* to be affective and comradely, though not (as we shall see) holistic; although *universitas, communitas, populus, commune* and *corpus* could equally be used as colourless descriptions (like our 'society', not like our 'community').

These terms did not as a rule refer to 'the people' or 'the community' in the egalitarian and democratic senses such words convey now; they referred to the political community in whatever form this was currently perceived to exist. A king was usually conceived as part of this community, indeed essential for the welfare and even unity of the whole. *Universitas* and so on had a collectivist meaning only in the sense that they commonly referred to rights and obligations belonging to all members as such. Of themselves, these terms did not imply a collegiate form of government. On the other hand, jurists developed clear distinctions in the case of *lesser* bodies (villages, towns, cathedral chapters) between acts performed arbitrarily by a few individuals and those performed on behalf of the group with certain formalities; and again between acts which *could* be performed by individual members and those which required 'common consent' in the literal sense of deliberation in a general assembly. The latter included disposition of corporate property, election of rulers and, in the case of towns, law-making. And it is the case that much of this political language was *open* to being interpreted in a sense favourable to wider political consultation and consent. This had great future significance.

Civitas, although it could also mean city or city-state, was the closest there was to a standard medieval and Renaissance term for 'state'. Its usage signified, in the first instance, continuity with the language of the Roman past. Cicero, furthermore, gave the Middle Ages and the Renaissance the concept of the state (*civitas*) as a central factor in human affairs, the natural fruit of human rationality, discourse and mutual benevolence, the bringer of peace and protector of property, the agent of justice and focus of love and duty (*patria*) (Cicero, *On Duties* 1.16 – followed by Alcuin and others – 11.12, 17, 21; *Republic* 1.25). From Cicero and other Roman sources burgeoned the idea of the *respublica* or public domain as a distinct category in human affairs, in which were located those good things which affect all together (see *On Duties* 11.21).

As well as this rather positive idea of the state, Cicero also gave the Middle Ages and Renaissance a strategic link between the state and liberty in the sense of protection of person and property against violence and the lawless will of tyrant, savage, brigand or again (this was especially perceived in Italy) of magnates, the powerful ones. And he gave a language, a framework of educationally accredited rhetorical and literary concepts within which the desire for security, liberty, property and rights might be expressed. This comes out clearly in the delightfully pedestrian language of John of Viterbo, writing specifically about cities in one of the earliest statements of political theory from Italy (*c.* 1250):

A city is called the liberty of citizens or the immunity of inhabitants ... for that reason walls were built to provide help for the inhabitants ... 'City' means 'you dwell safe from violence' ('Civitas', id est 'Ci(tra) vi(m) (hab)itas'). For residence is without violence, because the ruler of the city will protect the lowlier men lest they suffer injury from the more powerful ... Again, since the home (*domus*) is for each person a most secure refuge and shelter, no-one should be taken therefrom against their will; nor is it reasonable that anyone in a town should be forced by violent fear and the like (*Digest* [2.4.18 and 2.4.21]).

Viterbo went on to paraphrase Cicero: 'Cities were invented ... so that each might hold onto his own, and no-one should be anxious for the safety of his goods' (ch. 3, pp. 218–19; cf. *On Duties* II, xxi, 73). This, one of the earliest examples of characteristically European discourse on the state, was a simple, insistent plea for the rule of law; and, if we look at the economic context in which it appeared, the strategic connection between liberty and commerce is not far below the surface. Thanks to Cicero, the Middle Ages already possessed the doctrine that the *civitas* (or *societas/communitas/multitudo civilis*) was the society natural to human beings on account of their reason and speech, along with the family (*domestica multitudo*). The emphasis may be summed up in the native term *immunitas* – legal immunity, containing glimmerings of what we now call negative liberty. The state is precisely (in Nozick's neo-liberal phrase) a protection association.

The concept of the state as a product of human nature and social skill was reinforced after *c.* 1260 by ideas taken from Aristotle's *Politics*, especially 1.1–2. Given the Ciceronian legacy, these were nothing like as 'revolutionary' as Ullmann and others have suggested (see bibliography, p. 201). People learned from both Cicero and Aristotle that, whatever the elevated status accorded to the clergy in sacred tradition, the *civitas* has a central role in human life. Equally important and new for the Middle Ages was Aristotle's conception of political science (*scientia politica*) as a distinct area of human understanding, indeed an 'architectonic' one, with its own store of knowledge and equipment of concepts and methods. It was of vital importance for the development of philosophy and *mentalité* in Europe (and beyond) that Aristotelian philosophy won the minds not just of a few outstanding intellectuals but of orthodox theologians, and so could become established in the university faculties of arts and theology. What a contrast with what happened in Islam where, after a brilliant renaissance, Platonic and Aristotelian philosophy were effectively marginalised by the orthodox religious teachers! There was to be no borrowing from non-Islamic sources on matters of principle or law.

Chiefly responsible for this move were the philosopher-theologians Albert the Great and his pupil Thomas Aquinas (*c.* 1225–74). They insisted that, since Christianity is the final truth, it can benefit from an investigation of whatever else is, or appears to be, true. This dovetailed with the syllogistic and dialectical method already prevalent in the schools: truth is known by comparing opposites and distilling what is right from each; the intellectual process is one of learning as well as of defending established positions.

The inspiration of Thomas Aquinas came from the preaching mission of the Dominican order, which in his case extended to a passionate determination to demonstrate both the reasonableness of

Christianity and the divine destiny of the human intellect – the harmony of faith and knowledge; he defended all this against a more 'fundamentalist' interpretation of Christianity (represented by Augustinian theology) and against those who followed the Muslim Averroes (Ibn Rushd) in teaching a radical disjuncture between the truths of theology and those of philosophy. What Aristotle had to say concerned natural science, the structure of the human mind and the created universe, about which theology was justly silent since its concern was the relationship between God and the human person or species.

The impact of all this on political thought was indirect. It meant that the character of the state and of human social and political relationships could be understood in a naturalistic way, through analysis of human nature, needs and desires. And such things could be known systematically because all nature – God's work – made coherent sense. What Aquinas and others took from Aristotle was not so much new doctrines as a whole new approach. If we compare writings on the papacy and the Empire before and after the absorption of Aristotle into political discourse we will observe a profound change not in doctrine but in the way it is expressed. To call this an 'Aristotelian/Thomist revolution' would not be helpful. Dante, Marsiglio and others did not follow Aristotle's prescriptions about the best polity. But Marsiglio was able to write the first modern systematic treatise of political philosophy in the belief that he was discovering the true essence of polity and authority. Political science had become part of the human being's creative exploration of the world.

Discussion of politics, both practical and philosophical, in Aristotelian language rapidly became a distinct political genre. Its most academic form was the commentary on the *Politics*; this flourished especially at Paris and, later, Cracow. Among the most famous were Thomas Aquinas' commentary on books I–III, completed by Peter of Auvergne, and those by Walter Burley (*c.* 1275–1344/5), by the famous natural-science philosopher John Buridan (1295/1300–after 1358), and – in a programmatic vein for a wider readership – by his still more famous pupil, the polymath and adviser to Charles V of France, Nicole Oresme (d. 1382).[2] On the other hand, philosophers who became intellectually involved in the great political issues of the

---

[2] Aristotle's *Politics* was translated into Latin by William de Moerbeke, *c.* 1260, into French by Nicole Oresme, 1371–4, and again into (humanist) Latin by Leonardo Bruni, 1438: R. R. Bolgar, *The Classical Heritage and Its Beneficiaries* (Cambridge: Cambridge University Press, 1958), pp. 508–11.

day – the constitutional conflicts in Italian city-states and northern kingdoms, and the church–state controversies in France and Germany– developed Aristotle's basic concepts of state, citizens, the good life, political prudence, mixed government, democracy and so on in many original ways with a direct bearing on contemporary events. In so doing, they were seldom 'Aristotelians' in a doctrinal sense: rather, they saw Aristotle as a storehouse of ideas out of which to construct their own models, a new language in which to express their own beliefs, which were themselves eventually shaped in the process.

Aquinas taught at Paris (1252–9), spent most of the 1260s with the papal court in Italy and then returned to Paris (1269–72). He was familiar with Louis IX of France, and so acquainted with the world of power as well as of spirituality and the intellect. His probable pupils included, among the best-known political philosophers of the next generation, Ptolemy of Lucca, Remigio de' Girolami and Aegidius Romanus (who in turn probably taught James of Viterbo); while John of Paris was a Dominican follower of Thomas, and Dante studied with the Dominicans at Florence. Aquinas' view of the state is set out in his theological compendium (*Summa theologiae* (*ST*)), of which the first part was written at Viterbo in 1266–8 and the second part at Paris in 1269–72 (especially in 1a/11ae, questions 90–105), in his commentary on Aristotle's *Nicomachaean Ethics*, written at Paris in 1271 (especially 1.1) and his unfinished commentary on Aristotle's *Politics*, probably written at Paris in 1269–72 (especially 1.1). It also appears in chapter 1 of the treatise *On Kingship* (*De regno*). (This, with the possible exception of chapter 1, was probably not Aquinas' work; it differs from his other writings in style, approach and, on important points, doctrine. It was, nevertheless, clearly influenced by Aquinas and was perhaps written by a pupil.)

Aquinas' discussion of the *civitas* and politics generally made available a whole new political language. He rehearsed with little development what Aristotle said about the origin and *raison d'être* of the state in human needs and the aspiration for the good life. But, while Aquinas' *civitas* translated Aristotle's *polis* ('city-state'), it is clear that he, like many after him, used it as we use 'state', as a wide, generic term to embrace also kingdoms and other politically autonomous units (see also below, pp. 108–9). Following Aristotle's argument in *Politics* 1.1–3, Aquinas argued that, since man is endowed by nature not with the physical attributes necessary to gain a livelihood but with reason and hands, one man cannot provide himself with all he needs. The division of labour is necessary; besides, different individuals possess different mental and manual skills. Lastly, the ability to 'use language, through which one person can express to another his whole mind' makes humans 'more communicative than any other gregarious animal', and proves conclusively that the human person is naturally constituted to live in society (*Commentary on (Nichomachaean) Ethics*, 1.1; cf. *On Kingship*, 1). This may seem obvious to us, it had been said before, and in bare outline was already familiar to people from Cicero. But Aquinas made two special points: first, society has a moral and intellectual function; human beings need each other's society not simply to maintain and propagate life, but to fulfil themselves as persons. Man's reason, which distinguishes him from other animals and constitutes his humanity, can only be developed 'in common'. This interdependence of mind and society is again suggested by the juxtaposition, 'man (*homo*) has a natural inclination to know the truth about God and to live in society' (*ST* 1a/11ae.94.2 *responsio*). Through this collective use of their rational faculties, human beings provide themselves not only with life but with 'a perfect sufficiency of life', thanks to the many branches of industry (*multa artificia*) – the technological argument for a larger community – and to the reinforcement of morality by the coercive power of the law (*Commentary on Ethics*, 1.1). Moral virtue is exercised and moral excellence developed in a social context. As *On Kingship* also put it:

It seems that the purpose of many persons being associated together is to live according to virtue ... which each person living separately cannot achieve; but a good life is one according to virtue; therefore the virtuous life is the purpose of human association (ch. 14).

There is a flavour of Benedictine and Dominican monasticism in all this.

Second, you simply cannot have a society without a government. This too was familiar from Cicero; but again Aquinas argued the point more systematically (*ST* 1.96.4 *resp.*; *Commentary on Ethics* 1.1; cf. *On Kingship* 1). Aquinas dovetailed this with Augustinian tradition by making a distinction (based on Aristotle, *Politics* 1.7.1255b and v11.3.1325a) between two senses of authority (*dominium*): slavery (or serfdom: *servitudo*) and the 'economic or civil subjection' of free persons 'for their own utility and good'. While servitude exists only because of the Fall of Man, civil subjection 'could have existed before sin' (*ST* 1.96.4 *resp.* and 92.1 *ad* 2; *Commentary on Sentences* 44.4.4 *ad* 1, *ad* 5). This meant that the state was part of God's original plan; indeed the distinction between state and society became unimportant.

From now on people could speak of 'political' or 'civil society', meaning society plus laws plus government.

Finally, the author of *On Kingship* invoked the Greco-Roman civic tradition which associated the highest grades of personal virtue with statesmanship. 'The good of society', which it is the king's task to secure, 'is greater and more divine than the good of the individual'. The government of the political multitude by one man is like the divine government of the universe. The just king will be rewarded with 'the greatest of earthly goods', namely 'a reputation for virtue'; and he 'will obtain an eminent place' in heaven (chs. 7, 9, 12).

THE COMMON GOOD

In general, documents and treatises suggest that rulers, subjects and theorists regarded political communities as having purposes. Some such purposes were at once moral and utilitarian; peace, unity and the common good were advantages which it was assumed to be one's duty to strive for. Others were distinctively moral: defence of the defenceless and provision for the needy were based on religious teaching; the good or sufficient life was emphasised after the recovery of Aristotle. Such purposes were stated in order to emphasise the duties of rulers and subjects, to proclaim the virtues of a ruler, or to provide a means of distinguishing between tyranny and good government. They stemmed partly from the church's view of government as installed by God for specific purposes, regarding which rulers could be held to account (*rationem reddere*). It rendered European notions of government, in Weber's terms, distinctively 'rational': government was a means to achieve definable goals and its validity could be assessed in the light of its achievement.

These goals themselves were stated in such general terms that few would dispute them: for example, peace and unity. In the Italian city-states, such values reflected the need to avert the bitter contests between political factions. In the northern monarchies, they justified increased royal control over the nobility and over property conflicts. In both cases, it was being suggested that government has a role above party and particular interest, that the state ensures a social order which will allow citizens of all kinds, including the clergy, to pursue their own callings. It was the task of king or council to ensure the smooth operation of the body politic. There is an overall unity coexisting with the diversity of subjects and members. Justice was frequently invoked, either in the sense of upholding existing rights, or in the sense of conferring justice where none had been before, for example on the poor or on turbulent regions. Procedural justice, a fair trial and so on, loomed large in medieval aspirations and complaints. The notion that individuals and groups should be permitted, or given, their just deserts was encouraged by clerical demands on behalf of the rights and properties of the church. With this went a general conviction that rulers may only act within the law (see below, pp. 152–5).

'The common good' (*bunom publicum, utilitas publica*) was the phrase most frequently used in official documents and philosophical treatises when referring to the goal or morality of government; it recurs regularly in all political writings. According to 'Aquinas', *On Kingship*, the very existence of a 'common good of many' makes government, in addition to society, necessary and natural (ch. 1). Rhetoricians urged devotion to *bonum commune* as a matter of virtue and honour, of 'true nobility' as opposed to mere nobility of birth. Of itself the phrase was of course vague enough, at times perhaps deliberately so, and open to a wide variety of interpretations. To say that some action was 'for the common good', or that a ruler should aim at the common good, was often tantamount to saying that this was just. No explicit distinction was made here – or perhaps intended – between material and moral welfare (Aristotle taught that they were interdependent).

'The common good' could refer to the need to maintain the fabric of society, a basis for good relations among people. It could refer to things like sound money; but often procedural justice and fair, 'equal' treatment of all before the law was what was meant. A judge or ruler must put aside private interests, he must not favour family, friends, the powerful or rich; to do so would be to pursue 'private' interests. The rhetoric behind this derived from Cicero. Another way of saying all this was to distinguish between the spheres of *civitas* and household. On the other hand, pursuit of the common good promotes 'friendship' among inhabitants – another goal of polity – because, as 'Aquinas' pointed out following Aristotle, friendship is based on community of interests; the people will 'love' a king who pursues the common interests, while tyranny (the pursuit of one's own interests and those of one's circle) will fall because 'what is opposed to the wishes of many (*votis multorum*) cannot last long' (*On Kingship*, 10). The common good could, again, be tantamount to 'peace'. Remigio de' Girolami (writing on Florence, 1304) preferred a common good (peace with neighbouring states) to an individual good (restitution of citizens' property seized by the enemy in time of war), on the ground that 'the good of the whole is greater than the good of the part' (*The Good of Peace (De bono pacis)*, p. 128).

A concept of the common good played a central role in Aquinas' social morality, though he was irritatingly spare with concrete examples. For him too, it meant the good of all members of a society, as opposed to one or a few – the principle of altruism extended within the bounds of a given state. Thus it is unjust 'when a ruler imposes burdensome laws on his subjects, which are aimed not at the common utility but rather at his own greed and glory' or again 'when burdens [sc., probably, taxes], even though directed at the common good, are unjustly distributed through society' (*ST* ia/iiae.96.4, *resp.*). Aquinas distinguished between just and unjust laws, between law in its proper sense and what merely claims to be law, on the basis of whether or not it 'refers to the common happiness' (*felicitatem communem*). Laws imposed for private gain or the glory of the ruler rather than for 'common utility' are unjust 'by reason of their purpose'; while precepts which refer to 'particular business' lack the character of law (*rationem legis*) not through their injustice but through their particularity (*ST* ia/iiae.96.4 *resp.* and 90.2 *resp.*).

Despite the sharp distinction between public and private, common good could refer either to the sum of individual goods or to what we would call truly collective goods such as defence of the realm; the two were not always clearly distinguishable since things like keeping the peace and a fair trial affected all. The tendency to call the sum of individual goods a 'common good' could go with a paternalist view: individual goods are the same for all *and* they are known best not by the individuals themselves but by those in authority. This was justified on the grounds of superior wisdom (see below, pp. 156–61). In any case, common good was part of the very idea of community (*universitas*, *corpus* and so on), and imposed corresponding moral constraints upon the ruler.

The introduction of Aristotle's notion of the *polis* was important because the classical Greeks did not recognise the distinction between state and society implicit in much Christian and medieval thought, from which limits upon what a ruler might do could be deduced. The range of economic and social policies pursued by medieval and Renaissance city-states fitted readily into an Aristotelian conception of government as aimed at the good, sufficient life and necessary to achieve this. Aquinas' view that political authority is required not only to repress wrongdoers but to coordinate the division of labour and other complexities in any human society reflected this. Most medieval states practised rudimentary economic policies. City-states, in particular, aimed to promote their economic security and increase their wealth by raising customs and restricting certain trades to their

own members under the craft-guild system, or alternatively conducting a more open policy favourable to a merchant oligarchy. They
concerned themselves with prices and employment, provided public
facilities such as market-places, water supply, sanitation and engaged
in sick and poor relief. These were not topics on which political
theorists had much to say, although they may have been implicit in
some discussions of the common good. It was commonly said that
rulers have a special duty to care for those in need, notably in biblical
categories (the poor, orphans, widows); city governments sometimes
provided facilities for charitable fraternities and hospitals. Ptolemy of
Lucca alluded to this function specifically:

It is opportune for kings and any state (*dominium*) to provide for the poor out
of the common treasury of republic or king. So it is that, in particular
provinces, city-states and boroughs, hospitals have been established ... by
the kings or citizens in order to relieve the need of the poor. This is found not
only among believers but among unbelievers. (II, ch. 15, pp. 299–301)

The redistribution of property, which could have been deduced
from Plato or Christianity, was barely spoken of except by fringe
groups; it had been fiercely condemned by Cicero. Justice in this sense
was partly channelled into the historical categories of the Fall and the
Second Coming of Christ: true justice had existed before the one and
would be restored after the other. After the revival of Aristotle, some
writers spoke of happiness (*felicitas*) as what the ruler should aim for,
and this, like *prosperitas* and common good, probably had a fairly
vague material as well as moral meaning. Buridan said that 'felicity'
rather than peace must be the state's aim, because things do not move
simply to be at rest (referring here to the theory of motion: v, q.3,
p. 252). Marsiglio mentioned the financial responsibility of the *civitas*
for the construction and repair of roads and bridges and for other
similar needs 'which it would be inconvenient and would take long
to enumerate' (*DP* 1.5.9). On a different – and, it must be said,
distinctively medieval-Christian, note – Aquinas suggested that Jews,
instead of being permitted to live by 'usury', might rather be 'com-
pelled to work to make their own living, as they do in parts of Italy'
(*On the Government of the Jews (De regimine Iudaeorum)*: d'Entrèves,
Selected Political Writings, p. 86).

Finally, the state had moral responsibilities. It was always supposed
to act as the executive arm of the church's teaching on morals and
religion; medieval rulers patronised the church and education. In
Aristotelian language, the state exists for the good life which includes
material sufficiency and moral virtue; moral regulation and education

are a normal concern of the *polis* and its rulers (see 'Aquinas', *On Kingship*, 15). As Aquinas put it, it is a property of law to 'induce those subject to it to their own proper excellence (*virtus*)'; 'the proper effect of law is to make those to whom it is given good' (*ST* 1a/11ae.91.1 *conclusio*). While 'a certain aptitude towards virtue is inherent in man by nature', nevertheless 'it is necessary that the actual perfection of virtue should come to a person through "a certain discipline"'. The state's role is to repress those 'prone to vices' by 'force and fear' both so that 'others can lead a quiet life', and also so that 'they themselves may thus eventually be led through habituation (*assuetudinem*) to do voluntarily what they previously did out of fear, and thus become virtuous' (*ST* 1a/11ae.95.1 *resp.*; *Commentary on Ethics*, 1.1).

<h2 style="text-align:center">LIBERTY</h2>

Liberty was a basic political value for many people throughout the Middle Ages and still more during the Renaissance.[3] It derived from the Frankish–Germanic ideal of the free man, from Cicero (e.g. *Republic* 1.31), and from St Paul's notion of spiritual liberty as the prize secured by Christ for the redeemed. It was summed up in Sallust's often-quoted remark: the good man loses his liberty only with his life.

Of course many kinds of subordination, including serfdom, were widespread. These were explained as one of the results of the Fall of Man. It was generally assumed, as passages in the *Digest* suggested, that liberty was a natural right in the sense that this was how God and nature had originally made us. The question was how far and for whom non-servile status could be vindicated in society and in law. It is interesting that, while the practice of communism (which like universal liberty was supposed to have been a feature of man's state of innocence) was advocated only by a few fringe groups and by short-lived mass movements like the Taborites, freedom of person made steady progress both as a principle and in many places as a practice.

There was a widespread striving to secure for oneself, one's family and descendants the social status of freedom. Freedom was widely understood as immunity from seigneurial justice. This could be acquired through membership of an immune community, such as a town; according to a German proverb, 'city air makes you free after a

[3] See bibliography, pp. 204–5.

year and a day'. Craft guilds too saw their right to corporate organisation, which gave their members economic security through an exclusive right to ply a given trade in a given area, as a form of liberty. The paradox was that this claim inevitably shut others out. The Roman and canon jurists were generally opposed to such compulsory guild membership (*Zunftzwang*) and asserted the right of individuals both to enter and to leave such associations as they chose, and to ply their trade outside them if necessary. This lawyers' doctrine of the prior rights of individuals in relation to corporations anticipated Enlightenment ideas about occupational and commercial freedom.

Basic attributes of freedom were the right to move where one pleased, choose one's marriage partner and profession, possess, buy, sell and inherit moveable property and real estate, enter into contracts and have recourse to the common law of the land. A peace treaty between the Teutonic Knights and the Prussians, drawn up by papal legates, called these faculties 'personal freedom in all its aspects' (*omnimodam libertatem personalem*).[4] The right of individuals to acquire property, including land, was hardly questioned. With land ownership, highly prized in itself, usually went specific obligations and rights; it was seldom absolute ownership. John of Paris defended the right of individuals to own property on the ground that the external goods of laymen 'are acquired by each person through art and labour ...'; but the ruler appointed by the community may decide property disputes and what each should contribute to common needs (ch. 7). Ockham, writing in the middle of the fourteenth century, regarded private ownership since the Fall as a right from God and nature ('the power of appropriating temporal goods to a person, persons or college has been given by God to the human race'); he noted that the right to own property for oneself presupposed the right to vindicate such possession in a court of law.[5]

While freedom was an attribute of individuals, it by no means led to legal or social individualism in a modern sense, for freedom and rights were very often assigned to individuals in groups. It was, for example, by belonging to a town or similar unit that you acquired 'liberties', these having been granted to the town and its citizens. In other senses, freedom had expressly political and collective, though not collectivist, meanings. Political communities had, by and large, the right to govern themselves and this was a kind of liberty which

[4] The Peace of Christburg (1249) in R. Philippi (ed.), *Preussisches Urkundenbuch*, vol. I (Berlin, 1882), part I, pp. 159–61.

[5] Cited by G. de Lagarde, *La Naissance de l'esprit laïque au déclin du moyen âge*, vol. VI: *L'Ockhamisme: la morale et le droit* (Paris: Editions Béatrice, 1946), pp. 177–82.

could be vindicated, by law or if necessary by force, against those seeking to suppress it.

In Italy there were further developments of the concept of freedom, especially in the political senses of communal independence and internal constitutional freedom from despotism or oligarchy – republican self-government. It was asserted, by those championing the political rights of the original full citizenry or of freely function-ing civic councils, that such open, elective, participatory 'popular' government (*a popolo*) was part of freedom itself. Liberty was a central political value in the Italian communes from the twelfth to the sixteenth centuries, and the preservation of republican liberty emerges as a chief concern from a large body of political writing in Italy, from the early rhetoricians down to the humanists. At Florence and elsewhere, liberty was a slogan and in public documents was identified both with popular government and with territorial independence: '*liberta, popolo e Guelfo*'. 'Liberty and the people', used as a slogan by urban revolutionaries, already echoed back to ancient times. On occasion, notably at Florence, freedom of speech in the sense of the right of citizens to speak their mind at public meetings was enunciated ('From liberty, a divine gift surpassing wealth, each acquires the power to say what he wishes').[6]

These ideas were fairly widespread and especially popular in the towns; they were also voiced by theorists. 'Bracton' stated a jurist's concept of liberty when he defined it as 'the natural power of every man to do what he pleases, unless forbidden by law or force' (vol. II, p. 28; cf. *Institutes* 1.3). Aquinas defined liberty in general as existing for one's own and not someone else's purpose. He made liberty the criterion of a legitimate regime: 'those who are made sons of God through the Holy Spirit' may submit only to a government 'which is directed towards the welfare (*utilitas*) of the subjects and does not take away their liberty' (*Commentary on Sentences*, d.44.2.2, *ad* 1). He later said in effect that a free man can only rationally consent to being governed by another so long as such government is 'for the good of those themselves who are ruled, or for the common good'. Indeed since life in society requires unified rule and some are by nature better able to care for the common good, humans cannot refuse to be so governed (*ST* 1.92.4 *resp.*; cf. *On Kingship* 1). This rather modern – indeed Kantian – view of legitimacy was a political expression, as Aquinas makes clear, of Pauline thought.

[6] Florentine decree (1329), cited by R. Witt, 'The Rebirth of the Concept of Republican Liberty in Italy', in A. Molho and J. Tedeschi (eds.), *Renaissance Studies in Honour of Hans Baron* (De Kalb, Ill., 1971), p. 191 (cf. Cicero, *Republic* 1.31).

Ockham regarded liberty, along with property, as a natural God-given right of the human person in post-Fall society; he identified liberty as a central element in Christian teaching about the human person. In the public domain, it means the right of every political community to make its own laws and institute its own rulers. While charters and civic documents spoke of 'rights, liberties and privileges' belonging to, claimed by or conceded to particular communities, Ockham spoke of 'the rights and liberties conceded to us by God and nature'.[7] The idea of liberty was developed much further by the humanists (see below, pp. 131–5).

Medieval Europe has been characterised by many as a pre-modern society in which individuals were steeped and absorbed in communal life, for ill or good. A variant of this view, stemming from Gierke and repeated by Lagarde, is that it featured an unusual proliferation of tightly bound corporate groups, such as villages, churches, towns and guilds, and that these claimed so much of the personality of their members that people identified their interests and derived their morals from relatively small, autonomous collective bodies. According to such views, individualism developed out of the Renaissance and the Reformation. Research suggests that such preconceptions have to be modified. Amongst literati, the higher clergy and some of the aristocracy, the 'discovery of the individual' has been taken back to the twelfth century. Individuals were engaged in commerce and entrepreneurial or commercial capitalism was beginning to emerge. Persons of humble origin could choose a religious vocation and so effectively shape their own destiny as individuals. Marriage was – at least in some places – more freely entered into, and personal relationships more developed, amongst ordinary as well as superior folk, than used to be thought. There was individual landholding, accumulation and labour for profit.

If we look at political theory the picture is the same. It is true, and striking, that this period had no word for the individual: the individual is referred to, according to context, as *homo, fidelis, civis, subiectus, singularis persona* or just *quisque* ('anyone'). But whenever the subject was broached we find not just an awareness that individuals have importance in their own right but an (at least) intermediate view of the individual–community and individual–state relation, which accords the individual (when he, and it is seldom she, is mentioned) some independent meaning and right. This is especially clear in contractual formulae and in all that concerns the lord–vassal relation-

[7] Lagarde, *Naissance*, vol. VI, pp. 177–85.

ship, though especially at the higher social levels. This is exactly what we should expect if Christianity were taken at all seriously; and it is difficult not to conclude that the difference in religion marked off pre-modern European views of the individual from those prevalent in other societies. On the other hand, women and the unfree had very limited rights.

The statements of Aquinas on this subject are illuminating. They show on some occasions acceptance of a rather holist view, while on others he strongly asserts the separate existence of individuals and their partial autonomy from the state. It would appear that on the former occasions he is being Aristotelian – in accordance with the view that human beings as such cannot exist outside the political community – and on the latter Christian. On the one hand he said:

All who are contained in any community are related to it as parts to a whole. The part is what it is in virtue of the whole; therefore every good of the part is to be directed towards the good of the whole [*ST* Ia/IIae 58.3 *resp.*, and 58.7 *ad* 2] ... Since every man is part of a state, it is impossible for any man to be good unless he is well adapted to the common good [*ST* Ia/IIae 92.1 *ad* 3, and 96.4 *resp.*].

This clearly suggested that clashes between individual and collective interests were to be resolved in favour of the latter. Girolami remarked in a similar vein that the citizen is like a stone built into the city wall (*The Good of Peace*, p. 129). Moreover, in this Thomist view, the social and political nature of man meant that being good or virtuous is equivalent to being orientated towards the common good. The state stands to the individual as whole to part, so that 'the good of the part is referrable to the good of the whole'. Personal morality is interdependent with communal morality, justice itself being, on one definition, 'that which directs man to the common good' – and all the virtues are related to justice (*ST* Ia/IIae 92.1 *ad* 3; IIa/IIae 58.5 *resp.*). Thus Aquinas and some other scholastics using Aristotle implied, in the manner of civic humanism (see below, pp. 130–5), that personal virtue is inextricably bound up with one's contribution to the political society of which one is a member.

On the other hand, Aquinas seriously modified this on other occasions: 'The common good of a state and the individual good of one person (*bonum singulare unius personae*) differ not only in degree but in kind; for the logic (*ratio*) of the common good is other than that of the individual good, just as the logic of a whole is other than that of a part' (*ST* Ia/IIae 58.7 *ad* 2; cf. *ST* Ia/IIae 92.1 *ad* 3). Again, social wholes (state and family) have 'unity of organisation (*ordinis*) only, so that [they are] not one in a simple way' (*Commentary on Ethics*, I.I). Parts, that is individuals, can do things which are unrelated to the activity of the whole. These cautions derived from Christian thought: human acts do not necessarily have to be judged according to their value for the political community, but they always have to be judged according to their value in the eyes of God (*ST* Ia/IIae 21.4 *ad* 3). He warned against taking the body–church analogy too literally.

Again, when Pope Innocent IV based his famous prohibition of collective excommunication (1245) on the fictional nature of all social entities like colleges or nations, this was also an assertion of the moral and legal responsibility of individuals, based on theological doctrine. Reification of the community or common good as real wholes separate and independent from individuals and their interests was rare among theologians and explicitly rejected by jurists after about 1250. Much of the ardour expressed for the common good reflected the urgent need for greater political solidity in the face of social divisions, rather than an attempt to glorify state or community at the expense of the individual.

Finally, the philosophies of Duns Scotus and William of Ockham led them in different ways to emphasise the significance of individuals rather than species. Ockham affirmed the right of individuals, in relation to the community of the church and its rulers, to question and assess the validity of official pronouncements on doctrine.[8] Ockham's view of Scripture and of our human understanding led him to conclude that no-one has privileged knowledge of religious truth: all public authorities may err, the truth may be kept by *any* group or individual. One person, male or female, adult or infant, may at any given moment be the sole repository of divine truth on earth – like Mary at the time of the death of Christ, the single remnant of the infallible church. There has been much debate about whether Ockham applied his nominalist ideas (that only individual objects have real existence) to society and politics, and the consensus seems to be that he did not, at least in any systematic way (see below, pp. 72–3). His religious individualism was in part the result of his personal situation as champion of what he regarded as sacred truth against the great majority of his fellow-churchmen.

---

[8] On Duns Scotus, see *CHMPT*, pp. 536–7.

JUSTICE AND LAW

Political communities were conceived as standing in a special relationship to justice and law.⁹ These were sometimes viewed virtually as the practical and theoretical expressions of the same thing; law being not merely what a ruler or assembly decreed but something almost sacrosanct, both as the 'nerves' of society and with a strong presumption that it was not merely law but also right. Maitland's famous remark rings true: for the Middle Ages 'law is the point where life and logic meet'. 'Bracton' stated that 'right (*ius*) and law (*lex*) mean the same'; law 'especially means a just command which orders honourable deeds and prohibits the contrary' (vol. II, p. 22, trans. E. Lewis). *Ius* could refer not only to a right relation between parties, but to a quasi-Platonic structure or order among different classes of being.

Law lies behind and above political authority; it is what establishes political authority ('law makes the king' (*lex facit regem*: Bracton, *On the Laws and Customs of England* (*De legibus et consuetudinibus Angliae*), vol. II, p. 33) both by defining the terms of royal succession and the scope of the royal office, and by telling the king what he should do, how he should act. Thus law was generally conceived as morally superior to those who applied it, including the king, and implementation of the laws constituted the chief goal of monarchical or any other government (see below, pp. 152–5). Here public belief and academic theory were in agreement. Marsiglio saw law as the first and fundamental requirement, the basis, of human society; lawgivers and governments are there to ensure that laws are effective. While insisting that only coercive commands qualify as law, Marsiglio insisted no less that conformity with justice was an essential quality of law (*DP* I.10.5–6).

It was through law that moral values were transmitted to human society. This outlook had of course a classical parentage in the Stoic theory of natural law which underlay the late-Roman philosophy of law, summarised in the opening parts of the *Digest*. Medieval thinkers explored in depth the relationship between transcendent and actual law. All actual laws were supposed to partake in *ius*; through the processes of legislation and *reformatio* there were constant attempts to make them reflect it more accurately. In this way the second part of the Decalogue dominated medieval social and legal thought. It forbade crimes against person and property, and so provided the

---

⁹ See bibliography, p. 205.

mould in which civil society and respect for individuals was cast. The medieval lawyers professed to apply the universal and eternal principles of justice to the minutiae of their cases. The great scandal of Machiavelli was that he subordinated justice to the state.

Justice could refer to objective norms such as the Ten Commandments and the classical virtues (*honestas* and so on); or, again, to 'subjective' rights, honours, liberties and privileges, which belonged to particular groups or individuals on the basis of custom or charter. These included the respective status of lords and serfs, the rights and liberties of towns, and rights such as those enumerated in the English Great Charter of 1215. To a certain extent these objective and subjective aspects coincided: not to murder, steal, commit adultery, bear false witness meant respecting the persons, properties and good names of others. When justice was defined, following the *Digest*, as 'to give to each his due (*ius suum cuique tribuere*)', this could refer to either aspect, but especially the subjective ('*his* due'). Philosophers and theologians tended to emphasise objective justice; jurists and William of Ockham tended to emphasise subjective rights.

A striking feature of medieval thought was the conviction that what was due to one on the basis of objective justice, as well as particular subjective rights, acquired or inherited, could be vindicated by legal process, by requested reform, as redress of grievances, or finally by armed force. Hence the widespread litigation and the juridical reasons often given for military conflict. There was a special problem when a small man wished to vindicate his claim against a magnate. Sometimes royal jurisdiction expanded at the expense of feudal justice to form an alliance between the crown and those of middle rank. Equality before the law was insisted upon in urban reform movements. In Italy the law sometimes imposed harsher penalties on the noble or rich than on the poor citizen. Legal equality was a centrepiece in Leonardo Bruni's eulogies of the constitution of Florence

All our laws point in this one direction, that there should be *paritas* and *equalitas* for the citizens in their dealings with each other; in this consists pure and true liberty ... Our laws strive so far as possible to depress the *supereminentiam* of individual citizens and reduce it to parity and *mediocritas*. (*Espistolary Description*, 1413, ch. 8).

By this he seems to have meant both that all citizens have equal access to juridical process and that there are no special legal privileges for men of high rank or status. Machiavelli singled out social equality as a great advantage the Swiss and south German city-states had in comparison with their Italian counterparts (but then he knew the Italian cities better).

Public opinion and philosophy were largely at one about the authority of custom (*consuetudo*: unwritten law). At this point law was inextricably bound up with the people (*populus*), and with each particular people in the different forms custom took over Europe. For, as Roman law (*Digest* 1.3.32) put it, custom derives its authority from its capacity to represent the true, considered will of a people, since what they have done many times over generations must be seen as their will. Here the jurists of imperial Rome had slipped in a clear echo of the Republic: custom stands for the deliberative 'vote' of a people over time. On this basis Aquinas argued that custom could override written law (*ST* 1a/11ae 97.3). Similarly in the church, tradition was regarded as one authoritative source of right belief and practice.

The argument from custom was taken a stage further when some constitutional theorists appealed to history, to the practices of a past which was no longer living in people's memory, as a source of information about what should and should not be done in the state (for example, Lupold von Bebenberg: below, pp. 101–2; Fortescue, *In Praise of England's Laws* (*De laudibus legum Angliae*), ch. 17: *MPI*, p. 86): an argument much more fully developed in sixteenth-century France and later in England. In this period history played the greatest part in debates about the constitution of the church. This was due to the very nature of Christian faith, based as it was supposed to be upon an authoritative past, namely the life and death of Christ, to which must be added the constant Christian belief that the early church, at least the very early church, was in some ways morally and religiously pure and should therefore serve as a model for relations among believers and for the structure of the Christian community. (The same is broadly true of Islam.) Debate about the Christian past became a question of urgency when from the fourteenth and fifteenth centuries, increasing numbers of believers were confronted with what they thought to be corrupt church practices. The church had, clearly, diverged from the true way, and one method of recovering the true way was to go back to a less corrupt period – to the 'primitive church'. Existing church institutions themselves might, as many small sects began to say of the papacy and episcopate, be corrupt or deviant; thus one had to scour the New Testament and other early documents to find out exactly how the Church was supposed to be organised. This line of criticism is found in Marsiglio, Wyclif and the Hussites. One response by orthodox Catholics, like Thomas Netter and Juan de Torquemada, was to begin to argue that the church's constitution had indeed changed, but that this was a development rather than a deviation, to enable the church to cope with greater numbers, a worldwide flock and so on. Historical argument abounded during the conciliar controversy (see below, pp. 177, 180), when conciliarists initiated a critical reassessment of the whole history of the church, finding therein ample evidence that councils had played a much more important role in earlier times. Therefore they should do so now.

Aquinas' theory of law was original and has turned out to be the one part of medieval political philosophy which still remains relevant, at least for many in the Catholic world, to political discourse today. It is the lynchpin of Thomist political philosophy. Aquinas' own rather brief remarks were extended and developed by the neo-scholastics of sixteenth-century Spain; whence they provided a starting-point for the theory of international law developed by Grotius and the theory of natural rights formulated by Locke. But during the later Middle Ages and early Renaissance, Aquinas' specific doctrines – as opposed to his general adoption of Aristotelian language – were taken up by few outside his own Dominican order; in the 1430s an eminent jurist complained that other jurists had failed to recognise the potential of Aquinas' theory of natural law.[10]

Aquinas' treatment of the law of nature and of law in general (*ST* 1a/11ae 90–7) was related to his conception of the political community and of the human being as a social and political animal. He divided law into eternal, natural, divine (the principles of the Old and New Testaments), human (man-made positive law including the civil laws of states and much of canon law) and the 'law of sin'; it is the eternal, natural and human that concern us here. Law for Aquinas, was a cosmic principle; and its manifold varieties are each, except for the law of sin, in their own way expressions of the mind of God. Aquinas' *lex* and *ius* are a good deal more formidable than our 'law' and in different contexts can embrace justice, rights, norm, regularity, principle, even order, structure (*lex naturae* as 'the natural order' and so on). Aquinas began his discussion of law by saying, in a rather revealing analogy between the state under its ruler and the universe under God, that the whole 'community' of the universe (*tota communitas universi*) is 'governed' by the reason of God in a law-like way, with regularity and justice (*ST* 1a/11ae 91.1); the rational principle (*ratio*) exists in God 'as in the sovereign of society' (*sicut in principe universitatis*), suggesting a play on the cosmic undertones of a

---

[10] A. Black, 'Panormitanus on the *Decretum*', *Traditio* 26 (1970), pp. 440–4.

standard term for society. Reason is the basis of all law. Eternal law is
the means by which the divine wisdom of the supreme craftsman
(*artifex*) always moves and directs every object and every act in the
created world (*ST* 1a/11ae 93.1). All other laws (normative orders)
derive from this, just as inferior administrators derive their principles
of political action (*ratio eorum quae sunt agenda in civitate*) from royal
precept and manual craftsmen the *ratio* (scope, rationale, principles) of
their art from the architect.

Aquinas' discussion of natural law (*ST* 1a/11ae 94) expressed his
philosophy of the human person and civil society. In the universe,
according to Aquinas, every being has its proper purpose, position
and essence ordained by God, and, consequently, its corresponding
'law'. Beings created with reason (humans, angels) are in the very
special position that they participate in this primary divine attribute;
such a being 'becomes itself a participator in providence, providing
for itself and others' (1a/11ae 91.2). God conveys his image, namely
understanding and will, to man by enabling man to share in God's
own specific activity; the knowledge 'of what is good and what evil'
is 'nothing other than the impression of the divine light in us' (1a/11ae
94.2). This striking adaptation, to say the least, of Genesis 3:5 and 22,
where acquiring knowledge of good and evil is an essential part of the
Fall of Man, justifies the cliché that Aquinas saw human nature as
damaged but not destroyed by sin. 'Grace does not take away nature
but completes it' (*gratia non tollit naturam sed perficit*); ordinary human
instincts and the more enlightened praxis of paganism remain valid
for a Christian world, just as the philosophy of Aristotle does for the
Christian theologian.

Natural law, then, is 'nothing other than participation in the
eternal law by a rational creature'. This is the character of conscience:
it makes man a participatory citizen of the universe. The human
being has three levels of natural inclination or 'law': the first, which
he 'shares with all substances' is for self-preservation; the second,
which he shares with all animals, consists in 'the mingling of male and
female, the rearing of children and suchlike'; the third, peculiar to
humanity, is, in words of truly Roman simplicity, 'a natural inclination to know the truth about God, and to live in society'.

Aquinas' attempt to state the relationship between natural and
human law (in modern language, between justice and law) was also
striking and is seen by some as a major contribution to the philosophy
of law. He began by asking whether natural law can vary from place
to place (*ST* 1a/11ae 94.4). He concluded, in the spirit of Aristotle, that
only very general principles can be laid down as valid everywhere

and at all times, and that, in practical as opposed to scientific matters, the more specific the principle the less generally valid it is: for example, one should repay debts (or invested capital), but not if this is going to be used as a means to fight one's own country. From 'harm no-one', one may derive the more specific principle 'do not kill', and from that specific penalties for murder: these vary, legitimately, from one society to another, and not all killing even is wrong (war and capital punishment are justifiable).

Such a summary of these brief passages does not do justice to the spirit and nuances of Aquinas' thought. For nearly everything he said about politics, including his views on just rebellion and the just war, was coloured by this understanding of the relation between the moral and the practical, of the need to translate principles into practice and the near impossibility of doing so with philosophic precision. In Aquinas, the philosopher humbly lays down his task at the feet of the practitioner. His statements often sound deceptively dull; they are in fact the fruit of a unique wrestling with abstract principle to elicit practical guidance, and serve as a constant reminder of the amount of practical art that goes into every moral act. Obviously Aquinas took much here from Aristotle; and there is a good deal of Stoicism here, and of the spiritual cadences of *Romanitas*.

Aquinas' discussion of human law was also far-reaching, while at the same time it wove together many of the most important strands in contemporary thought (*ST* 1a/11ae 95–7). Human laws are necessary since without them human society could not exist (and without society human beings could not exist). They consist in a further particularisation of the general precepts of natural law; what happens here is that, in addition to each individual specifying natural-law principles by applying them to his or her own moral decisions, each state (*civitas*) lays down its own laws as it thinks appropriate. For example, while murder and theft are forbidden by natural law, what counts as murder and theft, and how they are to be punished, is determined by each state severally. Thus human laws may vary considerably from one state to another and still be perfectly legitimate (1a/11ae 97.1), just as there may be a legitimate diversity of forms of government (95.2). There is, furthermore, scope both for changing human laws and for improving them over time (97.2). The development of human laws requires effort, inventiveness and skill (91.3 *resp.* and 95.1 *resp.*).

Aquinas had spelled out his criteria for the validity of laws at the beginning of his whole discussion of law, and these apply to human laws: they must have regard to the common happiness (90.2 *resp.*);

they must be laid down either by society as a whole or its representative (90.3 *resp*.); and they must be published (90.4). Aquinas gave prominence to the sovereign *qua* legislator in any legal system. Again, it is the purpose of laws in general to 'lead those subject to them to their own proper virtue' (92.1 *resp*.) and 'make them good'; this is true of human law as well. But Aquinas affirmed in a somewhat liberal spirit that it would be oppressive if all acts that are morally wrong (sins) are made crimes.

Ockham spoke of natural law or right (*lex/ius*) in a way which some have seen as original but which is very difficult to interpret. Some things are clear. He spoke – as some others did – of natural right as constituting a basis for moral claims by persons, regardless of social or political status. Perhaps because of the Franciscan poverty dispute, he tended to see natural right in terms of individual entitlement. And, in particular, God has given all humans two specific rights which they have by nature, regardless of whether they are Christian believers or not: freedom and property. Property rights depend in practice upon the right to vindicate one's possession in law (*ius fori*). Ockham used the language of 'rights and liberties', which was used in charters and the like to describe positive rights conferred upon or claimed by groups or persons, as a way of describing 'the rights and liberties granted to us by God and nature'. The idea of subjective rights inhering in persons in a remarkably 'modern' sense seems first to have been developed by canon-law jurists in the twelfth century. 'The everyday use of *ius* to mean a right, a rightful power, infected the language of the canonists when they came to write of *ius naturale*' (Tierney). It may be possible to see in Ockham a notion of the human laws of states (civil and criminal laws) as formed by the sum of individual rights. As Lagarde puts it:

Human society, by the interplay of conventions, pacts, argeements, concessions, transfers, gifts of every sort, which have followed one another without interruption since the beginning of time, has witnessed the birth and disappearance of innumerable *particular rights* which taken together constitute *the civil law* . . . The whole of public and private law, therefore, is summed up in a complex of particular rights.[11]

(This is an interesting anticipation of the philosophy of Robert Nozick, for which Lagarde may take credit even if his interpretation of Ockham is exaggerated.)

---

[11] Lagarde, *Naissance*, vol. VI, pp. 179–209 at p. 208; cf. A. S. McGrade, *The Political Thought of William of Ockham* (Cambridge, Cambridge University Press, 1974), pp. 177ff.

This concludes the general picture of the sorts of political concepts and values current in European discourse. It has inevitably been selective and also wide-ranging. There was indeed no single 'medieval' or 'Renaissance' system for the theory of politics any more than there was for political practice. There was a diversity of languages, political doctrines and preferences.

2

CHURCH AND STATE

The medieval problem of church and state was a version of the perpetual question facing a religion which claimed to be in the world but not of it, which preached about morals and social order yet refused to be identified with any particular such order.[1] The medieval-European church–state relationship was unique, and 'the West' had a problem not so acutely felt elsewhere, because of the particular way Christianity had become institutionalised there, and the sort of polities which, partly as a consequence of this, had developed there. On the one hand, the church was in theory and largely in practice coterminous with society as 'the association of the faithful' (*universitas fidelium*), 'Christian society' (*societas christiana*), 'the Roman church' or 'the Christian republic'. On the other hand, both secular and ecclesiastical authorities were deemed to be of divine institution. The papacy was credited with the moral and spiritual leadership of a community of peoples in which kingdoms, duchies, city-states and other bodies were the actual units of government. Incidentally, this sometimes meant that it was possible for political, and on occasion religious, dissenters to find a haven.

In the form in which we find it in the middle of the thirteenth century, the debate went back to the late eleventh century, and lasted until, with the Reformation, the church ceased to be coterminous with society. The papacy's spiritual authority and actual power had been expanded by the reform movement associated with pope

[1] See bibliography, p. 202.

42

Gregory VII (1073–85). The ensuing 'investiture controversy' had focussed upon whether pope or king had the right to appoint bishops, who were not only spiritual leaders but frequently royal ministers as well. Secular and church functions were intertwined at all levels. Various compromises, subject to re-negotiation, were reached. No less contested were the boundaries between lay and clerical jurisdiction, royal and church courts: what categories of persons and offences came under which? During the twelfth and early thirteenth centuries, when great lawyer-popes had legislated for the whole of Europe on a wide range of topics including certain aspects of property rights (where marriage or legitimate birth were concerned, for example), the efficiency of the papal courts and the energy of the papacy as a legislature went some way towards realising the ideal of western Christendom as a juridical unit. But kings like Henry II of England had insisted that criminous clerks should be punishable in lay courts. The papacy aimed at international hegemony and constructed a formidable judicial and bureaucratic system. But it needed economic and educational resources with which to maintain and replenish its hierarchy. And from the later thirteenth century the fiscal obligations of clerical subjects to kings, and of laymen generally to the papacy, became a matter of intense dispute. At the same time the development of academic institutions and disciplines meant that intellectual enquiry acquired a certain momentum of its own.

Popes claimed authority to depose rulers for sin or injustice; as Hugh of St Victor put it, 'The spiritual power has to institute the earthly power and to judge it if it turns out not to be good. But it itself is instituted originally by God, and when it deviates it can be judged by God alone.'[2] The king of Germany was especially vulnerable because as Roman emperor he was crowned by the pope; after a bitter conflict, Innocent IV deposed Frederick II (1245). But his attempts to promote the papacy's political position in Italy led him into factional local politics, which debased the currency of the spiritual realm. Church–state relations now entered on a particularly troubled time. The papacy's weapons were excommunication and interdict, whereby a refractory ruler could be declared a social outcast, or a whole region denied access to divine favours. Kings and princes possessed physical coercion and intimidation but also, increasingly, a wide measure of popular support.

The church–state dispute was about where the boundary lay, and about who, if anyone, had the authority to say where, in a disputed

---

[2] *De Sacramentis* II.II.4; cf. John of Salisbury, *Policraticus* IV.3.

case, it lay. One ancient and for a long time dominant doctrine, sometimes called 'dualist' or 'Gelasian', held that, in the words of pope Gelasius I (496),

Christ ... separated the offices of both powers according to their proper activities and their special dignities ... so that Christian emperors would have need of bishops in order to attain eternal life and bishops would have recourse to imperial direction in the conduct of temporal affairs.[3]

From this and various New Testament sources it was deduced that, while the church was superior in principle and purpose, the state was also founded by God. But this clearly left much to interpretation in a society where intertwined secular and church authorities were each busily asserting their rights, and where eternal salvation and law and order were equally urgent matters. Murder, theft and false witness affected both eternal salvation and social order. And to what extent did superior moral authority justify, in the last analysis, a political overlordship?

The hierocratic (papalist or theocratic) view held that Christ had empowered Peter and the apostles to judge the sins of all believers regardless of their rank. It was a cardinal innovation of Gregorian hierocracy that the king was a mere layman and therefore, in church matters, as much a subject of pope and clergy as anyone else. As for the scope of subject-matter, it was for the pope, as the supreme human agency delegated by Christ on earth, to determine what counted as sin and what, therefore, fell within church jurisdiction; certainly any form of injustice counted, so that appeal could be made from secular judges on that ground. The scope claimed by the papacy is indicated by Innocent III when, in justifying his attempt to mediate between king John of England and Philip Augustus of France during the latter's successful conquest of Normandy, which John held in fief from Philip, he declared (1204) that he could not judge regarding the fief but only regarding sin (*ratione peccati*); and promptly went on to say that, since in this instance peace had been disrupted and an oath broken, sin was after all involved (*Novit* in *CIC* II, 243–4; cf. *Per venerabilem* in *CIC* II, 714–16: Tierney, *Crisis*, pp. 134–8). It came to be said that the pope possessed both spiritual and temporal power – both 'swords' – in essence, but that temporal power, that is, physical coercion, was only to be exercised by lay rulers. The point here was that, although the division was divinely ordained, popes could hereby claim the right to direct kings as to how, in particular cases, temporal power should be used for spiritual ends. Kings were thus said to rule

[3] *CHMPT*, pp. 288–9.

not on their own authority but by a 'right of administration'. This reduced them, theoretically, to the status of provincial officials. Largely due to the influence of canon law and the canonists, this became the prevailing view during the twelfth and thirteenth centuries.

Hierocracy corresponded to a streak of idealism in many people so long as the actual exercise of ecclesiastical authority remained of a high standard. But by the later thirteenth century, in much public opinion, this was no longer the case. Kings and princes had considerable moral authority in their own realms and considerable actual control over their local clergy; besides, even though nothing much of this was yet articulated by theorists, the practical world of local politics often corresponded much more to a secular outlook.

Specific issues in international and local politics were closely bound up with the debate. The emperor Frederick II had confronted the papacy with the prospect of a Romano-Germanic Empire based in Germany and Sicily and capable of mounting a pincer movement to control central Italy and the papacy itself, ruled indeed by an emperor who was religiously tolerant and perhaps neo-pagan in outlook. The papacy sought alliance with the kingdom of France. But conflict between France and England in the 1290s led both monarchs to seek extra revenue sources and to tax their clergy. The papacy clashed with Philip IV of France on this and other issues, but subsequently made its peace with France, moved to Avignon (1309) and, under John XXII, entered into a final struggle with the German Empire, from which France benefited considerably. Under these circumstances, England found difficulty in paying papal taxes.

Yet, far from being confined to the immediate issues at stake, these debates reached to the very core of authority as such. The clashes of Titans tested the foundations upon which each rested. Popes appealed to councils to judge a king, kings to councils or parliaments to chide and judge a pope. That the question of fundamental legitimacy was at stake comes out even in the ironical remark of a French envoy to a masterful pope: 'your sword is verbal, ours is real'.[4] The modern European idea of the state and the modern European states system were in part generated by the church–state dialectic.

It has been argued, by Ullmann and others, that Aquinas' 'new' theory of the state based on Aristotle worked as a catalyst transforming the way people looked at the relationship between church and state. But, as we have seen (above, p. 20), the idea of the *civitas*

---

[4] Thomas Walsingham, *Chronica Monasterii S. Albani* (Rolls Series, London, 1863–76), vol. II, pp. 197–8.

as the product of nature had been present for a long time. On the other hand, one cannot deny that the debate was transformed in the decades following the rediscovery of the *Politics*; but not so much in the sense that new positions were stated but in the philosophical sophistication with which the range of positions was defended. There had been advocates of secular independence and superiority before; and some now used Aristotle to support papal supremacy. Even so Aristotle's insistence on the self-sufficiency of the *polis* and its close involvement in the good life probably gave added confidence to those favouring the independence or superiority of the state.

Aquinas' position is problematic. In his *Commentary on the Sentences*, written in 1253–5 before he knew the *Politics*, he seemed at first merely to restate the dualist position: 'in those things that pertain to the civil good, the secular power is to be obeyed rather than the spiritual' (II, d.44, q.2, a.3, *ad* 4). God has already determined who should do what. Yet paradoxically he added: 'unless perhaps the secular power is joined to the spiritual, as in the pope, who holds the apex of both authorities, spiritual and secular'. This ambiguity or self-contradiction has been variously explained; one possibility is that hierocratic doctrine had been so emphasised by recent popes and canon-lawyers that Aquinas felt obliged not to dismiss it. (He allows only that the pope, not the clergy in general, holds both powers.)

If, as I have been assuming, Aquinas was not the author of *On Kingship*, he initiated no new development in the theory of church–state relations. Chapters 14–15 of *On Kingship* do in any case suggest a striking adjustment, based on Aristotle's notion of the state. Human beings and the state are parts of a cosmos in which all things have purposes outside themselves. Therefore, anyone in charge of something must 'not only preserve it unharmed but also guide it towards its goal'. But these two functions can be separated; thus the carpenter has the job of repairing a ship, the pilot that of getting it to port. In human life, the doctor preserves a person's health, the household manager supplies the necessities of life, the teacher teaches the truth, the moral educator seeks to make one live according to reason. And man has a further goal outside himself, final beatitude, for which he needs 'care by the ministers of Christ's church'.

All of these functions are required in a human community. Adapting Aristotle, 'Aquinas' insists that the purpose of human community is not just health, affluence or knowledge but virtuous living. Otherwise, the king could be (merely) a doctor, economist or teacher. Strangely, but significantly, 'Aquinas' does not at this stage mention the possibility of his being a moral educator; he momentarily sidesteps that implication. Instead, he goes on to point out that the final purpose is not virtuous living, but rather the enjoyment of God. If this were attainable by human effort, it would be the king's job to direct humans towards this end. But in fact the 'king' in this respect is Christ alone, whose task is analogous to the ship's captain directing the shipwright, and to the civic militiaman directing the arms smith. Now Christ is king and priest, and so are all Christians. So that 'spiritual things should be distinct from earthly', the *ministerium* (service, administration) of this kingdom has been entrusted to priests, and especially the pope 'to whom all Christian people ought to be subject just as they are to Jesus Christ'. Since the purpose of the priesthood is to lead humans to the greater good of heaven, 'in the law of Christ kings ought to be subordinate to priests'.

This passage has perhaps been overlooked because it is at first sight platitudinous. Not so the following chapter.

Since therefore the purpose of the life, by which we live well in the present, is heavenly beatitude, it belongs for that reason to the king's office to attain the good life for society (*vitam multitudinis bonam procurare*), in such a way that it is compatible with the achievement of heavenly beatitude: that is, he should command what leads to heavenly beatitude and forbid, so far as possible, what does not. And the way to true beatitude, and obstacles to this, are known from the divine law, the teaching of which belongs to the office of the priests ... A king, therefore, having learned the divine law, should make it his special task to see that the society subject to him lives well. This task (*studium*) is divided into three: first, that he establish the good life in the subject society; second, that he preserve what has been established; third, that he moves forward what has been preserved to better things (*ut conservatam ad meliora promoveat*).

This allocation of functions gives far more to the king than would any hierocrat, and seems to go beyond the traditional 'dualist' position, tilting the balance in favour of the civil power. The king is taught by priests, but it is he who commands and forbids what promotes or obstructs the journey to heaven. There is here a concept of improvement, not certainly economic but moral and spiritual, as a function of government; furthering the church's work through endowment, perhaps. Indeed the conversion of peoples from above, reform of the church and no doubt crusade would all appear to be legitimate royal functions under this rubric. Anyway, it is now unequivocally stated that the chief function of the king, 'having learned the divine law', is to secure the good (moral) life for his subjects.

THE PAPACY, FRANCE AND THE EMPIRE

The application of Christian-Aristotelian ideas began in a French context. In 1296 pope Boniface VIII attempted to prevent Philip IV ('the Fair') of France from taxing the clergy and their lands; he issued a forceful decree forbidding secular rulers to tax clergy without papal consent and the clergy to pay such taxes, under pain of excommunication and, in the case of clergy, deposition. Philip IV promptly forbade the export of all currency, thus cutting off one of the major sources of papal revenue. The dispute, which gave rise to a series of treatises including the pro-secular *Dispute between a Priest and a Knight* (*Disputatio inter clericum et militem*: *MPI*, pp. 567–74), was patched up. But in 1301 Philip had the bishop of Pamier arrested and condemned for treason; bishops were normally regarded as under papal jurisdiction. Boniface responded indignantly by reasserting papal authority over kings in church matters and summoning the French bishops to Rome to discuss Philip's conduct. Philip pre-empted Boniface by, first, circulating a forgery in which the pope was made to claim that the king was subject to him in civil matters as well, so as to inflame public opinion against Boniface; and, second, dramatically assembling the three Estates of the realm at Paris (February 1302) in what some see as the first meeting of the French Estates General. The nobles and commons denounced Boniface and withdrew recognition from him as pope. The bishops requested an explanation from Boniface; only about half of them attended the Rome synod, which proved abortive. Boniface now issued the famous decree *Unam sanctam* (November 1302). This gave official sanction to the hierocratic doctrine that

Both [swords] are in the power of the church, the material sword and the spiritual. But the one is exercised for the church, the other by the church, the one by the hand of the priest, the other by the hand of kings and soldiers, though at the will and suffrance of the priest. One sword ought to be under the other and the temporal authority subject to the spiritual power.

A king can be judged by a pope, but a pope can only be judged by God:

Therefore, if the earthly power errs, it shall be judged by the spiritual power, if a lesser spiritual power errs it shall be judged by its superior, but if the supreme spiritual power errs it can be judged only by God not by man. (*CIC* II, 1245–6: Tierney, *Crisis*, p. 189)

Once again, Philip went onto the offensive. He summoned an assembly of bishops and barons, denounced Boniface as heretical and criminal, and demanded that he be tried by a general council of the church (June 1303). Two theologians of Paris University gave their opinion at this time, broadly in favour of the Crown: the anonymous author of *Two Sides of the Question* (*Quaestio in utramque partem*), and Jean Quidort de Paris (*c.* 1240–1306), a Dominican, who wrote *On Royal and Papal Power* (*De potestate regia et papali*). Philip was excommunicated and Boniface was planning to release his subjects from their oath of allegiance; but Philip decided to use force. An attempt was made to arrest Boniface; after some kind of scuffle this miscarried, but Boniface died shortly afterwards. The affair died down and pope Clement V issued a clarification of *Unam sanctam* to the effect that the bull in no way altered the position of the French church and monarchy. In 1309 the papal court moved to Avignon where it remained until 1377; from the middle of the century its attitude towards France was amicable, indeed pliable. The affair was a signal victory for the lay power.

It gave rise to a flurry of theoretical writings. The hierocratic position was defended and developed by two remarkable theorists: James of Viterbo (Jacopo Cappucci: *c.* 1260–1307/8), whose *On Christian Government* (*De regimine Christiano*) was written in 1301–2, and Aegidius Romanus (Egidio Romano/Colonna or Giles of Rome: *c.* 1243–1316), whose *Ecclesiastical Power* (*De ecclesiastica potestate*) was written in 1302. Aegidius' treatise in particular 'formulated the ideology that lay behind Boniface VIII's pronouncements'. They based their argument upon the extensive claims made by the popes of the previous two centuries for ecclesiastical and especially papal power in temporal matters and over secular rulers; some such claims had the added authority of having been included in canon law. But they built these into a coherent doctrine, partly by putting it all in the context of a detailed theological consideration of the church as a community, partly by using Aristotelian ideas and also, in Aegidius' case, a novel theory of property developed from Augustine. Both men were members of the order of Eremitical Augustinians, both had studied at Paris (Aegidius probably under Aquinas, James probably under Aegidius), and rose to be archbishops. Aegidius had been Philip IV's tutor, and was to serve the king again in his prosecution of the Templars. We will consider here also the papal-hierocratic ideas of theorists in the early years of the Avignon papacy, expressed partly in connection with the dispute between pope John XXII and Ludwig of Bavaria (see below, pp. 55–6), notably Augustinus Triumphus (Agostino Trionfo of Ancona) (1270/3–1328), whose massive *Summary on Ecclesiastical Power* (*Summa de potestate ecclesiastica*) was finished in 1328, and Alvarus Pelagius (Alvaro Pelayo) (*c.* 1275–1349) whose *Lament of the Church* (*De planctu ecclesie*) was composed between 1330 and 1340.

Here was the climax of medieval papalism as a political theory; yet these most far-reaching claims ever made for the papacy came at the time when its political power was most in question, and indeed during and in the wake of its first major and public defeat. According to these authors, Christ had given the pope 'fullness of power' (*plenitudo potestatis*). This meant, first, that a duly elected pope could not be called to account by any other human authority; second, that the church through the pope possessed *both* 'swords', spiritual and temporal power: for he was the representative of God, or Christ, on earth. All ecclesiastical and secular rulers derive their authority from the church, require papal legitimation and can be judged by the pope if they are defective. As Triumphus put it: 'The power of the pope is greater than every other by virtue of its causal superiority, because its power is the cause of every other power, examining, confirming and judging it.'[5] The one reservation was that the pope was obliged to delegate to others the actual exercise of temporal (physically coercive) power: this division was decreed by Christ because clergy ought not to use violence, and it was demeaning and distracting for them to be involved in the sordid details of secular affairs. And even so the pope can exercise temporal power 'in certain cases'. Here a clear distinction was made between underlying *auctoritas*, which church and pope held in both spiritual and temporal spheres, and *exercitium* or *executio* which kings had in temporal affairs: between, as it were, policy-making and day-to-day management. This brought clergy and pope rather close to Plato's philosopher-kings. James of Viterbo argued that the pope had prior possession of (*praehabet*) temporal power, which he held 'in a superior, more honourable and more outstanding way' than a secular prince.

For he does not have it in such a way as to exercise its tasks directly, except in certain cases, but he does its tasks in a nobler way, by commanding (*imperando*), directing and using its tasks for his own end. The temporal power is, therefore, said to pre-exist in the spiritual as to its first and highest authority, though not as to its immediate execution generally and as a rule. (II. 7, p. 236)

This was not a 'separation of powers' because it was always for the spiritual power to decide in what kinds of case and in what particular instances it should intervene, call a secular ruler to account, or issue a directive to him.

[5] Cited by Michael Wilks, *The Problem of Sovereignty in the Later Middle Ages* (Cambridge, Cambridge University Press, 1963), p. 69.

Without this divine institution and approval transmitted by the priesthood, typically in the form of coronation, kingdoms, said Aegidius of Rome, lack true righteousness and are therefore (as Augustine said) no better than robber bands. Indeed not only political authority but the ownership of property depends in principle upon the claimant being in a state of grace, so that if the church excommunicates a ruler his title to *dominium* or rightful lordship lapses (I. 4–5 and II. 7, 12: *MPI*, pp. 112–15, 574–9). The nature of the clergy's and the pope's spiritual authority means that, and requires that, they judge temporal office-holders whenever these deviate from the purposes of a Christian society, about which the clergy are more fully informed than any prince. They may also issue specific commands to rulers. The pope can depose and replace an erring or disobedient secular ruler (I. 5: *MPI*, p. 579).

Now both Aegidius and James knew of and accepted the general world-view of Christian Aristotelianism. Aegidius had composed one of the earliest and most influential Aristotelian political treatises, *The Rule of Princes* (written in 1277–9, translated into French *c*. 1286, and circulated very widely in many languages throughout our period). Here he spoke of a natural 'impetus' amongst humans towards 'the community of the (city-)state'; human life involves 'living politically according to certain laws' (III, part 1, chapter 2: fols. 237r–9r). This too was slotted into and used to clarify hierocratic doctrine, as James of Viterbo in particular showed. 'Temporal power derives its existence, materially and *inchoative*, from the natural inclination of humans, and thus from God', while '*perfective* and formally it derives its existence from the spiritual power, which is derived from God in a special way' (II. 7: *MPI*, p. 581). The spiritual power stands to the temporal as [Aristotelian] form to matter: without the approval of the spiritual power no secular authority can be 'true and perfect' (II. 7: *MPI*, p. 582), just as divine grace perfects the world of nature. But nature is independent of grace, and secular of church authority, in principle only. As François de Meyronnes put it, 'Just as the political virtues are formless unless subjected to the theological virtues, so the principate of temporal affairs is formless unless subject to the prince of spiritual affairs' (cited Wilks, *Problem*, p. 126). Furthermore, said James, nature provides man with authority over man, but only the church can legitimise the authority of Christian over Christian (II. 7: *MPI*, p. 583). Aegidius argued that the relation of clerical to lay power is determined by the priority of soul in relation to body, and of spiritual to physical in the cosmos generally (*Ecclesiastical Power* II. 6). James, on the other hand, incorporated the view of Aristotle and Aquinas that the state does indeed have a spiritual purpose, namely the virtuous life 'which is primarily a matter of the soul': this virtuous life is itself subordinated to the 'ultimate and supreme end of man'; 'natural beatitude' has to be oriented towards 'supernatural beatitude', of which the clergy have cognisance (II. 7: *MPI*, p. 584). In other words, the coming of Christ altered the terms of secular legitimacy. Therefore, spiritual rulers have to direct the secular.

Finally, the human being's true kingdom or *polis* is the universal church. It is the church which is *societas perfecta*, the 'highest and most inclusive' human society (Viterbo II. 4: *MPI*, pp. 182–4). And human and Christian society must be arranged according to the cosmic principle that all multiplicity and diversity are 'reduced to singularity'. In this way the constitution of human society on earth faithfully mirrors the order of the universe which is governed by a hierarchy under God in such a way that, as the now very influential Pseudo-Denis (a sixth-century mystical theologian from the East) had said, the inferior powers are always mediated by the superior (Aegidius II. 5: *MPI*, pp. 578–9). All powers emanate from above in a series of graded ranks, the superior always transmitting capabilities to the inferior: this is the principle of 'hierarchy'. The qualities of spiritual unity and of the underlying authority of priesthood and pontificate can only be realised in practice through the juridical subordination and constitutional accountability of Christian kings to the papacy.

The response made by king Philip, his advisers and others who wrote in support of the king, was, in the first instance, to appeal to 'the custom of St Louis [sc. Louis IX] and his predecessors', and to repeat the traditional arguments for Gelasian dualism, supported by biblical texts and interpretation. The king should obey the pope only in spiritual matters, just as the clergy should obey the king *in temporalibus*; the king is supreme in temporal matters. According to the *Question*, this corresponded to the nature of man with his soul and body, his two-fold life and two-fold culture (*duplex civilitas*) (*CHMPT* pp. 403–6). The king may tax the clergy because it is he who protects their material property from theft by others: 'when you hand over a little to the king, you are paying for your own safety, since he saves all your property from being lost' (*MPI* p. 573).

This was all very well, but it was by now essential for defenders of dualism to demonstrate how one could decide whether a contested topic (such as clerical taxation) lay in the king's or the pope's domain. Both the anonymous *Question* and John of Paris tried to be much more specific about exactly where the boundary between the two jurisdictions lay without either admitting that the pope could decide, or making what would have been a novel assertion that the king could do so. The *Question* argued that disputes could be decided by simple recourse to law: the pope does not have temporal power except 'occasionally' (*casualiter*), that is 'in certain cases defined by law' (such as peace, perjury, usury), 'incidentally', that is in temporal cases with a spiritual aspect (such as dowry) and 'indirectly' (for example, in a matter regarding a fief where an oath is involved).[6]

John of Paris approached the problem in a similar way but broke a lot more new ground. He was one of the first openly to recognise that such dualism could only be made to work by identifying much more precisely the constitutional relationship between the civil and ecclesiastical powers. And he based this on the crucial proposition that the clergy's temporal power derived not from any coercive or proprietorial authority (*dominium*) inherent in their clerical, episcopal or papal status (as Aegidius argued), but from their universally acknowledged 'right of preaching': they might influence others, lay people, to act in specific ways in the temporal sphere and with regard to temporal property. It was in this sense that their temporal power was 'indirect'. He based his denial of *dominium* to the clergy on the argument that church property is properly speaking the property not of individual office-holders but of the church as a community: the pope, therefore, is not a 'lord' but an 'administrator' (manager). And he made a further distinction between authority to pronounce on matters of principle, for example that usury is a sin, and authority to judge specific disputes involving property. The former is the domain of ecclesiastical judges (as part of the 'right of preaching'), the latter pertains to secular judges.

The constitutional relationship is further defined as follows. If a secular ruler (he is speaking here, as a matter of fact, of the emperor) commits an ecclesiastical crime, the pope is entitled to bring his moral influence to bear on that prince's subjects and to encourage them to depose him. Similarly, the *Question* stated that the pope could 'absolve vassals from their oath of allegiance, or rather declare them absolved, in a case of [a prince's] heresy or contumacy against the Roman church' (p. 133). John of Paris argued that, if a king commits a temporal misdemeanour, it is in the first instance for 'the peers of the realm' to correct him. Correspondingly, more or less, if the pope commits a spiritual misdemeanour, it is in the first instance for the cardinals to act 'on behalf of the whole clergy'; if that fails, they may

[6] J. A. Watt, 'The *Quaestio in Utramque Partem* Reconsidered', *Studia Gratiana* 13 (1967), pp. 411–54 at pp. 435–7.

invoke the help of the secular arm. A prince is permitted to use his influence to encourage the cardinals, and eventually he may coerce people at large, through physical means and confiscation of property, to withdraw allegiance from a defaulting pope (John of Paris, ch. 13). John supported Philip's decision to cite Boniface before a church council. Neither the *Question*'s nor John's moderate support for the French monarchy involved any real break with traditional theology or canon law.

John of Paris was the only royal supporter who brought in Aristotle. Indeed he began his treatise by following Aquinas closely on the naturalness of both society and government (chs. 1, 3, 5), which he interpreted, contrary to Aegidius, to mean that secular authority cannot draw its legitimacy from the church. But his most telling point against Aegidius, which had nothing directly to do with Aristotle, was to go on to say that the superiority of the spiritual power in the order of being did not make it superior in jurisdiction or in temporal matters. This equally plausible version of hierarchy gave separation between the two powers a metaphysical basis. Both stem from a higher power, God, independently of one another; and this higher power has also demarcated their respective spheres of authority. 'The priest is superior in spiritual matters and conversely the ruler is superior in temporal matters, even though, absolutely speaking, the priest is higher in proportion as the spiritual is higher than the temporal' (ch. 5). It is like the power of a general in relation to that of a father, or again the authority of a moral teacher in relation to that of a doctor. They are simply different kinds of authority. The secular power, albeit of a lower order, has its own independent sphere of competence because – and here we can see the influence of Aristotle – it is concerned with something 'good and desirable in itself', with something not purely material: the life according to virtue (chs. 5, 17).

The next episode in the church–state debate arose out of conflict between popes and German king-emperors, but other states and the question of clerical-lay relations generally were also involved. It generated the most original political writings of the later Middle Ages, by Dante, Marsilius, Ockham and Nicholas of Cusa. This was no coincidence, for the whole political order of Europe, as well as the prospects of Germany as a nation-state along French or English lines, were involved.

The circumstances were as follows. After the debilitating interregnum of 1250–72, Rudolph of Habsburg was elected emperor with papal support (the first Habsburg emperor: 1272–91). He was followed by Adolph of Nassau (1291–8), but he was deposed by the princes in favour of Rudolph's son Albrecht of Austria (1298–1308). He was followed by Henry of Luxemburg (1308–13). After his death there was a contested election as a result of which both Ludwig of Bavaria and Frederick of Austria claimed the Crown. Ludwig defeated Frederick at the battle of Mühldorf (1322) but pope John XXII refused to recognise him as emperor. This dispute dragged on until Ludwig's death in 1347.

Behind all this lay rival visions of Europe as an international community of states (see ch. 3) and rival bids for hegemony within Europe. The papacy was determined to frustrate the expansionist tendency within the German imperial monarchy. Previously, the popes had built up alliances among Italian cities. Now they sought alliance both with the French monarchy, which had an interest in increasing its influence and control in regions along its eastern frontier with German territories, and with Charles of Anjou who had established Angevin rule in southern Italy. Within Germany itself, some princes wished to increase the powers of the central monarchy, and to pursue the traditional imperial objective of securing support for this end and a measure of international authority, by controlling or gaining the allegiance of northern and central Italian states. Milan and Padua were in the main pro-imperial, Florence and Venice pro-papal. Other princes wished the monarchy to abandon imperial ambitions and be reduced to a mere figurehead within Germany. This latter group was the natural ally of both the papacy and France; it included the prince-elector-archbishops of Cologne and Mainz. Rudolph of Habsburg, Albrecht of Austria and Frederick of Austria belonged to this camp, while Adolph of Nassau, Henry of Luxemburg and Ludwig of Bavaria pursued a strong monarchy and international power. This brought them, especially the last two, into conflict with the papacy.

When Henry of Luxemburg launched his Italian expedition (1310–13), the papacy supported Robert of Anjou against him, and he died under threat of excommunication. This episode inspired Dante's *Monarchy* (*Monarchia* (c. 1313): see also below, pp. 96–100). Pope John XXII supported Frederick of Austria against Ludwig of Bavaria, and refused to confirm Ludwig as emperor or to crown him; instead he cited him to appear at Avignon to have his title to the throne examined and even forbade him meanwhile to exercise royal powers. Ludwig refused and was excommunicated (1324); he in turn accused John XXII of heresy. The pope declared Ludwig's subjects absolved from their oath of allegiance to him. It was in these circumstances that Marsiglio completed and published his *Defender of the Peace* (*Defensor pacis*) (1324) anonymously. He joined Ludwig on his expedition into Italy from 1327 to 1330, when Ludwig had himself crowned at Rome and had John XXII deposed and replaced with a new pope. Ockham joined Ludwig's court about this time and stayed thereabouts during the ensuing years of controversy; he himself died shortly after Ludwig.

The dispute between Ludwig and John XXII was also tied in with a doctrinal dispute between a number of Franciscans who denied that Jesus or his apostles had ever owned anything, even in common, and the great majority of churchmen who, in rejecting this interpretation of the New Testament, were also concerned to uphold the clergy's right to ownership. It was on this question that Ludwig and his supporters condemned the pope for heresy; there was indeed some connection between the right of ownership and the right, also claimed by Ludwig's opponents, of clergy to exercise temporal, coercive jurisdiction. Both were forms of *dominium*. More obviously, the dispute involved the internal constitution of the German monarchy and of any German state or states that might emerge. The papacy used its acknowledged right to crown the emperor-elect to claim a right of confirmation and, by witholding this, to weaken both imperial authority and royal authority in Germany itself. It did this to considerable effect during Ludwig's reign. Indeed it was the relative success of the Franco-papal policy of weakening the Empire and creating a power vacuum along Franco-German frontiers that helped strengthen relations between Ludwig and England. And it was when French hegemony had been temporarily neutralised by Crécy and Poitiers that the centrifugal electors could finally be persuaded to agree to a settlement of Germany's constitution in the Golden Bull of 1356. In return for forgoing foreign claims, this excluded the papacy from any role in the electoral process, and established the majority principle among the seven electoral princes. This made possible a rapprochement between German king-emperors and the papacy, which lasted for centuries, and brought to an end this phase in the church–state controversy.

Dante (see below, pp. 96–100) used Aristotle creatively to argue that, if we follow through the argument from human needs to politically organised society, we find that these needs can only properly be met through a universal society with a unified legal and political order maintained by the coercive and executive authority of a single 'monarch' or 'world overseer' (*curator orbis*). The establishment of the universal empire is necessary if the goals of philosophy are to be achieved, that is, if humans are to be able to develop knowledge and become wise to their full potentiality (as Aristotle had said, approximately, of the city-state: *Monarchy*, III.15). Such a universal polity arose not only out of the need for peace and justice, as advocates of the Romano-Germanic empire had long argued, but also out of the need for human fulfilment in the moral and intellectual spheres. This civil power has a role in remedying the effects of sin by educating humankind and by establishing the real unity of the human race. Dante's 'empire' was *the* social setting where alone human beings could find fulfilment as moral and intellectual beings. More than ever before, the papacy was thus presented with an opponent which had some of the features and capabilities claimed for the church. The 'emperor', as the conveyor of liberty and peace, was God's personal representative on earth. The purpose of imperial government is to obtain for us 'the beatitude of this life, which consists in the functioning of our own virtue, and which is symbolised by the earthly paradise' (*Monarchy* III. 16). Dante located this earthly paradise between purgatory and heaven as the garden of Eden restored, for which humanity was destined by nature in God's original creation; it is here that in the *Divine Comedy* (*Divina Commedia*) Dante finally meets Beatrice (*Purgatorio* 28–33).

Dante thus established a parallelism between papacy and empire: man, alone among all beings, 'is directed towards two ultimates' – towards earthly paradise 'through philosophical texts ... in accordance with [his] moral and intellectual energies [sc. justice, prudence, etc.] (*per philosophica documenta ... secundum virtutes morales et intellectuales*)'; and towards heavenly paradise 'through spiritual texts [sc. Scripture] ... in accordance with the theological virtues [sc. faith, etc.] (*per spiritualia documenta ... secundum virtutes theologicas*)'. The two are correlated in so far as 'this mortal felicity is in a certain manner orientated towards the immortal felicity'. 'The temporal kingdom does not receive its essence nor its energy – its authority – from the spiritual'; it may none the less be enabled to 'function more energetically (*virtuosius*) through the light of grace' which God provides in heaven and the pope on earth (*Monarchy*, III. 4). The emperor should revere the pope as a first-born son; on the other hand, he may make good deficiencies in the spiritual power (*Letters* v). Dante supplied no further details on this relationship, but it is clear enough that the emperor is junior only in a moral sense; juridically and politically they are intended to be simply separate. The pope's authority is purely religious, and the political and the religious are entirely distinct. Perhaps the relationship between pope and emperor was meant to be like that between king and archbishop.

Dante's conception of the whole human species as a single social and cultural entity with all human persons engaged in the same mental and moral purpose, meant that the Roman church and papacy were now faced with a new kind of theoretical counterpart. There was, however, nothing secularist in this view: could one imagine a mind more religious than Dante's? Dante personally thought that the right relationship between the universal polity with the emperor and the universal church with the pope was clear enough and reserved his fiercest barbs for those who, like Boniface VIII and John XXII, wilfully misunderstood it (*Purgatorio* 16, 29, 32).

MARSIGLIO

Marsilius of Padua (Marsiglio dei Mainardini: 1275/80–1342/3) studied medicine at Padua University, practised as a doctor in Italy and taught in the arts faculty at Paris. He had also served with Matteo Visconti of Milan, head of a powerful pro-imperial league in northern Italy. His *Defender of the Peace* was published in 1324. When his authorship became known, Marsiglio sought the protection of Ludwig of Bavaria at Munich (1326), anticipating John XXII's condemnation of the book as heretical (1327) for its attacks on papal authority. From then on Marsiglio served as adviser to Ludwig and probably also continued to practise medicine. He was especially influential during Ludwig's expedition to Italy (1327–30), and the manner of Ludwig's coronation in Rome, of John XXII's deposition and the election of a new pope owed much to Marsiglio's ideas. 'The *Defensor pacis* had the fortunate privilege of being immediately put into practice in the historical and political reality of its day, albeit for a short time.'[7]

Marsiglio states as his purpose the establishment of peace and the removal of civil discord from all cities and kingdoms. Aristotle, in his *Politics*, diagnosed the causes of social conflict and prescribed remedies; but there is one 'special and very concealed' cause unknown to him, namely the interventions by the clergy and especially the papacy in political affairs, and their claims to jurisdiction in civil matters over secular rulers (*Defender of the Peace* I. 1, pp. 3–4; cf. p. 108). Italy in particular has been torn apart on this account (pp. 2, 101–10). The Roman bishops' claims to fullness of power, the 'oligarchical laws'

---

[7] Jeannine Quillet, *La Philosophie Politique de Marsile de Padoue* (Paris: J. Vrin, 1970), p. 14.

they have made exempting clergy from civil jurisdiction and citing laymen before their own courts, are based upon a 'fallacy', an intellectual error which people have not had the courage to oppose (pp. 395, 420; compare Hayek's view of 'socialism'). Marsiglio's invective is restrained and carefully worded: the Roman bishops will persecute (he would know) any who speak against their aim of unjustly possessing temporal property and 'burning desire to rule (*ardenti desiderio principatus*)' (p. 103; cf. p. 398); they want to take over 'the coercive jurisdiction of all kingdoms' (p. 113). What stirred Marsiglio most was the plight of Italy, devastated by war and filled with strife and hatred by the popes:

Cut back is the restorative succession of progeny, consumed their substance, households are disrupted and subverted, cities once great and famous emptied . . . fields uncultivated . . . and, most utterly lamentable of all, divine worship there has almost wholly ceased, churches and temples being deserted and lacking guides or curers of souls (pp. 422–3).

It reminds one of Virgil's lament over another Italian civil war.

It is Marsiglio's intention to remove such 'perverse opinion' (p. 3) concerning the temporal power of the clergy from men's minds, to direct men towards peace (p. 1). For it was his duty to use the intelligence God had given him to expound the truth and help the oppressed (p. 5); he will imitate Christ in 'teaching the truth by which the said plague of civil governments may be extirpated from the human race and especially from Christian peoples' (pp. 4, 109), by providing 'certain conclusions and much-needed testimonies for citizens, both as rulers and as subjects' (pp. 6 and 500). The third section of *The Defender* consists of a summary of how his conclusions can be applied in practice.

Marsiglio intended to remedy the ills of all states, whether city-states or kingdoms. He wrote in general terms about the right distribution of authority among human beings as such; in this sense his work was philosophical, intended as an exposition and supplementation of Aristotle for the world as it now was. Much of the argument in the first part of *The Defender* refers specifically to a city-state milieu, not unnaturally for an Aristotelian, and here Marsiglio drew on his knowledge and experience of Italian city-states in his own day, sometimes with remarkable perception. But, taking the work as a whole and bearing in mind Marsiglio's later writings in which he explicitly referred back to the arguments of *The Defender*, it is clear that all this was supposed also to be applicable to larger states, whether kingdoms or the Empire (which nominally included the

'Italian kingdom' with its city-states). Marsiglio repeatedly referred to John XXII's attacks on Ludwig, to whom the work was dedicated, and to the conflict between Boniface and Philip IV (e.g. pp. 335–6). He believed that the papacy was intent on subduing or destroying the Empire, and he wanted to warn all other rulers that they would suffer a similar fate: the doctrines used against Ludwig would be turned upon them (I. 19.8–13, esp. p. 109; cf. pp. 3, 113, 338, 398, 403). He was fully aware of the way the papacy was prolonging the imperial vacancy by refusing to crown Ludwig, as a means of inserting its own power into the vacuum (pp. 398, 406, 494; cf. pp. 107, 114).

But there is no need to see a conflict between Marsiglio's desire to restore order to Italian city-state politics and his devotion to the Empire, or indeed his concern for the stability of the civil power in Christendom generally. For all of these purposes it was necessary to demonstrate where the basis of legitimacy lay and to refute the claims of the clergy. This required a restatement of what the state is and how it is constructed. Papal intervention had been a significant factor in Italian civic politics for some two centuries; Matteo Visconti and other Italian rulers had already, like Ludwig, suffered the embarrassment of excommunication and deposition by the pope. There was a yet more direct link between the Empire and Italian *signori*: Henry of Luxemburg and Ludwig appointed local rulers as 'imperial vicars'. By this means the lord acquired a legitimate title for himself and his heirs, and the emperor secured their allegiance. Marsiglio ascribed ultimate authority to 'the association of citizens or the people', and definitely implied that on occasion they wield this authority in person. To square this with the current situation in the Empire and in kingdoms, and even in many Italian states, where Marsiglio obviously assumes that no less legitimate an authority is embodied in the present rulers, one has to forget Rousseau and keep in mind the medieval notion of representation as equally valid when it is tacit or has been expressed in the distant past (see below, pp. 123–6).[8]

Marsiglio's method of argument and style of writing are both

---

[8] Quillet, *Philosophie*, pp. 11–19 and ch. 3 states the position well; see *DP*, ed. C. W. Prévité-Orton (Cambridge, Cambridge University Press, 1928), pp. 409, 415, 417 notes. Michael Wilks 'Corporation and Representation in the *Defensor Pacis*', in *Studia Gratiana* 15 (1972), pp. 251–92, puts the case for an 'imperial' interpretation, arguing that 'the people' sometimes refers to the princes of the empire. Nicolai Rubinstein, 'Marsilius of Padua and Italian Political Thought of his Time', in *Europe in the Later Middle Ages*, ed. J. R. Hale, J. R. L. Highfield and B. Smalley (London: 1965), pp. 44–75 and Quentin Skinner, *Foundations*, vol. I, pp. 57–65, argue that it should be read as an anti-oligarchical, pro-communal-democratic statement in the context of the Italian cities.

remarkable. More than anyone, he was inspired by reading Aristotle to think his own thoughts. Like Aristotle, he argued from what human beings are like to the fact that they have certain needs which can only be met in a certain kind of community. But his analysis of human nature is both more all-embracing and more abstract than Aristotle's. First, he does not differentiate between free-born citizens on the one hand and barbarians and slaves on the other as having different levels of social and political potentiality. Rather, he draws a distinction between humans in general and those 'corrupted by nature, habit or perverse affection'; since this distinction is used to argue for majority voting and his whole argument rests on the scientific–naturalistic supposition that 'nature does not in most cases fail', it is clear that only a fairly small minority, not predetermined by race or class, falls into the latter category.

Marsiglio's argument is more abstract than Aristotle's in the sense that he regarded *all* states, not only city-states, as examples of the kind of polity to which humans are driven by their natural needs and tendencies; above all, he laid down a particular derivation of power and constitutional model as applicable to all states, indeed as the exclusive basis of legitimate authority generally. Aristotle did not argue that any particular constitution alone was legitimate, nor that all legitimate power had to originate in a particular way (even though Marsiglio did cite an argument of Aristotle's that collective decisions are usually better than those taken by small groups or individuals as if it supported his own case).

Here Marsiglio was a profound innovator. For he held that, by means of syllogisms resting upon self-evident propositions, one could arrive at a definition of constitutional rectitude valid for all peoples and all times, and indeed for the church itself, since it proceeded from human nature. It was, none the less, a definition which may at first sight appear more specific than it really was, due to Marsiglio's use of tacit representation. It could be squared with a great many different actual forms of political authority. Perhaps the only thing it ruled out was what Marsiglio was most concerned to rule out, namely the exercise of coercive jurisdiction by anyone other than the duly constituted government, in particular by the clergy. Marsiglio's originality lay in marshalling so much moral and philosophical force behind civil authority, correctly held. His mode of argument came to dominate European political thought, as we see in Hobbes, Locke and Rousseau. Further, while Marsiglio did not present his argument in the form of a systematic examination of empirical facts, he claimed that his whole case rested upon self-evident truths about human nature and was supported by *inductio sensata*. He argued from experience and *inductio*, for example, when discussing elective and hereditary monarchy (I. 16, esp. pp. 77–9); and he frequently appealed to the manifest experience of papal intervention in politics (e.g. pp. 42, 339).

Marsiglio appealed to Aristotle as an authority when establishing the basis for legitimate coercive jurisdiction (*DP Dictio* I), and to Scripture when refuting clerical–papal claims (*DP Dictio* II). Indeed the whole work is rather like a Gothic cathedral of which the choir and nave are in different styles. But, while he shows the utmost respect for philosophers in general and Aristotle in particular (e.g. pp. 12, 41), his views are developed in the first instance not by what others have said but, as he puts it, 'by certain ways discovered through human ingenuity' (p. 6). Marsiglio's theory owed as much to the civic experiences of northern and central Italy and the corporate political culture of Latin Europe as to any intellectual precursor. But it was essentially new.

His style is like that of no other medieval Latin writer. He wrote with *gravitas* in rather complex Latin, avoiding obvious or familiar words. The way he anticipates possible misconceptions and is very precise about to whom a certain power or characteristic is to be ascribed, gives his work at times the feel of a constitutional document (e.g. p. 24). He presents great rolling phrases of minute exactitude in which every word is calculated. It reads like the slow march of an inexorable force.

Marsiglio's clinical detachment when referring to Christian beliefs in *DP Dictio* I emphasises the distinction between philosophy and theology; it may also suggest a certain scepticism towards the totality of prevailing religious beliefs. His medical background and practice come out in his treatment of papalism as a 'disease' (pp. 3–4) and of the state as a living organism (pp. 8, 69–70). He compared priests to doctors in that their prescriptions are non coercive; indeed 'Christ in and during his life on earth called himself a doctor, not a ruler or judge' (p. 187; cf. pp. 169, 177, 203).

Marsiglio starts by clearly stating his aim (I. 1). He defines 'kingdom' as 'moderate monarchy' (*monarchia temperata*) either in a single city or in a state composed of several cities (I. 2). In order to determine 'what the state (*civitas*) is in itself and what it exists for', he considers 'the origin of civil association' in, first, the expansion of nuclear families into villages. In the nuclear family the 'elder' can dispense justice at his own discretion, pardoning homicide, for example. In the village, he must rule 'by the common dictate of reason' in accordance with social norms; injuries must be punished to avoid 'war and the splitting-up of the villagers'. As the population increases, new villages arise and human skills and crafts are developed: 'the necessities of life and of the good life were all provided for by the reason and experience of humans; and then the perfect community called the *civitas* was instituted, with distinctions between its parts' (I. 3). The aim was that 'those living in a state (*viventes civiliter*) should not only live, as beasts and slaves do, but live well, with leisure for the liberal tasks pertaining to the virtues of the practical and speculative soul'. The pursuits of justice and philosophy are 'liberal' in the sense that they do not arise strictly from material needs.

Marsiglio now establishes as his first premise:

> the beginning (*principium*) of all that is to be proved, which is by nature spontaneously held, believed and agreed upon by all: namely, that all humans, not deprived or otherwise impeded, desire by nature the sufficient life.

The same is true for animals 'as anyone can plainly see by induction from sense experience (*inductione sensata*)'. The good life for humans is two-fold: one aspect is 'temporal or worldly', the other 'is habitually called eternal or celestial'. It is concerning the former that 'the glorious philosophers' have acquired virtually complete understanding and proof. Marsiglio gives two particular reasons why political society is absolutely essential to a satisfactory human life. Because humans are 'born naked and unarmed', we require a diversity of crafts that can only be found in a relatively large community. But also – a point not made by Aristotle – because humans are 'made up of contrary elements', 'among men thus brought together there arise arguments and quarrels which, if unregulated by a norm of justice, would cause wars, the splitting-up of people and thus finally the rupture of the state'. There must, therefore, be 'a rule and a guardian or maker of just acts' (i.e. a judicial system), some means of repelling injury from within and without (a police force and army), and a treasury to finance common needs and the repair and maintenance of common property. We also need 'teachers' (*doctores*) to cater for the needs of the future life (I. 4).

Marsiglio turns next to the 'parts' or 'offices' of the state which, following Aristotle, are identified as agriculture, manufacture, the military, finance, priesthood and 'the judicial or counselling' part (I. 5). The 'causes' of the offices are, first, the 'minds and wills' of individual men; nature produces men with inclinations for the different skills required for a sufficient life. The 'efficient cause', which

actually determines which individuals should engage in which callings, is generally speaking the 'human legislator' (I. 7). Marsiglio
looks in greater detail at the priesthood (I. 6) and the judiciary or
'ruling part' (*pars principans*) (I. 8–9). The aim of the priesthood is 'the
disposition of human acts, immanent and transitive, as demanded by
knowledge and desire, so that by these the human species may be
directed towards the best life in the world to come' (p. 21). We need
'teachers of the [evangelical] law and administrators of the sacraments
in accordance with that law' to counsel us about what to do and avoid
in order to obtain happiness hereafter (p. 24). Although Marsiglio is
usually concerned to distinguish sharply between earthly and
heavenly welfare, occasionally he suggests that the same factor may
affect both. Thus worshipping God also promotes 'welfare in the
present life' (pp. 13–14); the truth that he, Marsiglio, will teach, 'leads
to safety in civil life and no small benefit in the eternal' (p. 4; cf.
p. 501); and the priestly office, in so far as it means teaching divine
law, requires a knowledge of all the skills discovered by mankind,
most of which can be had from 'the wonderful [Aristotle] and other
glorious men' (pp. 24–5). This suggests that Marsiglio had some idea
of religion in the ancient-Roman sense (like Machiavelli later).

The ruling part (government, or prince) derives ultimately, like all
the other parts and 'especially the priesthood', from the divine will
acting 'through human minds, to whom he has granted the determination (*arbitrium*) of the institution' of the ruling part. But it is the
ruling or principal part in the further sense that it derives authority
(from, as we shall see, the human legislator) to institute all the other
five parts. Aristotle regarded the priests as one of the six parts of the
state, but it was Marsiglio's idea that the judicial or ruling element sets
up all the other parts and determines their personnel. All this partly
reflected widespread practice in medieval cities, where important
aspects of civic life and administration were conducted through
craft-guilds, but it also clearly formed an opportune basis from which
to argue for the subordination of the clergy to the secular ruler.

Since the ruling part's function is 'to regulate human civil acts', its
'cause' may be identified as a rule (*regula*) which, whether statute or
custom, is called law. Law may be defined (I. 10) 'in itself' as that
which tells us what is 'just or unjust, useful or hurtful'; or alternatively as a 'coercive command' indicating what acts will be
punished and rewarded in the present life: the latter is 'the most
proper meaning' (p. 38). Here as elsewhere (e.g. I. 3), Marsiglio
stressed the distinction between precept and coercion, in accordance
with his intention of demonstrating that the role of the clergy is to

counsel but not to command or coerce. Yet Marsiglio acknowledged the importance of non-coercive rules; and unjust rules lack an essential element of law. The passage is important.

Hence not all cognitions of just and useful civil [acts] are laws, unless a coercive command has been given that they should be observed, or they have been passed in the form of a command, even though such true cognition is required for a perfect law. Sometimes indeed false cognitions of just and useful civil [acts] are made [and] a command is given that they be observed . . . as we find in the countries of some barbarians, who make it be observed as just that someone who commits homicide should be absolved from guilt and civil punishment upon payment of a certain price . . . hence their laws are not altogether perfect. For although they have the requisite form as commands compelling observance, they lack the requisite condition as proper and true orderings of just [acts]. Under this meaning of law are included all rules concerning just and useful civil [acts] that are instituted by human authority, such as customs, statutes, popular decrees (*plebiscita*), decretals and all similar things. (p. 39)

Laws are an essential part of the polity both because they embody 'civil justice and common welfare' and because they ensure the stability of, especially, a hereditary ruler (I. 11). For both reasons princes must rule according to the law which 'is and ought to be the formative element (*forma*) of the principate' (pp. 37, 45–7).

What, then, brings laws themselves into being? 'The legislator or first and proper effective cause of law [is] the people or association of citizens or its weightier part (*populum seu civium universitatem, aut eius valentiorem partem*)' (p. 49). In supporting this proposition (I. 12–13) against all the arguments in favour of government by one or a few wise, Marsiglio takes us back to the 'self-evident' propositions that 'all men seek the sufficient life and shun its opposite', that 'nature is not found wanting in most cases' to which he adds that 'no-one knowingly harms himself' (pp. 55, 51, 53). It follows that the common good will be what most people desire: legislation by the people or their weightier part will, therefore, have good results, whereas legislation by one or a few may well not be for the common good (p. 53). This argument is striking for its identification of the common good as the sum of individual interests.

Next, the majority are not only better intentioned, they are also wiser and more judicious than any partial group, even of the wise. For many persons of lesser intelligence can make a better judgement than a few of greater intelligence due to the cumulative factor of numbers (p. 57; based on Aristotle, *Politics* III. 11). The majority may or may not be wise or expert themselves, but they can recognise wisdom in others and in the proposals put by others; they can therefore use the advice of better-informed persons and they can make sensible judgements about legislative proposals brought before them by panels of experts (pp. 57–9). Besides, 'every whole is greater than its part' (pp. 51, 56). Laws which all have made will be better observed because 'each one seems to have imposed it on himself'; such citizens are free because not under the legislative dominion of others (p. 52). Individuals may err, and everyone may err – in will or understanding – sometimes, but

the majority of citizens are neither ill-disposed nor lacking in judgement with regard to the majority of topics and most of the time. For all or most are of sound mind and reason and have the right desire for polity and for those things that are necessary for its conservation, such as laws, statutes and customs, as has already been demonstrated. For although neither every individual nor the great multitude of citizens is a discoverer of laws, nevertheless every individual can judge concerning what has been discovered and proposed to him by someone else, and discern what should be added, taken away or changed. (I. 13.3, p. 56)

The people or association of citizens or their weightier part also have the authority to elect the ruling part (I. 14); Marsiglio thought that kings and princes generally, including the emperor, derived their authority from this source (see below). It is, consequently, the people who have the ultimate authority to 'institute the other parts of the state', including the clergy (p. 61). And they have the task of correcting and deposing a ruler (I. 15; cf. p. 18). After discussing the advantages and disadvantages of elective and hereditary government (I. 16) with more specific reference to the Empire (p. 77), where the question was as live an issue as in many Italian states, Marsiglio expressed the need for any city or kingdom to be 'unified in number', not necessarily through one-man rule but through having, whether in a monarchy, aristocracy or democratic 'polity', a single chain of offices, law-courts and administrative officials (I. 17). Otherwise, 'among the citizens [there will be] faction and opposition, war and splitting-up, and finally corruption of the city' (p. 92). Although he postponed the question of world government (p. 94), Marsiglio illustrated the character of civil unity, resting as it does on people's willing submission to one government, by the manner in which 'Rome and Mainz and other cities are numerically one kingdom or empire' (p. 95), thus clearly implying that the empire in its present form was legitimate.

The weight of Marsiglio's reasoning in *Distinctio* I bore precisely on the point that was central to medieval controversy and discourse:

DATE: 05/11/1998 TIME: 12:46
TILL: 0018   NO: 18186573
CASHIER: Lisa G

DESCRIPTION	QTY	AMOUNT
Barcode: 9780521386098		
POLITICAL TH;BLACK,	1	11.95 A
TOTAL	1	£11.95
CREDIT/DEBIT CARD		£11.95

VAT A @ 0.00% (£11.95): £0.00

the ultimate source of legitimate authority. By narrowing this question down to coercive authority, Marsiglio was able to construct a sequence of reasoning which at every stage excluded any opportunity for justifying the independent authority of any group such as the clergy. Authority in the state cannot be claimed on the basis of wisdom or superior knowledge of the purpose of earthly life; a ruler cannot legitimately be judged or deposed by special persons or groups in the name of abstract justice, since the human legislator has a unique entitlement to do just that. Marsiglio in effect constructed two lines of argument from human nature. One leads, as it also did in Aristotle, Aquinas and the papalist James of Viterbo, from nature to the sufficient life for humans and thence to the civil association (state). The other leads from human nature to the human legislator (the community as a whole) and thence to law, the government, the other five 'offices' of the state, and the judicial and administrative structures. Here both the chain of command and the derivation of legitimacy are strictly unitary. This second line of argument, which is not found in Aristotle or anywhere else, derives from those elements in human nature which make us prone to conflict. What we have is something like the idea of the modern state.

Distinctio II builds on the conclusion that coercive and legislative authority can only belong to the people or those to whom they assign it (p. 104). The Roman bishop and clergy generally

> have not, and ought not to have, any real or personal jurisdiction whatever over any bishop or priest ... [nor do they] collectively or individually hold such jurisdiction over any prince or principate, over any civil community, college or person of whatever status. (pp. 113–14)

Marsiglio proceeded to refute supposedly scriptural arguments that pope and clergy could wield powers of jurisdiction with legal penalties either over lay persons or over the clergy themselves (II. 3–4). Contravention of divine law (i.e. sin), while it may be confessed to a priest, is actually remedied by the offender's contrition and remitted without priestly mediation by God himself. This removed much of the *raison d'être* of ecclesiastical authority. But Marsiglio now went onto the offensive by applying in the church virtually the same criteria for legitimate power as in the state. 'The church' is most properly defined as 'the association of faithful believers' (p. 117), and, as in the secular sphere, it is they, acting as a body, who hold or entitle others to hold all powers pertaining to ecclesiastical order.

As in the civil sphere, this association of all may empower others to act on their behalf, notably the secular power itself now doubling in the role of 'faithful human legislator with no superior', or, especially in matters involving the whole church, a general council. First, in local matters falling within the jurisdiction of a single state, the faithful human legislator is the local civil government. Second, the whole association of the faithful (*universitas fidelium*) worldwide, or a general council representing it, may establish a universal faithful human legislator to act on its behalf in matters of public ecclesiastical law and administration – namely, the emperor. Marsiglio speaks of the emperor as the legitimate representative, and therefore in terms of legal and political authority the equivalent, of the human legislator or association of citizens, and, in the ecclesiastical sphere, of the 'faithful human legislator' or universal body of believers. Thus in all matters requiring public action, legal penalties or rewards, property, appointments to church offices, action is to be undertaken not by the clergy themselves, but by whomever the church as a whole has empowered (p. 170). Marsiglio here refers us back to *Distinctio* I. 15, and presumably meant to justify this by arguments similar to those used to justify the *civil* jurisdiction of the community as a whole.

As for the clergy's role, Marsiglio's answer is quite clear: it is, first, to advise and teach people about what they ought to do or shun in order to attain eternal beatitude. The penalties and rewards attached to divine law are mainly enforced by God himself alone (p. 186). In so far as the divine law requires penalties or rewards on earth, these, since they affect people's public status and lives, cannot be meted out by anyone other than those entitled to jurisdiction – the association of the faithful citizens. Excommunication, involving as it does, in a society where all are believers, deprivation of membership of the political community (*civilis communio*), can only be legitimately imposed by the association of the faithful, or by a judge set up by them or their weightier part, with coercive power to expel people from the community (p. 170). Similarly,

judgement of heretics, schismatics or of any unfaithful whomsoever, and the power of constraining them and exacting from them a penalty or temporal sanction, belong to the prince alone on the authority of the human legislator (*potestas solius principantis auctoritate legislatoris humani*). (p. 202)

In non-ecclesiastical matters, the clergy 'are themselves subject to ... the jurisdiction of the judges who have the coercive power to punish transgressors of human law'. Marsiglio's anticlericalism comes out in this proposed discrimination against criminous clerks: they ought to have known better, and should therefore be punished more severely than ordinary citizens; 'the priest sins more gravely, and should therefore be punished more fully' (p. 182). Those who (like Ludwig's opponents) claim jurisdiction for unauthorised persons and issue decretals as if they had the force of law, are guilty of conspiracy, political schism, and treason – the ultimate crime 'because it is committed against the principate, even the supreme principate [sc. the emperor], with a view to dividing it and so leading inevitably to the dissolution of every polity'. They should be punished by death (p. 469).

The clergy's other function is to administer the sacraments; they are empowered to do this by their divine vocation but they are entitled to do so in a particular place only by those who have authority to allocate the offices of the state, namely the human legislator or, by delegation, the ruling part. It is, therefore, for these to 'institute' the clergy (p. 263).

The immediate effective cause (*causa factiva*) is or ought to be the entire multitude of the faithful in that place through its express choice or will, or he or they to whom the said multitude has granted authority over such acts of institution; it pertains to the same authority legitimately to remove any said official from such offices ... In communities of the faithful that are now perfected, it pertains solely to the human legislator or multitude of the faithful of that place, over which the minister to be promoted shall have responsibility, to elect, determine and present persons to be promoted to church orders. (II. 17.8–9; pp. 293–5; cf. pp. 337–8)

In this passage, quasi-legal and constitutional in its precision and exclusiveness, it could not be made much clearer that benefices are in the hands of the civil community or civil ruler, who may remove as well as appoint. Distribution of church property for the support of 'evangelical ministers and other needy persons' (*personas miserabiles*) also lies in the hands of the legislator (p. 301). Education and the conferring of degrees should be under the control of the secular authority (p. 341). The conclusion to the whole work is that every single aspect of legal and political authority and of coercive jurisdiction belongs exclusively to those to whom it was assigned in *Dictio* I. 12–13, that is, to the association of citizens or its weightier part (*Dictio* II. 30.8).

Marsiglio's work of demolition is not quite complete. Having thus defined the role of the clergy, he goes on to argue that Christ made no distinction in status or power between different ranks of clergy, all of whom have, from their sacramental ordination, the same capacity to perform the Eucharist and hear confessions. Later some were made bishops or pope purely on human authority and for administrative convenience. Therefore the highest authority even within the non-coercive, teaching and preaching sphere is the general council; its primary functions being to determine disputes about the meaning of scripture and to enact rules for ecclesiastical observance (p. 310). The derivation of the council's authority follows the same pattern as that of government in general, and of ruler or emperor in ecclesiastical legislation proper: it comes from the community at large. Thus Marsiglio's general council is allied, as in the policies of Philip IV and Ludwig, to state authority. This was justifiable on the grounds that both council and emperor derive their authority from the association of faithful; Marsiglio found precedents in the ecumenical councils of the late Roman and Byzantine church. The resolution of theological disputes belongs 'only to the general council of all the faithful, or of those who have the authority of all the faithful' (p. 310). In Marsiglio's ecclesiastical polity, the general council plays a role similar to that of the citizens' association in the state: it alone may interpret or dispense from its own decrees; the Roman and other bishops derive their powers from it. His purpose is, once again, to exclude the pope and clergy from any decisive say.

The general council is the ultimate *church* authority; its powers, though supreme over anyone else's in interpreting divine law, are not coercive. Rather, it is 'the authority of the faithful human legislator with no superior' which turns decisions of a council into coercive commands, and may enforce excommunication or deprivation of office against those who dissent. The council is convoked 'only on the authority of the human legislator with no superior, or of him or those to whom such power has been committed by the said legislator' (p. 327). The human legislator determines the composition of the council and ensures that those summoned attend until business is completed. This human legislator could of course be the association of faithful citizens; but the added phrase 'with no superior' suggests that Marsiglio here had in mind secular monarchs, such as the king of France and the German king-emperor, acting to be sure on an authority conferred upon them by the believing people at large.

Marsiglio finally concludes:

A subject people and any individual member thereof can learn from this book what kind of ruler or rulers it is right to establish ... If these things are understood, kept in mind and diligently observed ... a kingdom and any other temperate civil community will be preserved in a peaceful state ...; by these means those who live in a state (*viventes civiliter*) will acquire sufficiencies for life on earth, but without this they will be deprived thereof, and they will also be poorly disposed for eternal blessedness. (pp. 500–1)

In theory Marsiglio conferred ecclesiastical authority on the association of the faithful; but in practice, and increasingly in the way he
uses his own terminology, he seems to be conferring key powers
upon the secular prince, and especially the emperor. When he said
that 'the human legislator or the prince acting on its authority' can
determine the way popes are elected (p. 331), this was a nice inversion
of John XXII's attempts to manipulate the imperial succession. Marsiglio intended to provide the intellectual means by which Ludwig
could overcome John XXII.

The means he provided would have led to a complete change in the
church–state relationship in Europe. Many of his ideas were indeed to
prove attractive later, for example to Thomas Cromwell, architect of
the Henrician Reformation in England.[9] Marsiglio's ecclesiastical
views, with the exclusion of priests from all avenues of political
power and so much ecclesiastical power given to the prince, suggest
again that what we have here is the prototype for a new kind of state.
Marsiglio used the derivation of public power from the people as the
principal argument for disallowing any form of clerical jurisdiction,
and for imposing princely–popular jurisdiction on the clergy. It was a
very unusual argument in his day; it should not be taken either as a
'logical conclusion' to Aristotelian thought (which could equally well
be aristocratic) or as typical of an 'ascending' theory of power (there
being plenty of advocates of 'ascending' power, in both state and
church, who did not share Marsiglio's anticlericalism).

What Marsiglio said of the Empire was meant to be equally
applicable to the Italian communes, in whose milieu his theory was
born (see below, pp. 123–6). The church–state controversy had
provoked the question of who should hold any kind of power, and
on whose authority anybody rules. Constitutional questions were
becoming philosophical ones, thus making possible much greater
departures from current norms. And Marsiglio's was one of the most
original of such theories. His response to theocracy was a self-
determining state based on the formal sovereignty of the people.

OCKHAM

William of Ockham (Occam, in Surrey, England: *c.* 1280–1349),
probably the most difficult medieval theorist, started out at Oxford
as a logician and philosopher concerned with the philosophy of

[9] G. R. Elton, 'The Political Creed of Thomas Cromwell', *Transactions of the Royal
Historical Society*, 5th series, 6 (1956), pp. 69–92. *DP* was translated into English
c. 1535 (*CHMPT* p. 422n.). Marsiglio's *Lesser Defender* was written to prove that

knowledge, the qualities of mental concepts and language, and the relations between universals ('man') and particulars (Peter, Ahmed, Chou, Miroslav). He concluded that universal concepts are mere 'names', 'vocal breaths' (*flatus vocis*), referring to nothing except every particular member of a category, whence 'Ockham's razor': 'entia non sunt multiplicanda praeter necessitatem [roughly: there should be a minimal use of abstractions]'. This led him to question the worth of some philosophical concepts which had entered the vocabulary of scholastic theology, and pope John XXII summoned him to Avignon on a charge of suspected heresy (1324–8). Yet Ockham's 'nominalism' did not lead him to doubt or disbelief. Rather, his passionate commitment to Christianity was expressed in his Franciscan vocation and, within the Franciscan movement, his dedication to the cause of absolute, 'apostolic' poverty (which had been formally condemned by pope John XXII in 1323). In 1328 Ockham and his friend Michael of Cesena, minister-general of the Franciscans and also an adherent of total poverty, anticipating their own condemnation by John, took refuge at the court of Ludwig in Munich. From then on Ockham devoted his immense intellectual energy and acumen to the defence of apostolic poverty, Ludwig's cause and the independence of the Empire against the Avignon papacy. Ockham's works on ecclesiastical and political authority mostly date from the late 1330s and early 1340s, the time when Ludwig and his supporters were negotiating most vigorously for a constitutional settlement in Germany. His most systematic work, the unfinished *Dialogue*, was written *c*. 1334–42 (McGrade, *Ockham*, pp. 17–22). Ockham became involved in the question of church–state relations partly because he loathed the Avignon doctrine of papal temporal power but also because of his own personal religious predicament: what he believed to be the scriptural, true and essential doctrine of apostolic poverty, the implications of which ran counter to the attitudes of the vast majority of churchmen, was condemned by the pope but upheld by the emperor. This forced Ockham to reconsider and re-evaluate the extent and the very nature of the authority of pope and clergy, on the one hand, and emperor and lay powers, on the other.

Ockham's views are often obscure and difficult to identify because of his tireless exploration of every possible theoretical position. There has been much controversy about the connection, if any, between

marriage and divorce were within the legal competence of the lay prince; cf. *DP* III.2.19. Cf. H. Stout, 'Marsiglio of Padua and the Henrician Reformation', *Church History* 43 (1974), pp. 308ff.

Ockham's theory of knowledge and his political ideas.[10] He insisted that there was a clear distinction in principle between spiritual and temporal spheres and authorities, between the prescribed, 'regular' functions of pope and clergy, on the one hand, and those of emperor and other lay rulers, on the other. And he was clear about the distinctive origin and source of secular political authority. Here, rather than following the neo-Aristotelian view, he said that after the Fall God had given humans two powers, to set up rulers and to appropriate individual property, thus linking this question to the poverty dispute. Therefore both these powers belonged to human beings as such, regardless of whether they were Christians or not (*Tyrannical Rule (Breviloquium de principatu tyrannico)* III. 13, p. 113; *Imperial and Papal Power (De imperatorum et pontificum potestate)* c. 11: *MPI* pp. 606–15 at p. 610).

Furthermore, all rulers derive their power from 'their people' (*Dialogue (Dialogus)* I. 6.8, p. 514). All legitimate political authority, the principal purpose of which is 'to correct and punish wrongdoers', rests upon voluntary consent. Humans can, of their own intelligence and for their own purposes, construct autonomous systems of right and their own laws. There is perhaps a parallel here with *homo faber* (man the maker–craftsman) in Renaissance thought. The state or city (*civitas*) is the focus of a human environment that may vary from place to place.

All mortals hold from God and from nature the right of freely giving themselves a head, for they are born free and not subjected to anyone by human law; whence every city and every people can establish law for itself. (*Breviloquium* in *MPI*, p. 161)

It was, therefore, also perfectly legitimate for all peoples to subject themselves voluntarily to the Roman Empire.[11]

Ockham linked this to man's intrinsic liberty which we derive from God, first as our natural condition, then again as part of the Gospel's 'law of liberty'. It was in the very nature of proper political authority to be exercised over free persons, and there was a world of difference between this and the 'despotic' authority of master over slave. Proper political authority is 'ministerial' that is, it serves the public utility and the interests of the governed and not the private interests of the ruler, precisely because free persons could not

---

[10] McGrade, *Ockham*, pp. 28–43; Brian Tierney, *Origins of Papal Infallibility 1150–1350* (Leiden: E. J. Brill, 1972), pp. 206–10.

[11] For this and much of what follows, see especially McGrade, *Ockham*.

rationally (as we would put it) submit to any other kind of authority (*Imperial and Papal Power c.* 7, 13: *MPI* pp. 609, 613).

The related point upon which Ockham insisted time and again was that pope and clergy as such have no claims over either temporal possessions or temporal jurisdiction. And, as in the poverty dispute, his clearest argument comes from the New Testament: Christ and the apostles did not have, and refused to have, any civil jurisdiction or political power: 'no-one fighting for God entangles himself in secular business' (2 Tim. 2:4). Christ and the apostles showed by their own clear examples that they recognised the authority of secular rulers and specifically the emperor over themselves; and Christ would not wish his stand-in (vicar), the pope, to have more power than himself. If pope and clergy possess temporal goods, and whenever they exercise temporal jurisdiction, they do so like anyone else by the gift of the people, and emphatically not 'by Christ's ordination'. Such 'customs' can be revoked by the people or the emperor, depending on who sanctioned them in the first place (*Dialogue* I. 6.8, p. 514 and III/ii. 3.22, p. 954). Ockham, like Marsiglio, equated temporal with coercive jurisdiction, so that his argument here denied the papal and clerical claim that ecclesiastical sentences, such as excommunication, could have any legal force without the sanction of the secular authorities.

In principle, the pope is superior to the emperor in church matters, and the emperor to the pope in temporal matters: the pope can judge an emperor for heresy, and the emperor can judge a pope for murder. Moreover, at the very end of the *Dialogue*, the 'master', probably expressing Ockham's own opinion, argues that, since the pope is subject to the emperor in coercive jurisdiction, and since two supreme judges in the one society of the faithful would give rise to endless quarrels and wars, there must be but one supreme judge – and that must be the emperor:

That supreme judge is not the pope; the pope cannot hold such a position. Therefore the pope must be judged by that supreme judge, which is the emperor, who by right is the ruler and lord of the whole world ... Therefore the emperor is to judge the pope for every kind of crime. (*Dialogue* III/ii.3.17, pp. 947–8).

This may only have been meant as a tentative conclusion; but it seems to be as close as Ockham ever came to a clearcut statement of the constitutional relationship between pope and emperor.

Even if this did express Ockham's settled opinion, such a statement was for Ockham only preliminary and provisional. For all that has been established so far is that the pope is superior in religious matters, and the emperor in secular matters, 'regularly'. What may be done 'in certain instances' (*casualiter*: occasionally) is, for Ockham, quite another matter. *Casualiter*, that is, if the pope is in error (as in the poverty dispute), the emperor may summon a general council to judge him on a spiritual issue; and if the council decides erroneously, then doctrinal and moral authority devolves upon others – Ockham's own experience of church authority may again have pointed the way here. And it is not just the emperor and princes who supplement the failings in papal rectitude but *any believing Christian*, even a woman or baby, who in fact upholds the truth as revealed by Scripture and reason. Ockham relied here upon the example of Mary at the Crucifixion. Church authority devolves upon the laity as such; they, as much as the clergy, are Christians.[12]

And *casualiter* pope and clergy have an exactly parallel right and duty to intervene in temporal matters when necessary, for example when injustice has been done and not rectified, due to the ineffectiveness or negligence of the competent secular judge. If it is necessary to 'supplement justice', the pope may act in any matter even affecting laymen and secular affairs. This principle of subsidiarity runs right through Ockham's proposed solutions to constitutional questions of all kinds (*Dialogue* iii/ii.2.11, p. 913 and iii/ii.3.22, pp. 954–6; *Imperial and Papal Power* c. 10: *MPI* p. 611).

Constitutional rights and functions within the society of the faithful are thus extremely complicated. It would not take a legal expert to see that, on Ockham's terms, appeals could be made from any church court to its civil counterpart and vice versa, and that the process could be unending; and it might not take a constitutional expert to see that neither church nor state has a constitution which can be relied upon to work. The stark fact is that Ockham threw the whole liability for judgement and political decision-making back onto the individual conscience.

He is not unaware of the dilemmas he has thus created. For he goes on to ask who determines when 'regular' has to be replaced by 'occasional' authority. And it is here that the sting comes. Such occasions arise – whenever they arise: that is, whenever pope, council, etc. err, or whenever emperor, princes, etc. fail to remedy injustice, then public utility and evident need require supplementary authorities to act.

How do we know when the pope is in error or when justice has

[12] Tierney, *Origins*, pp. 230, 233; McGrade, *Ockham*, pp. 48–74; Jürgen Miethke, *Ockhams Weg zur Sozialphilosophie* (Berlin: Gruyter, 1969), pp. 538ff., esp. p. 546n.

not been done by secular rulers? We know in the same way that we know anything: by true faith in theological matters, by educated judgement or 'wisdom' in temporal matters. And who possesses these qualities? Whoever possesses them. *Casualiter*, in cases of faith, it may be any group of faithful, like the Franciscan minority, or a single Christian, male, female or baby. *Casualiter* in cases of temporal justice and public welfare, it may be no constituted authority but 'the wisest men, most sincerely zealous for justice, without any exception of persons [i.e. considerations of office or rank], whether subjects or rulers, whether poor or rich, if they can be found'. Papal misdemeanours may be judged by 'learned men', and indeed by 'any individual' (*Imperial and Papal Power* c. 13, 15–16: *MPI* pp. 613–15). Ockham's point seems to be that right and wrong will be obvious to any sincere and well-intentioned person; but we cannot predict who, of whatever status, is going to be right in a particular case. He himself as usual stated the dire conclusion: 'perhaps it is impossible to give a fixed general rule for these special cases'.

It is interesting that, while in the last resort ecclesiastical authority reverts to any individual believer, secular authority reverts to the wise. This is surely because faith is equally accessible to all, while in mundane matters special qualities, albeit subjective, still count. Thus it is Ockham's ecclesiastical theory which points more in the direction of modern democratic thinking.

We do not know, then, where in any particular case true authority resides. Ockham has turned constitutional questions into epistemological and psychological ones. He has taken the pursuit of truth and justice beyond the point where they can be attained by any legal or political process. The authority of the emperor as much as that of the pope, and of all potentates – although Ockham insisted that all such authority was in principle monarchical – turns out to be riddled with holes. For Ockham, the respective rights and duties of pope, emperor, clergy and princes dissolve into questions about the capabilities of individuals. By pursuing the rationale of the ecclesiastical polity to its uttermost, Ockham seems to have discovered, despite himself, that it could not really be a polity at all, if it were to be true to its own principles of divine truth and human rationality. He was really, though he did not set out to be, an anti-political thinker, an anarchist individualist, a meticulous deconstructor of church and polity.

Ockham's political writings, as one might have expected given his personal predicament, strongly upheld the right to dissent, inner freedom and the right to free expression. As he said in the preface to his last work: 'one evident reason or one authority from Scripture reasonably understood will move me more than the assertion of the whole world of mortal men' (*Imperial and Papal Power*, Preface: *MPI* pp. 606–7).

Despite the difficulties in interpreting Ockham, we find consistent statements as to the ultimate sovereignty of the individual conscience, informed by simple faith and intelligent judgement. Church authority comes from Christ, and secular authority from God via the people, but neither originator intended to set up a power that could act against truth or justice, or override the judgement of right-thinking persons. This dovetails with Ockham's insistence upon 'rights and liberties', corporate and individual, as the atoms of the social and judicial system, which it is the duty of rulers to maintain (see above, p. 40). Some of the problems raised by Ockham would be removed if social institutions did not claim authority on theology or other intellectual matters. But this would not remove the problem of the *moral* fallibility of all institutions and persons.

Ockham's insistence that legitimate political power can be exercised only over free persons, while supported by Aristotle's distinction between political and despotic rule, was inspired above all by the idea of liberty in the New Testament. Authority which robbed people of the spiritual liberty given by Christ could not be legitimate; and an authority which demanded that they believe or behave contrary to Scripture or reason was doing precisely that. In other words, the supremacy of the individual conscience followed from Ockham's interpretation of the New Testament. In him the church–state controversy inspired an original statement of individual rights. None of this should surprise us, coming from an ardent follower of St Francis and a diligent reader of the New Testament; and it would be hard to deny that the spirit of philosophical nominalism was blowing here too.

What we now call being an intellectual seems, in Ockham, to grow out of an uncompromising religious mentality. It is refreshing to find that, when nowadays the connection is so often made between liberty and the right to be wealthy, this first major European exponent of liberty and rights was dedicated to total poverty. Ockham constructed his libertarian argument from a need to defend the absolute poverty of the son of God, and the right of others to follow that example. Not that one should imagine a direct lineage from Ockham to modern liberalism. His political works were read by very few. They provided, none the less, encouragement and arguments for many different types of criticism of papal and clerical authority. But the ethos and tone of Ockham's writings, the spirit of restless questioning until one encountered a bedrock of Scripture or reason, affected the whole climate of later medieval theology, philosophy and university teaching. And these fed into ways of thought that would later issue from the cliffs of time as a torrent of civil liberties.

Looking at this burst of intellectual activity from *c.* 1250 to *c.* 1350 one can conclude that the non-ecclesiastical origin, purpose and legitimacy of secular political authority were now justified and explained by reference to a coherent set of ideas. The dualism of 'flesh' and 'spirit' had definitely been modified to admit of an area that was ethical but not ecclesiastical: there was a legitimate society that was not a church. This is true both of moderates like John of Paris who, in delimiting the spheres of church and state, wished to deny that the latter derived from God via the former; and also of secularists like Marsiglio who moved the boundary much further, denying the clergy any authority to enforce law on their own. The difference between these lay chiefly in their conceptions of what the church was: moderates still held that its purpose was to guide mortals to heaven by teaching and discipline which, to be effective, had to be public and enforceable; kings must permit the clergy and their courts to enforce their decisions by excommunication.

Since no-one thought that jurisdiction came to kings from themselves or their predecessors, advocates of secular independence tended to say that it came from the people. But this was not because they had, as Walter Ullmann and others have repeatedly suggested, read this in Aristotle. Aristotle's remarks in favour of some form of rule by the many (moderate *demokratia* or *politeia*) were scattered, nuanced and guarded; he argued just as strongly in favour of other forms of government. Medieval statements of ultimate popular sovereignty were schematic, abstract and sometimes based on mythical history in the Ciceronian manner. Aristotle may have helped ward off church sovereignty over the state by showing that an alternative philosophy of humanity and state to that propounded by monastic culture, Neoplatonic theology and canon law, was possible. To call Dante or Marsiglio 'Aristotelians' is to underestimate their originality. The uses made of Aristotle even by hierocrats suggest that, just as in a later age people took masonry from ruined abbeys for everyday purposes, so publicists used Aristotle's works as a quarry for the advocacy of many causes.

WYCLIF

During the fourteenth century, the kingdom of England, her government and people alienated from the Avignon papacy by its diplomatic and financial support for the French, was achieving something like *de facto* autonomy in church affairs. After the 1350s, senior church appointments were largely in the hands of the Crown and appeals from English courts were generally disallowed. The last major medieval theorist of church–state relations, John Wyclif (d. 1384), was an eminent Oxford scholastic theologian. In the early 1370s he was employed by the English Crown, under John of Gaunt's influence, to argue the case for royal taxation of the clergy, and for practical limitations upon the papacy's power over the English church and its wealth. Wyclif's theological compendium, begun in the same years, dealt in its early sections extensively with the question of divine and civil authority (*dominium*). Wyclif also began a translation of the Bible into English and promoted 'poor preachers' to carry his evangelical ideas to ordinary people. As the heterodoxy of his views on theological as well as political questions became clear, he fell from royal favour; but, despite his suspected if unintended influence on the Peasants' Revolt of 1381, he was allowed to continue living and writing, voluminously, as a parish priest.

Wyclif held that the only human group that had spiritual significance was the true church, consisting exclusively of those predestined to salvation, 'the community of the just'. It alone had a legitimate claim to spiritual authority. But, since no-one except God knew who these persons were, this group is unrecognisable, and therefore non-institutional. What is commonly called 'the church' – the clergy, bishops and papacy, and the identifiable community of baptised Catholics – is but an institution of human contrivance with no divine sanction.[13] Yet another reason why in its present form such a church cannot be authoritative is that it has, as any study of history clearly shows, changed radically over time and today stands in desperate need of reform. Wyclif reinterpreted sacred history: the church's best period was before Constantine. Since then the clergy had grown in status, power and wealth, especially since the eleventh century when (Wyclif correctly observed) power became increasingly concentrated in the papacy: this was corruption. Yet, according to Wyclif's understanding of Scripture, salvation is in fact available to all true believers quite independently of the clergy and their minist-

[13] Cf. Howard Kaminsky, *A History of the Hussite Revolution* (Berkeley, Calif.: University of California Press, 1967), esp. pp. 25–9.

rations, through faith, the reading of Scripture and personal sanctity. There is, therefore, no need for any group or institution calling itself the church to exercise coercive jurisdiction.

Wyclif too made a connection between authority and property. This was crucial because one of his chief aims, for both political and religious reasons, was to discredit clerical titles to wealth and land-ownership, except as a voluntary recompense for their services granted by lay people and subject to re-possession if abused. This supported the Crown's case in negotiating with the papacy, but Wyclif's arguments went much further than the English authorities required: they justified a wholesale expropriation of church properties on the grounds of abuse and corruption. For, in the first place, all *dominium* – property-ownership and jurisdiction – is given by God on condition of one's being in a state of grace: this is because, Wyclif rather tortuously argued, nature bestowed goods on human beings in common, private property was introduced by God only as a remedy for the sin of Adam, and now Christ has redeemed human beings from sin by his grace. But we have absolutely no means of knowing who is in a state of grace.

In the second place, Wyclif said that the church militant here on earth, being composed of humans, still requires some visible organisation. And, in the absence of any identifiable spiritual community or authority, this is nothing other than the kingdoms and other states which make up ordinary human society throughout Christendom. There is no special divinely ordained religious organisation among Christians, and therefore for practical purposes the public religious affairs of Christians are to be managed by those who are in any case, by clear biblical precept, their legitimate rulers in other matters: the civil authorities. By this theological route Wyclif arrived at a position comparable to Marsiglio's. This would remove much that was distinctive about western Christian civilisation as compared with, say, eastern Christendom or even Islam. The church (*ecclesia*) was equivalent to the polity (*regnum, respublica*); 'the supreme heads of the church militant were the actual secular rulers' (as Kaminsky puts it).[14] Wyclif used the conventional division of society into those who pray, fight and work (except that he put the first last!) to explain how lords, commons and clergy respectively should each fulfil their distinct tasks for the common good; but with the new implication that the military order, headed by the king, was in the driving-seat.

Wyclif applied his rigorous equation of dominion with grace to

[14] *History*, p. 32.

ecclesiastical authorities but not to secular rulers. One argument with which he justified this (which could be traced back to the Anonymous of York, *c.* 1100: *MPI* pp. 562–6 at p. 565) was that priests represent Christ's manhood while kings represent his divinity.

The upshot was that, given our ignorance about who is in a state of grace and therefore about who has an absolutely valid title to property and jurisdiction, dominion in all its forms is under the disposition of the king. Clergy hold their possessions by the will of the ruler; this achieved one immediate purpose of his political works by showing that the clergy could indeed be taxed by the state. But far beyond this, since the clergy had obviously abused their possessions, they should be generally expropriated. Furthermore, since the realm is the church and the king is God's only visible representative on earth, it is the king's duty to carry out that reform of the church which is so pressingly needed. Wyclif looked forward to a *reformatio* as a spiritual renewal for both clergy and laity, for which dispossession of the clergy was a prerequisite.

It is not difficult to see that, in certain basic respects, Wyclif provided a link between Marsiglio and Ockham, on the one hand, and the Protestant Reformation, on the other. His restatement of the nature of religious life, of the sources and means of salvation, was organically connected to a shift in the boundaries between church and state which amounted to pushing the church off the political map altogether. There was a remarkable convergence between the practical conclusions – notably, subjection of clergy to king – reached by Marsiglio and by Wyclif.

It was the writings of Wyclif which provided the intellectual framework for the ecclesiastical and social revolution which took place in Bohemia from the 1390s. Wyclif gave the vital element of theological legitimation and intellectual coherence to the religious reforms initiated by Jan Hus, during the initial stages of which king Wenceslas' support facilitated that 'revolution from above' for which Wyclif had looked in vain in England.[15] In the event, the moderate Hussites established a reformed national church, with Scripture and liturgy in the vernacular and under royal leadership, which survived until after the German Reformation and in some ways resembled the *ecclesia Anglicana* of the sixteenth century.

The extreme Hussites (or Taborites) suggested another path that

---

[15] Michael Wilks, '*Reformatio Regni*: Wyclif and Hus as Leaders of Religious Protest Movements', ed. Derek Baker, *Schism, Heresy and Religious Protest, Studies in Church History*, 9 (Cambridge: Cambridge University Press, 1972), pp. 109–30 at pp. 110, 124–8.

Wycliffite political theology might take: they came to believe that the hitherto unidentifiable church of the elect was at last manifested, in millenniarist fashion, here and now in their own communities and city-states, with mass conversion to evangelical spirituality and redistribution of both wealth and powers of leadership among the elect community. Here the barriers between church and state were down, but this time it was the Taborite priests who assumed the authority of magistrates. Millenniarism was indeed papalism turned on its head; and during the brief life of these regimes a new kind of holy republic was experienced.

TORQUEMADA

Looking at Europe as a whole, it is remarkable how Wyclif ended his life in obscurity at the very time when the 'great schism' between rival popes (1378–1417: below, pp. 170f.) gave kings and rulers a practical choice as to which, if indeed any, pope to recognise as legitimate. For the disputed election of 1378 made it possible and often necessary for people to choose which 'allegiance' to 'adhere' to. And most often it was the secular rulers who set in motion the machinery, such as a national church synod, for taking such a decision, and frequently exercised great influence on the outcome. Again, in the late 1430s and the 1440s many European princes, great and small, including the emperor and the king of France, remained neutral, this time between a pope-dominated council and a council-dominated pope. They were gradually persuaded to restore allegiance to the Roman papacy but only through far-reaching concessions which gave many secular rulers a great deal more say in senior church appointments and more control over ecclesiastical revenue, officially sanctioned in concordats. Such was the confusion of religious authority, jurisdiction and finance threatened by the schisms that for long periods the management of church affairs, notably appointments, judicial proceedings and revenues, was partly nationalised, that is, conducted at a national-territorial level by a combination of princely and clerical authorities. The diplomacy of the schism and the conciliar crisis found popes and bishops of different opinions persuading, cajoling and bribing rulers in order to get them to adopt a given allegiance and even doctrine.

The papacy's changed situation and policy were partially reflected in the writings of Cardinal Juan de Torquemada (Johannes de Turrecremata: 1388–1468), the last significant theorist of the pre-

Reformation papacy. From the 1440s he proposed what he called a 'middle way' between papalist and secularist doctrines of the church–state relationship (*Summary on the Church* (*Summa de ecclesia*) II. 113–115 and *Commentary on the Decretum* (*Commentarium super toto decreto*) d. 96, c. 6 and 10). He stated that the pope 'by right of his sovereignty' (*principatus*) does indeed have 'some jurisdiction in temporal matters in the whole Christian world', but that this is limited to the purposes of 'direction of the faithful towards eternal salvation, the correction of sin and the preservation of peace'. The pope (as John of Paris had once said) is administrator, not lord or proprietor of church property. Torquemada appeared to follow Dante when he said that papal sovereignty is concerned with the supreme felicity which men attain through the theological virtues, while secular 'power' (*potestas*) aims at the political felicity attainable through the moral virtues. But Torquemada added that, since the former is of a higher order, it is the pope's legitimate function 'to direct, regulate, prescribe and give laws to the secular power, by means of which it too may be directed towards eternal felicity'.

All of these apparent concessions to dualism turn out to be largely a form of words (although some have seen here an anticipation of Bellarmine's 'indirect' theory of papal temporal power). For Torquemada proceeded to reclaim for the papacy all the powers which had been contested over the previous two centuries, emphasising, it is true, especially those relating to international affairs and which might be needed to face Islam and Hussitism. In true Roman style, he conceived the papacy as having ultimate responsibility for the historical survival and well-being of Christendom. The pope can depose rulers for negligence and absolve subjects from their oath of allegiance; he can raise taxes from the faithful to defend the faith and prevent invasion; he can deprive apostate rulers of their temporal dominion (this with an eye on Bohemia); he can declare war against infidels, heretics, tyrants, misappropriators of church property and disturbers of the peace; he can exercise temporal powers during an imperial vacancy; and he can inflict both temporal and spiritual punishments on Jews. Thus Torquemada's appeasing preface, made in the spirit of diplomacy, veiled a restatement of Innocent III: the papacy may intervene, it would appear, whenever 'spiritual' interests seem to require it.

The actual church–state relationship in most of Europe from about 1350 till the Reformation was articulated by no theorist. It was alluded to in private by diplomats; one finds traces of it in public documents, as when in the early 1460s pope Pius II, in a plea for peace preparatory to a crusade, confessed that 'in such matters we are not able to coerce so much as to request'.[16] But the ideas of secularists like Marsiglio and Wyclif, while not unrealistic, were far from being implemented and were in fact officially denounced by lay as well as clerical authorities. Theorists were either ahead of or behind events.

[16] Cited by R. Haubst, 'Die Reformentwurf Pius des Zweiten', *Römische Quartalschrift* 49 (1954), ch. 8.

3

EMPIRE AND NATION

This was a period when the distinctive features of the modern
European states system first appeared and began to evolve. At few
times has the very nature of the international order been so contested.[1] In feudal society persons of various ranks acquired authority in
certain matters, such as raising armed fores, judging disputes, making
laws and disposing of vacant properties. A king's domain shrank and
expanded depending on his hold over neighbouring nobles. Beside all
this was the parallel hierarchy of church office-holders. During the
high Middle Ages there were numerous divisions of authority, yet at
the same time strong impulses to concentrate power wherever possible in the interests of law and order and dynastic ambition. Towns
carved out, where possible, their own legal, fiscal and economic
domains. They in turn were sub-divided into craft-guilds and quarters. The village unit often retained some collective rights over
agriculture and minor disputes. The tendency towards a division of
political powers between different levels – Empire and papacy,
kingdom, county, domain, diocese, city, guild and village – was
recognised to some extent by jurists in their discussions of the limited
rights of self-management that could be ascribed to corporate bodies.
But these horizontal divisions of authority got little support from
either philosophers or humanists; Ptolemy of Lucca was unusual in
listing 'region, province, city or borough' and again 'kingdom, city,
borough or any college' as instances of political society (II chs. 7–8).

[1] See bibliography, p. 203.

All over Europe judicial and military powers were exercised simultaneously at a number of levels. In England and France powerful monarchies were emerging. Germany, on the other hand, was an extreme example of the division of powers between levels: emperor, territorial princes, cities, lesser nobility, small towns and villages; while in some German lands dynastic princes were becoming territorial sovereigns. In central Europe, the kingdom of Poland stood on its own; the kingdoms of Hungary and Bohemia were dynastically intertwined with German politics: yet in Bohemia an ethnic as well as a territorial dimension was also developing. In northern and central Italy, power gravitated towards the new mercantile and industrial centres of Venice, Genoa, Florence and so on: city-states ruling a hinterland (*contado*). The wide borderlands between the expansionist power of Capetian France and the German-speaking Rhineland were continually contested. Power, and eventually legitimate power, could crystallise at various points in the old feudal ladder: around the king in some places, a duke, lord or city in others.

Attempts were made, on the other hand, to create confederations, such as the Rhineland league (1254), the Flemish cities and the Hanseatic League of North German towns. The Rhineland League offered protection to 'rich and poor, clergy and laity, Christians and Jews'.[2] The Flemish and Hansa had a central Diet. But they lacked cooperation and failed to incorporate the countryside. The Swiss Confederation was uniquely successful in creating, by very gradual stages, an alternative to the usual state development: authority delegated upwards from rural communities and towns to an alliance or league (*foedus*). Part of its success lay in the combination of town and countryside. The founding treaty of 1291 was a carefully drafted legal document based on the principle of mutual aid; the three rural communities swore to come to the defence of each other if attacked. They proclaimed their right to be ruled by their own native magistracies and customary laws, to independence from the local Habsburg lords and to recognition as immediate vassals of the Empire.[3] Contemporary thinkers ignored all these developments; there was no theory of federation in the Middle Ages.

---

[2] Ed. F. Keutgen, *Urkunden zur städtischen Verfassungsgeschichte*, in *Ausgewählte Urkunden zum deutschen Verfassungsgeschichte*, ed. G. von Below and F. Keutgen, vol. 1 (Berlin, 1901), pp. 80–9.

[3] Bernard Guenée, *States and Rulers in Later Medieval Europe*, trans. J. Vale (Oxford: Basil Blackwell, 1985), pp. 212–16; Susan Reynolds, *Kingdoms and Communities in Western Europe, 900–1300* (Oxford: Oxford University Press, 1984), pp. 238–40.

INTERNATIONAL SOCIETY

In what sense was Europe or Latin Christendom, from Poland to
Ireland, Sicily to Iceland, an international community? The general
consensus is that internationalism was on the decline, and membership of a national or local unit was what increasingly counted. Yet
the canon law of the church remained at least in some sense a truly
international law. Supranational legislation by popes and councils and
the Roman courts' appellate jurisdiction covered important matters
relating to social status and property: excommunication, legitimation
of bastards, matrimony, inheritance and dowry.

That the church was an international, indeed universal, society
nobody questioned: it was an article of faith. All human beings ought
to be Christians and all Christians belonged to a single society: the
body of Christ. But the question remained, how this was to be
operationalised. The body of Christ was a moral and spiritual unit in
virtue of a shared faith. It was virtually unanimously agreed that the
church was a juridical unit in the sense that religious and moral
matters were subject to the canon law of the church and to the church
courts. This law was modified by the papacy or general councils
acting with the pope, and the ultimate judicial appeal was to the
Roman courts. This was the basis for those who said that all mortals
should be subject to the Roman church. Thus in addition to a
common religious language and liturgy, 'the church' always referred
to a legal community with a single formal organisation. Non-
believers, heretics and schismatics – such as Jews, Moslems and Greek
Orthodox – were *ipso facto* excluded from this 'universal' society.

We have seen how the further politicisation of the church was kept
in check by the doctrine of 'render unto Caesar the things that are
Caesar's, and unto God the things that are God's', and by the material
and moral power of secular rulers in Europe (chapter 2). But the
papacy continued to call for crusades ('wars waged on direct papal
initiative for the sake of the faith')[4] against the infidel, not so much
now to recover the holy places but to defend the vulnerable eastern
borders of Christendom against Islam. Such calls were not very
effective; the Ottoman Empire continued to make gains. Largely
unsuccessful attempts were made to reunite the eastern and western
halves of Christendom in the face of the common threat. When in the
1420s and 1430s the Hussite rising in Bohemia threatened great
swathes of Germany and central Europe, it called forth a collective

[4] Frederick H. Russell, *The Just War in the Middle Ages* (Cambridge: Cambridge
University Press, 1975), p. 195.

response at least from the emperor and some German princes. In the middle of the fifteenth century, in response to the successful establishment of a Hussite kingdom in Bohemia and the fall of Constantinople and many Greek islands to the Turks, humanists and others, especially in the ambience of the restored papacy, spoke of *respublica Christiana* (the Christian commonwealth) as identifying common interests for which princes as well as pope were responsible in the face of 'common enemies' (*hostes communes*), meaning heretics and Turks. Common social and political principles, such as benevolent monarchy, were supposed to operate at every level of this *respublica*. These ideals were summed up in the policies and writings of pope Pius II (1458–64: the humanist Aeneas Sylvius Piccolomini); he sought in vain to generate enthusiasm for crusades against Hussite Bohemia and the Ottomans. Such ideals were especially popular in Spain where, with the Reconquest virtually complete, religious nationalism was seeking for new ways to assert itself and expand.

Besides the church, the concept of Rome itself provided some sense of transnational citizenship for all Western Christians. The Empire proper might be territorially constricted, but the notion that all belonged in some sense to a universal 'Roman empire' remained strong even in the absence of a transnational secular government. Theology, ethics, medicine, all branches of philosophy and science, canon and 'civil' (Roman) law were studied, taught and authoritatively interpreted in self-governing corporations – which eventually appropriated the generic term *universitas* (corporation) – immune from interference by local rulers, among scholars who felt themselves members of a world of learning which transcended national and sometimes even religious boundaries. The chief sources of intellectual inspiration – the Latin authors Cicero, Seneca, Sallust, Livy and the Greek authors Aristotle, Plato, Galen, Ptolemy – belonged to an unbounded community.

Moreover, just as the ancient Romans had succeeded in incorporating other peoples in their rule by extending to outsiders civil rights such as intermarriage and commerce, so the inhabitants of Europe (their self-styled successors) shared a wide range of social *moeurs* and treated one another as social equals. Germans, Englishmen, Frenchmen, Italians and others were able to do business together thanks partly to their shared *Romanitas*. Latin was a lingua franca; Roman law was 'the common law' (*ius commune*). Not that it was adopted as the current legal code, but it provided a common basis of legal criteria, procedures, principles of codification and notions of justice whenever, as was often the case in an expanding mercantile society, existing local, tribal or national codes stood in need of development. A common understanding of property rights, contract, commercial transactions, not to mention honour, facilitated the growth of Europe-wide commerce which was still expanding in the fourteenth century (to be sure, Europeans also traded with Muslims and Russians).

Behind Roman law stood the principles of the law of nature (embodying roughly the ten commandments), and the law of nations (*ius gentium*): this referred to property rights, the sanctity of promises and principles of justice to be observed in buying, selling, lending, borrowing, letting and hiring. This made it much easier for Lombards, Jews and others to do business in many different places. Economically, Europe was a partially international community with a degree of interdependence in money-lending, capital investment, the cloth trade, metals and luxury goods. The institutions of this international commerce included the individual merchant houses and companies, which acquired facilities from and served foreign princes; the German Hansa, which acquired facilities for German merchants throughout Europe and beyond; and the unique stonemasons' craft which sought to regulate architecture and the building trades on a partly international basis.

The papacy claimed a right to regulate the international political order by authoritatively resolving disputes between otherwise sovereign rulers or states in order to prevent war. The preservation or restoration of peace had always been regarded as a moral duty of Christians and especially those in authority; to induce others to make and keep the peace was a primary task for bishops and above all the papacy. Over and above that, the pope, or emperor, occasionally claimed authority, as supreme arbiters of the Christian people, to compose quarrels between sovereign princes, or others, and to impose a peaceful settlement through legal channels. The canon lawyer Hostiensis (writing in the 1250s) denied the right of Christians to wage war upon one another at all, on the grounds of Christian love and the universal kinship of Rome. Others suggested that declaration of war should be limited to pope and emperor.[5] Innocent IV, in legal commentaries written while he was pope (1243–54), said that the pope could impose a judicial settlement with the force of law; so that any subsequent violence would be illegitimate. In practice, however, during the later Middle Ages popes were able to act only as arbitrators: 'not by reason of our authority, but by

[5] For this and much of what follows, see Russell, *Just War*.

reason of the power given to us by the two parties', as someone put it.[6]

A more widespread and realistic view was embodied in the theory of the 'just war'. This theory originated in St Augustine and underwent significant development by Aquinas and medieval canon-lawyers and later by the neo-scholastics and Grotius. It distinguished, in the first instance, between what could and could not provide legitimate grounds for one party to engage in war with another. First, rulers and subjects have a moral duty to examine the rights and wrongs of a dispute before taking up arms; and, second, as Grotius later emphasised, the declaration, conduct and conclusion of war itself should be regarded as a para-legal process. In Russell's words, war must be conducted as 'a procedure for legal redress of grievances that was invoked by the aggrieved authority when more normal procedures were of no avail'.[7] Once the grounds of the dispute have been removed, whether by victory or by negotiation, the conflict must cease. Rules for the treatment of prisoners, non-combatants and so on fitted logically into such a quasi-judicial view. It was of course universally asserted that treaties must be observed (*pacta sunt servanda*).

In the second place, war could only be declared by a legitimate authority, namely the sovereign (*princeps*). This was the aspect of just-war doctrine most explicitly developed and most widely disseminated during the high and later Middle Ages. Some canonists tried to restrict this category to kings, emperor and pope.[8] But for the most part it became agreed that the declaration of a just war belonged to any autonomous ruler on the ground that he had no superior to whom to appeal in pursuance of his claim; Aquinas used the neo-Aristotelian concept of the state to support an existing consensus among jurists. This outlawed violence between mighty subjects and the feudal vendetta. It was an attempt to define the role of war in the emerging international order of Europe. And it completed from above the concentration of legitimate political authority in the sovereign state and its government.

During the early fifteenth century, an attempt was made to revitalise the ideal of a universal, supra-national church. The general councils of Constance and Basle were international assemblies both for religious purposes and for the purpose of restoring peace. All Catholic nations were supposed to be represented there. The Council

---

[6] English chronicle (1344), cited by R. W. Southern, *Western Society and the Church in the Middle Ages* (Harmondsworth: Penguin, 1970), p. 149.

[7] Russell, *Just War*, pp. 86 and 268.   [8] Ibid., pp. 139, 220.

of Basle (1431–49) played a part in negotiating an end to the religious and nationalist wars between Hussite Bohemia and her German neighbours, and helped persuade Philip of Burgundy to make peace with Charles VII of France at Arras (1435). An attempt was also made to transcend the principle of nationality itself within the council: whereas Constance had been organised into sub-committees consisting of 'nations' (in which most discussion took place), Basle chose instead 'deputations' organised according to their subject matter (one was devoted to peace), and in these persons of different nationality were deliberately mixed. National differences did not cease to plague the Council. Reflecting on this arrangement, the leading conciliar theologian Juan de Segovia reaffirmed the ideal of an undivided *oikumene*: nations can learn from one another by studying each other's different customs. *Curvitas* (crookedness or deviance) makes humans love those close by to the exclusion of those farther away. But

those incorporated into the general council become members of the universal church ... One person cannot say to another, 'You are not from Italy, Spain, France or Germany' ... Out of the intermingled multitude, forced almost daily into one another's company, is born true love for people of all nationalities ... so that, brought together by a kind of pleasure, they explore more wisely the true, common good.[9]

These church councils were remarkable attempts at conducting inter-state diplomacy through a regular and putatively impartial forum.

The papacy meanwhile made a serious attempt at the rival Council of Ferrara-Florence (1437–45) to reunite the Greek Orthodox and other eastern churches with Rome. After the fall of Constantinople (1453), both Segovia and Nicholas of Cusa argued that the differences between Christians and Muslims should be settled not by force but by theological debate and examination of one another's faiths. This accorded with the view of those who held that infidels may legitimately own property and exercise political authority even over Christians. For, as Aquinas put it, the divine law, which distinguishes between believers and unbelievers, does not invalidate human law 'deriving from natural reason', and government (*dominium et praelatio*) is based upon the latter (*ST* Ia/IIae 10.10

---

[9] *Historia gestorum Generalis Synodi Basiliensis*, in F. Palacky, E. Birk and C. Stehlin (eds.), *Monumenta Conciliorum Generalim Seculi XV* (Vienna–Basle, 1857–1935), vol. II, pp. 133–4; cf. pp. 40, 45–7.

resp.). Ockham pushed this point further and suggested that an infidel world emperor might again be desirable.[10]

THE DEFENDERS OF EMPIRE

Apart from this religious community, the other focus for aspirations towards international unity and authority was the Empire. Its rulers and their apologists regularly claimed some kind of inter-state authority as such. Roman in name, it had since the tenth century been in the hands of the ruling dynasties of Germany, the king of Germany being crowned as emperor by the pope. As titular rulers of 'the Italian kingdom', they claimed over the Italian city-states rights which had been defined, after prolonged conflict between the emperor Frederick I and the Lombard league, in the Peace of Constance (1183). Apart from this, their 'imperial' powers were largely nominal even in the old 'middle kingdom' of Lotharingia-Burgundy; although one should not wholly discount the influence which such a honorific title might, under certain circumstances, command.

After the collapse of the Hohenstaufen dynasty (1250), the German electoral princes succeeded in ensuring that no new dynasty capable of impinging seriously upon their own territorial sovereignty would emerge. German kings were rendered incapable of becoming effective rulers in Germany itself outside their own domains. Yet during the papal schism and conciliar crisis (1378–1450), Sigismund of Luxemburg (elected 1410, crowned 1433, died 1438) played a considerable role in Europe-wide church affairs, in virtue of his still acknowledged position as defender of the church (*advocatus ecclesie*). From the middle of the fifteenth century the Habsburgs became *de facto* hereditary king-emperors at a time when princely sovereignty within German lands seemed secure, and when imperial aspirations outside Germany were, like the aspirations of other princes, based mainly on dynastic claims. Yet the career of Charles V (emperor 1519–56) demonstrates that the Roman ideal of imperial hegemony lived on. On these occasions, religious controversy seems to have revealed a fragility in other polities and restored some credibility to the emperor's role (see also above, pp. 54–6).

During this prolonged crisis in an institution central to European Christian society's self-image, and also a powerful focus for allegiance and proto-national sentiment in Germany, the internationalism of the Empire was defended by some remarkable theoreticians. Some were

[10] McGrade, *Ockham*, p. 102.

idealists who wanted to convert people to a universal polity; others were constitutional writers anxious to secure for Germany the unity and stability enjoyed by other kingdoms. The impact of Aristotle's philosophical approach here was considerable. In the tracts written between *c.*1250 and *c.*1281 by Jordan of Osnabrück and Alexander of Roes (*MPI* pp. 440–1, 466–7) it was claimed that divine dispensation had allotted the empire to the Germans via Charlemagne. The contrast with Engelbert and Dante could not be greater. Here for the first time the empire was rationalised as an institution necessary for the well-being of the human race. These were not merely defensive apologists; they felt they had something positive to offer. We are presented with an institution which we can recognise as an international authority in a modern sense. Certainly no-one thought a world ruler should have anything like what we consider governmental powers. It was generally assumed that his powers would be less extensive than those of an ordinary medieval prince. Rather, he would supplement the existing jurisdiction of princes and cities, providing a right of appeal from king or prince to imperial court, a judicial process whereby an emperor could compose disputes between rulers without resort to war.

Engelbert of Admont (or Volkersdorf: *c.*1250–1331), a Benedictine abbot, had studied philosophy at Padua. His *On the Rise and Conclusion of the Roman Empire (De ortu et fine Romani imperii; fine* has a double meaning: purpose and end) was written in 1307–10, when the king of Germany and emperor-elect, Henry VII of Luxemburg, was preparing an expedition to Italy (see above, p. 55). Engelbert was the first to ground the argument for empire on the new range of political concepts and arguments available from Aristotle. He also relied upon Plato for the authority of the wise (chs. 3, 5), upon Cicero for the origin of kingship (ch. 2), and upon the New Testament, Roman history and St Augustine for the legitimacy of the empire (chs. 11–15, 17).

Engelbert's crucial step was to argue that the goals and norms ascribed by Aristotle to the *polis* (city-state) could only be realised fully in a world-wide monarchy (Aegidius Romanus had said they could be fully realised in a kingdom). The development of kingship in general is described and analysed in both Ciceronian and Aristotelian terms, illustrated and supported by Roman history (chs. 1–6). The question of world government is introduced via a discussion of different kinds of kingdom: just and unjust, large and small (chs. 7–13).

First, regarding the moral aspect, we are told that the Romans acquired new territories because they were better able to defend their peoples; those whom they conquered came to see that 'Roman rule (*imperium*) over them was tolerable, modest and fair'. Thus 'the Roman Empire acquired other kingdoms and dominions through voluntary subjection ... subjection by force became subjection by consent (*voluntatem*), so that they obeyed and were subject no longer through coercion but voluntarily, and they accepted of their own will the Roman laws which had been imposed upon them' (ch. 11: cf. Thomas Hobbes, *Leviathan*, ch. 20). The Roman Empire was, therefore, just.

Turning to distinctions between communities according to size, we have (1) the household, (2) the village, (3) the city, (4) 'a whole nation (*gens*), which is a community of a single language, fatherland, customs and laws', and (5) 'the community of a kingdom with its people scattered among villages, cities and distant and remote nations, subject to one king and lord' (ch. 12); (4) presumably refers to the Germanic tribes such as Saxony, (5) to *Germania* as a whole. Greatness (*magnitudo*), however, can be defined either in spatial, territorial terms, or in terms of royal excellence (*virtus*). And such *virtus* is to be measured in terms of both justice and power (*potentia*); for 'justice directs power and power turns justice into (effective) judgement ... so that justice directs and decides what is just, while power executes and defends what is just' (ch. 12). The greatness of a kingdom depends upon a combination of these two qualities. Engelbert's point here may have been to draw attention to the gap in the effective authority of the German kings.

Engelbert next discussed four possible combinations – just and large, unjust and small, just and small, unjust and large – in relation to their capacity to bring happiness (*felicitas*). This is defined as sufficiency or absence of want, tranquillity or absence of pain, and security or absence of fear. These in fact also constitute true liberty (ch. 9). Now small kingdoms lack sufficiency, and unjust ones lack tranquillity. Consequently, 'only the just and large kingdom can be happy, since it alone knows how to be self-sufficient *and* secure'. Magnitude itself does not make a kingdom just, but it makes it possible for it to be just; for justice requires power. Thus 'the larger and more powerful a kingdom, the more just it will be able to be, supposing love and zeal in the ruler' (ch. 13).

Engelbert now, finally, addresses the question 'whether it is better that all or most kingdoms of the world should be subject to one kingdom or empire, such as the Roman' (ch. 14). He based his answer upon the considerations of peace, order (*ordinatio*) and happiness. He finds that the reasons which give rise to and justify kingship in human societies also justify kingship for the community of mankind. Kingship, or monarchy, within particular kingdoms arises from nature and is achieved through art and reason by application of the universal principle of subordination of the many to the one. The peace and common good of mankind can only be attained in a worldwide commonwealth:

Thus also the many kingdoms of the world and their well-being are orientated (*ordinantur*) towards one natural kingdom and empire, as the particular good is towards the common good of all kingdoms and nations, the private to the public, the greater to the greatest, and parts to the whole in nature. (ch. 15)

Happiness in this life depends upon hierarchical organisation: for the happiness of individuals is orientated towards that of the household; this towards 'another greater and more common happiness, that of the city'; and this in turn is related to 'the greatest happiness, that of the kingdom' –

So the ultimate and highest happiness is that of the empire, to which the happiness of nations and kingdoms is orientated ... The safety and happiness of all reside in the happiness of the empire, for this is the universal and thus the one, ultimate and best happiness. (ch. 17)

So much for the argument from Aristotle. Engelbert also produced an argument from Cicero, based on Cicero's celebrated definition of a 'people' as a group bound together by consent and a common law.

Where there is one divine and human law and one concordant consensus of the people about that one law ... there we find one people and one commonwealth (*respublica*). And where there is one people and one commonwealth, there we necessarily find one king and one kingdom. But in all the world there is but one true divine law, namely one true worship of the true God; and but one true human law, namely the canons and laws consonant with divine law [he means the current canon and Roman-civil laws] ... And there is but one consensus of the people about that divine and human law, namely the Christian faith; and but one people, namely the Christian people ... and therefore but one commonwealth of the whole Christian people. (ch. 15)

This then is in effect a religious argument for international polity. The specifically Christian character of Engelbert's international community is underlined by his argument that unity under imperial rule will assist in wars against 'paganism' (ch. 18). The closing chapters (21–4) are apocalyptic: the Empire is destined to disappear just before

the coming of Antichrist, an event already foreshadowed by kingdoms today withdrawing from the Empire. There is an enchanting
gloom about this conclusion.

Dante Alighieri (1265–1321) combined in his life and person politics,
philosophy and poetry. His *Convivio* and *Monarchy* are works of
philosophy, drawing on contemporary developments in neo-
Aristotelian thought. It is as if James Joyce had written on the
philosophy of language. Dante was, at least by modern 'western'
standards, a profoundly political poet, to be counted among the
visionary reformers of society and *moeurs*. His participation in the
politics of his native Florence from 1295 to 1302, when the commune
was undergoing crises in its constitution and alliances, and his acute
sense of loss after he was exiled for supporting the Ghibelline-
imperial cause against pope Boniface VIII, show his civic patriotism
as well as the unity of public and private in his mind and fortunes. For
him, the categories 'medieval' and 'Renaissance' seem superfluous:
the inspiration of his thought was Christian and Aristotelian but the
way he used both to make an argument for universal polity, and the
kind of polity he conceived that to be, were original. Dante wrote his
masterpiece on universal government, *Monarchy*, during Henry VII's
expedition into Italy (1310–13), which he fervently supported and to
which he attached an apocalyptic meaning very different to that
suggested by Engelbert. In 1310 he addressed to Henry three passionate yet thoughtful letters in which rhetoric verges on poetry. His
vision of the Empire had been outlined a few years earlier in *Convivio*
IV, and was given final expression, with a touch of desperation, in
several passages in the *Divine Comedy*, written some years later,
notably in *Purgatorio* 6, lines 85–151.

The essence of Dante's argument for universal empire under one
ruler turned on the nature of the human species and of philosophy:
the act of understanding is our ultimate goal and the characteristic
activity which defines our species (*Monarchy* I.3). In a passage of some
originality, Dante suggested that philosophy is a collective activity
which can only be carried out properly by the human race as a unit.

The proper task of the human race (*genus*) taken as a whole is always to
actualise the whole power of the potential intellect, first in contemplation
and second and consequently in act. (*Monarchy* 1.4)

By virtue of this single goal of the good life (*vita felice: Convivio* IV.4),
there exists a single human civilisation (*umana civilta*) and devotion, a
'universal religion of the human species' (*Convivio* IV.4, 6); attainment

of this goal is 'mortal felicity', symbolised by the earthly paradise of Eden restored (*Monarchy* III.16: above, p. 57). Therefore, the human community being a kind of whole (*humana universitas est quoddam totum: Monarchy* I.7), it is appropriate for there to be a single polity for all men.

The claims of empire are not limited to Italy and Germany nor indeed to Europe (see *Letters (Epistolae)*, VII.31). 'The world is our *patria*' (*On the Vernacular (De vulgari eloquentia)* I.6); why should there be one *civilitas* at Florence, another at Rome (*Letters* VI.2)? This idea of the unity of human mental activity, knowledge and culture produced a case for universal rule at the very moment when state boundaries and perceptions of national differences were hardening (see below, pp. 110–11). Dante presented briefly and with powerful simplicity a radical alternative, based it would appear on philosophy rather than religion in the ordinary sense.

Dante also presented arguments for empire that were more conventional, but seldom without some twist of his own. The objectives of philosophy require universal peace ('the human race is most freely and easily disposed to its proper task when it is in . . . the tranquillity of peace': *Monarchy* I.4). He argued, like Engelbert, that the generally recognised need for political unity applies to the community of mankind (*Monarchy* I.5). He used common monist arguments, including analogy with God and the pope, to show that such unity required universal rule by a single individual (*Monarchy*, I.6–8 and III.16; *Letters* VI.2). Concord, on which human well-being depends, resides in unity of wills; but this can only be achieved if there is 'one will, which rules and regulates all the others into one' (*Monarchy* I.15; cf. Hegel, *Philosophy of Right*, 279–80). To attain our common goal, we need the 'authority' both of Aristotle, 'the supreme philosopher', and of the emperor. Aristotle's authority

is not repugnant to imperial authority; but the latter without the former is dangerous, and the former without the latter as it were weak, not of itself but because of the disorganization of the species.

The two should, therefore, be joined together (*Convivio* IV.6). Italy itself stands in desperate need of that peace which only a universal sovereignty can bring (*Letters* VI.1 and VII.1).

Similarly, the needs of judicial process require a worldwide polity and monarchy. For 'wherever there can be litigation, there must be adjudication'. There can be litigation between two rulers who are not subject to another sovereign. Therefore,

Either there will be an infinite process, which cannot be; or it will be necessary to come before a first and supreme judge, by whose judgement all quarrels are removed either mediately or immediately [sc. on appeal or as court of first instance]; and this will be the monarchy or emperor. (*Monarchy* I.10)

Dante argued, like Engelbert, that justice is greatest when joined to power; therefore there will be most justice in the world when it lies in the hands of the most powerful individual. He adds the absurd argument that the emperor, unlike all other princes, will have nothing to tempt him to greed 'since his jurisdiction is bounded (*terminatur*) only by ocean' (*Monarchy* I.11). Both 'written reason' enshrined in Roman law and Aristotle's philosophy are ineffective without a correspondingly universal law-enforcer (*Convivio* IV.9; *Purgatorio* VI.88–90). Indeed, only the emperor's law makes private property secure (*Letters* V.7). Dante's fiercest invective was aimed at lawlessness, especially in Italy, which he ascribes to the absence of imperial power (*Letters* VI.1; *Purgatorio* VI.85–151 and XVI.97–8).

A more startling claim for empire was that it would bring liberty and (this amounted to the same thing) just governments. Dante's argument here was that the world ruler loves and is loved by his subjects more than any other ruler because he has responsibility for the *whole* human race, acting as intermediary between men and all other princes (*Monarchy* I.11). Therefore under him human beings will exist not as a means to someone else's end but for themselves – this is what liberty means. And, since the world ruler wants men to be good, he will remove those deviant constitutions which prevent this – 'democracy' or mob rule, oligarchies and one-man tyrannies – and install in their place good government by kings, by the great and the good (*optimates*), or by 'those zealous for the liberty of the people' (*Monarchy* I.12; cf. *Purgatorio* VI.124–6).

Dante grounded belief in political liberty on the philosophical and theological doctrine of free will ('freedom of choice': *libertas arbitrii*). Indeed the salience of liberty as a *political* value derived from the unusual prominence he gave it in the whole scheme of human life; it is 'the greatest gift conferred by God on human nature; since through it we are made happy (*felicitamur*) as humans here, and through it we are also made happy as gods elsewhere' (*Monarchy* I.12; cf. *Purgatorio* XVI.64–84). Dante could now harness the Roman theme of republican liberty to the cause of worldwide monarchy (*Monarchy* II.1, 5). The Roman people earned the right to rule the world by liberating peoples from tyrants and usurpers. In shunning greed, 'neglecting their own interests for the sake of the public safety of the human race', and embracing 'universal peace with liberty', the Romans were a people 'born to rule', 'ordained by nature for empire', entitled by 'divine predestination'; as the birth of Christ in the Augustan age testifies (*Monarchy* II.3–7, 12). Observance of the (universal Roman) laws is 'the supreme liberty'; 'only those who voluntarily obey the law are free' (*Letters* VI.5). By removing tyrannical government and upholding the laws, the emperor makes his subjects free. Henry of Luxemburg would liberate Italy and indeed raise Italians to their proper role in the government of the empire (*Letters* V.2, 6).

The scope of the emperor's authority is limited by the very considerations which give rise to it. He has no authority over philosophy or science, only over matters in which human *choice* plays a part, as 'the rider of the human will' (*Convivio* IV.9; *Purgatorio* VI.88–99). Aristotle tells us what felicity is, the emperor enables us to pursue it. The emperor's authority is confined to the sphere of positive law. Dante illustrated this by a complex analogy with different kinds of craft in which skill (*arte*) and nature are combined in different proportions. It is in 'pure arts', in which nature does not determine human action, that the emperor rules: for example in questions of matrimony, servitude, knighthood and inheritance (though he cannot define gentility: *gentilezza*: *Convivio* IV.9). Provided people obey the laws, the emperor is 'servant of all'; he exists for the sake of the laws; 'the monarchy is bounded by the end prescribed for it in the making of law' (*Monarchy* I.12).

Finally, such universal rule does not mean empire in the conventional Roman (or indeed modern) sense but something a bit closer to confederation. Separate states and nations keep their own laws; the emperor acts not as a court of first instance but when municipal laws are defective, and on matters common to the whole human race (*Monarchy* I.14). On the other hand, it is clearly part of the emperor's function to discipline and depose bad rulers and install better ones.

It is clear that Dante was determined to press ahead with his vision of political unity regardless of any objections. In *Letters* V and VII and in the *Divine Comedy* his statements are apocalyptic and, of course, poetic. Henry is 'the peacemaking Titan ... the mighty lion of the tribe of Judah ... a new Moses who will snatch his people from the oppression of the Egyptians ... the sublime eagle ... a second Hector ... the lamb of God' (*Letters* V.1, 4 and VII.2). The messianic language of Virgil's *Fourth Eclogue*, long appropriated by Christians for Jesus, is transferred back again to its Augustan origins: 'new hope of a better epoch for Italy ... the realms of Saturn' are promised by Henry's advent across the Apennines (*Letters* VII.1). In the *Divine Comedy* this is developed into the symbol of the Hound (*Veltro*) who will come to

liberate Italy, drive out avarice and give peace to the world (*Inferno*
I.101; *Purgatorio* XX.10 and XXXIII.40). Henry's adventure had
collapsed but Dante's vision remained.

The next group of writings in support of the Empire was connected
with the conflict between Ludwig of Bavaria and the papacy from
the early 1320s till the late 1340s (above, pp. 54–6). The crucial issue
was now no longer an emperor's title to international authority but
rather the method of succession to the kingship of Germany. In the
Declaration of Rhens (1338) and finally in the Golden Bull (1356) it
was determined that the Empire was directly from God and that
whoever was elected king by a majority of the seven electoral princes
or their heirs could exercise the full rights of sovereignty without
need for papal confirmation; claims to overlordship in Italy were
tacitly set aside. The debate ranged over questions of German constitutional law and of church and state.

Lupold of Bebenberg (or Bamberg, of which he became bishop in
1353) (*c.*1297–1363), as a canon of Würzburg and doctor of canon
law, which he had studied at Bologna under Johannes Andreae,
supported the papal position up till 1338. It was probably pope John
XXII's obstinacy despite concessions offered by Ludwig that led him
in that year, like many others, to support Ludwig. He played a part in
Ludwig's negotiations at the Diet of Rhens, probably assisting
Baldwin, prince-archbishop of Trier and an imperial elector, who led
the estates in their support for the independence of the German
Crown. He may have helped draft the Golden Bull itself. Lupold's
The Rights of Kingdom and Empire (*De iuribus regni et imperii*) was
completed in 1340 and dedicated to archbishop Baldwin. It was a
systematic defence of the position of Ludwig and his supporters.
Lupold was concerned with the independence and stability of the
German monarchy rather than universal lordship; his approach was
thus poles apart from that adopted simultaneously on behalf of
Ludwig by William of Ockham.

Lupold's professed motive was 'fervent zeal for my fatherland,
Germany, and especially Germanic *Francia*' (ch. 19). He used legal
expertise to disprove the view, endorsed by two recent authorities in
canon law, Innocent IV and Hostiensis, that the person elected king of
Germany could not, since that same person was also emperor-elect,
exercise his sovereign rights until approved by the pope (chs. 8–13).
Here he took the unusual step, especially for a canonist, of basing his
argument chiefly upon natural equity as enshrined in custom –
meaning in effect national custom – 'the contrary of which cannot be

remembered' (*cuius contrarii memoria non existit*). He intends to prove that election of itself confers the powers of kingship and empire

by the law of nations and the general customs of western kingdoms and also by ancient histories and chronicles. Such proof by means of ancient histories and chronicles seems sufficient, especially in this matter which goes beyond the memory of men. (ch. 5, p. 178b)

His work is remarkable for a systematic reliance upon history, in other words precedent, as an authoritative source for settling constitutional questions. Lupold has been called 'the first systematiser of German constitutional law'.[11] His appeal to custom is analogous to Bartolus' reliance upon 'fact' (below, pp. 115–16).

Lupold's tract, then, was primarily aimed not at establishing the rights of the king-emperor as a universal monarch, although his particular claims to Italy and Burgundy were not abandoned, but rather, like Ludwig's diplomacy, at salvaging the integrity of the German Crown from the wreckage of imperial fortunes. His priorities are indicated at one point when he says that he will leave to others the question of the independence of the king of France (ch. 7). For this purpose, appeal to custom was more appropriate than argument from abstract philosophical principles, ancient Roman history or Roman law. Lupold began by refuting the argument that the role of the papacy in transferring the Roman Empire from the Greeks to 'the king of the Franks in the person of Charlemagne' gave it a right to scrutinise, approve or reject an emperor-elect (chs. 2–4, 16–18). Rather,

The person elected in concord by the electoral princes as king or emperor of the Romans can immediately by virtue of the election itself legitimately assume the name of king and administer the rights and goods of the kingdom and of the Empire in Italy and in the other provinces subject to the kingdom and Empire;

and he can do so whether elected unanimously or by a majority (chs. 5–6). Hence Lupold's insistence on the fully representative and imprescriptible status of the electors (ch. 5), and on the validity of a majority vote among them in view of their collegiate status (ch. 6). His argument that Charlemagne held the Kingdom of the Franks 'by paternal succession, according to the tradition and virtually universal custom (*more ac consuetudine quasi generali*) of all western Kingdoms, which then as now were nearly all held by succession through kinship (*per successionem generis*)' (ch. 5, p. 178b) suggests a preference for

[11] Hermann Meyer, *Lupold von Bebenberg* (Freiburg-im-Breisgau, 1909), p. 1.

hereditary succession, and a hint that Germany might one day adopt this in the interests of stability and continuity. This is confirmed by his insistence elsewhere that hereditary succession in western Kingdoms can be justified on the grounds of immemorial custom (ch. 15); and by his remark that in natural equity successors enjoy the same rights as those they succeed (ch. 7).

Lupold's relative indifference to old-fashioned imperial claims and his acceptance of the independence, in general, of other Kingdoms came out in several of the arguments he used to support the full sovereignty of the emperor-elect. It is, he said,

a general custom of all western Kingdoms, hitherto observed from time immemorial, that their kings in their own Kingdoms and regarding their own subjects exercise functions reserved by law to the emperor. (ch. 7, p. 183b)

On grounds of, again, 'custom or prescription from time immemorial', western kings legitimately exercise over their own subjects all the rights of sovereignty (*merum et mixtum imperium*) *immediate*, that is as courts of first instance. In other words, no case however grave is reserved to the emperor. Lupold's purpose in saying this was to argue by analogy for the complete independence of the emperor-elect from the pope. The emperor is not a vassal of the pope but holds his power immediately from God, just like other kings 'who today for the most part do not recognise the Roman emperor or any other superior in temporal affairs' (ch. 9, p. 187a).

What the emperor does have is 'mediated jurisdiction' over the subjects of other kings: that is, a right to act on appeal, or when justice has been 'neglected' or 'denied'. And over the kings themselves he has 'in cases of this kind' immediate jurisdiction. This meant, presumably, that he could hear a suit brought against a king by one of his subjects or by another king. These were quasi-technical terms for grounds of appeal and gave the emperor exactly the same kind of appellate power which Ockham claimed for pope over emperor and vice versa (see above, pp. 74–5). Thus there remains in Lupold a residual sense of a need for an international court of justice.

William of Ockham's writings on empire, composed at almost exactly the same time, were quite different in aims, method and doctrine.[12] He was concerned with the arguments for and against a

---

[12] These are contained in III *Dialogue* ii, probably written 1339–41 (extract in Lewis, *MPI* pp. 300–10, 495–500), *Eight Questions*, 1340–2, and *Tyrannical Rule*, 1341–2: McGrade, *Ockham*, pp. 20 n. 69 and 96–107; for comparison with Lupold, ibid., p. 97 n.

truly universal monarchy rather than with the constitutional situation in Germany. As ever, he wished to explore the matter exhaustively and with academic fairness. He argued from first principles and from Scripture, especially the New Testament. III *Dialogue* (*Dialogus*) ii book 1 discussed the arguments for and against having a single ruler for the whole world (*universitas mortalium*: not just the Christian world), and asserted that the emperor held his position directly from God, not by papal mediation. Book 2 discussed the emperor's jurisdiction in temporal matters and the separation between imperial and papal spheres of authority. Book 3 discussed the powers of the emperor over ecclesiastical goods and persons.

Ockham's conclusion was that, while the desirability of having a single ruler for the whole of mankind depended upon 'the diversity, quality and need of the times', nevertheless 'as a rule it is expedient that all mortals should be subject to a single ruler (*principi*) in temporal affairs' (III *Dialogue* ii, book 1, chs. 6 and 14). He argued that present-day emperors owed their position to their succession to the emperors of ancient Rome rather than to Charlemagne. Moreover Scripture and reason persuaded Ockham both that unbelievers can, in general, legitimately exercise civil authority and that Christ and the apostles accepted the pagan imperial authority of their own time. This exemplified Ockham's indifference to contemporary diplomacy, his willingness to distance himself from contemporary ideology and to ignore his own historical context in the search for basic principles.

After the promulgation of the Golden Bull of 1356, German monarchs abandoned territorial claims outside Italy based on their imperial status and the papacy tacitly accepted as emperor-elect the person chosen by the seven electoral princes. The issue of world government seemed dead and it was a very long time before the question of an international legal or political authority returned to the agenda of practical politics. Within Germany itself the position of the king-emperor was weak due to the mode of succession, as the electoral and other territorial princes built up their domains into sovereign principalities and were never going to permit the development of a national monarchy which would subordinate them. Nevertheless the ideal of a politically united Germany under a king-emperor and a national parliament (*Reichstag*) survived in popular sentiment and reforming circles.

The schism within the papacy from 1378 to 1417 and the ensuing contest over whether pope or council should hold supreme authority raised anew the whole question of the constitution of Christendom; this included the position of the emperor, especially when a renewed schism, this time between pope and council, was narrowly averted, partly by imperial diplomacy, in 1432–3 and actually broke from 1437 till the late 1440s. The possibility of an emperor playing a leading role in resolving these international ecclesiastical crises as defender of the church (*advocatus ecclesie*) was made a reality through the statesmanship of Sigismund, the last emperor of the house of Luxemburg (1410–37). He used his prestige and influence to persuade the ecclesiastical and secular authorities to convoke and support the Council of Constance (1414–18) and to ensure the election of an undisputed pope. He attempted with some success to play a mediating role at the Council of Basle, not least because he saw such a council as a forum of negotiation and a means of resolving the conflict, ostensibly religious but at the same time national, territorial and dynastic, between the Bohemian Hussites and their German Catholic neighbours. In 1433 Pope Eugenius IV crowned Sigismund emperor in Rome.

It was in this context that Nicholas of Cusa (see also below, pp. 178–83) wrote his *Catholic Concordance* (*De concordantia catholica*, CC), the third book of which, written in 1433, dealt expressly with the church's 'body, that is the holy empire'. Cusa saw the clergy, the secular powers and the Christian people as organically united, as complementary elements making up 'the whole, that is the church'. At this time he was supporting the council against the pope, and in the main the reform programme adopted by the council. But, like some other religious reformers in Germany, he saw reform as something that needed to be applied not only to the papal curia, with its notorious 'abuses', but also to what he saw as the unjustly fragmented and disorderly state of Germany and the 'Empire' itself. Given the organic concordance of the Christian polity, the same organisational principles – hierarchy and voluntary consent – which apply to the church and the clerical structure, apply no less to secular authority and the Empire.

Legitimate authority resides in offices ordained by God and filled through the voluntary consent of subjects (below, pp. 181–3). The imperial office is one of those divinely created powers which are a perennial feature of the Christian community (*CC* III chs. 1–2). Just as the Virgin Mary 'by free consent' gave birth to Christ who is God and man, so

true authority (*principatus*) should issue from the one uncorrupted church, or assembly of men, by most pure consent; not by any violence, not out of ambition or simoniacal depravity, but out of purity.

In the church's body (the secular order), which mirrors its soul (the priestly order), there is by right

a graded hierarchical order up to one prince of all, [proceeding] from the lowest simple laymen, who play the part of feet, through rulers, counts, marquises, dukes and kings up to the imperial head (*caesareum caput*). (*CC* III preface, p. 326 and ch. 1, p. 327)

The bodily or temporal aspect of Christian society is ordered like the spiritual; the emperor stands, like the pope, as 'one lord of the world supereminent over others in fullness of power' (*CC* III ch. 1, p. 327), as 'Christ's vicar' (*CC* III ch. 5, p. 354).

Cusa used the argument from consent to support his main practical claim, namely that the Empire is independent of the papacy and that choice of the ruler lies with the electoral princes. But for Cusa, like Marsiglio whom he had just recently read, this did not mean the consent of the governed here and now, but rather the consent originally given to the electors, first by the Roman people and later by the Germans, to exercise the power of election on their behalf (*CC* III ch. 4, p. 348). The electors, then, 'hold their fundamental power from that common consent of all, who were empowered by natural law to set up an emperor for themselves' (*CC* III ch. 4, p. 348). Like Lupold, he cited in support of this the history of the Roman Empire and the German monarchy (*CC* III chs. 3–4). He reinforced the historical argument by denying the authenticity of the Donation of Constantine (a ninth-century forgery, according to which the emperor Constantine was alleged to have given the papacy authority to rule in the West), not, as Lorenzo Valla was soon to do, by textual criticism but by inference from silence in contemporary and immediately subsequent sources (*CC* III.2). But above all natural right which underlies the principle of voluntary consent excludes the pope from any role in the election of an emperor. The person elected by the princes 'obtains everything . . . because he has the subjection of all and consequently the power of commanding (*imperandi*), which is the essence of empire (*imperii*)' (*CC* III ch. 4, p. 350). Unction and coronation by the pope do not affect the emperor's status and power; these are quite independent of and distinct from priestly authority (*CC* III ch. 4, p. 351; ch. 5, p. 353; ch. 41).

Regarding the international or inter-state authority of an emperor, Cusa emphasised the ecclesiastical aspect for, as we have seen, good reasons at the time. What sets the emperor apart from other kings is not any overlordship in secular law or politics; Cusa does not mention this. (In an interesting aside he reminds us that the emperor's rule is confined to Europe; this is no great drawback because Europe, though smaller than the rest of the world, has the greatest population, despite India's alleged '9,000 walled settlements': *CC* III, ch. 6 at p. 357). The excellence of imperial power is based, rather, on his Christianity, that is his acceptance of the laws of nature and the Old and New Testaments. It resides specifically in his role as 'defender of the church' with responsibility to implement decrees made by the clergy (*CC* III, ch. 7 at p. 361). And this function too derives not from succession to Constantine (the first Christian emperor) but rather, in accordance with Cusa's general theory of legitimate authority, from a fundamental transfusion of power by the Christian Roman people. He supports this view with extensive documentation from the first eight ecumenical councils. And he devoted a large part of book III to the emperor's role in general councils of the church (*CC* III, chs. 13–24).

The rest of the work concerns the emperor's secular role (*CC* III, chs. 25–40). This consists principally in presiding over and implementing the decrees of an imperial council, modelled upon the general council of the church. What he had in mind here was more or less the German parliament or Reichstag, although he does once allude to attendance by 'subject kings' as well (*CC* III, ch. 25, p. 421). And the reform which he has above all in mind for his native country was precisely an application thereto of the principles of conciliar government. The Reichstag should take its cue from the Council of Basle and meet every year. There should be a 'daily council', corresponding to the college of cardinals, of persons elected 'from every part of the kingdom' (*CC* III, ch. 12, p. 376). Such secular conciliar government is justified by 'the observance of ancient times, which will be clear to anyone who has read the acts of the kings and emperors' (*CC* III, ch. 25, p. 425). But it is above all a fulfilment in the imperial sphere of the principles of harmony and consent.

A very different kind of case was argued by Aeneas Sylvius Piccolomini (1405–64) in his *Origin and Authority of the Roman Empire* (*De ortu et auctoritate Romani imperii*), written in March 1446. Piccolomini's line of argument was modelled on Engelbert: he first explained why kingship developed, using the same passages from Cicero and the Roman historians (pp. 7–8), and then argued that these reasons postulate universal monarchy. Piccolomini argued for nothing less than a complete restoration of imperial sovereignty over all secular rulers. Shocked (he says) by those peoples and princes who claim independence from the jurisdiction of the Roman empire, he affirmed the emperor's authority as supreme court of appeal: he is to settle disputes between other kings, interpret doubtful points of law and temper the rigour of the law with equity and humanity (pp. 7, 16, 19, 22–3). Only the emperor can make law, presumably in the sense of the theoretically universal Roman law, and new dispositions to meet new contingencies (pp. 17, 19).

Such extravagant claims could hardly have been meant seriously by anyone as conversant with practical politics as Piccolomini; there is an element of playful and formal Latin prosody in imitation of Cicero. Indeed Piccolomini applied to Christendom republican ideals taken from Cicero: individuals ought to sacrifice their welfare for the common utility; the occasional miscarriage of imperial justice is justified by the elimination of disputes consequent upon imperial authority (pp. 16–19, 22).

But Piccolomini argued, in a Ciceronian style that is not without conviction, that the benefits of civil justice, and of kingship, will only be fully enjoyed when all kings are subject to one supreme monarch:

For when [the several kings] contended now over boundaries, now over jurisdiction, and there was nothing to stop quarrels save the sword, since no-one considered himself less than another, with wars seething and raging, neither cities nor provinces could associate with one another, which prevented that sweet and most agreeable interchange (*commercium*) of human society. But the benign providence of human nature, which by its own instinct tends to the best and never acquiesces in disorder either present or future, quickly intervened. By its help it was decided that individual [realms] should be reduced to a single sovereignty (*principatus*), called monarchy by the Greeks, empire by ourselves. (p. 9; see also p. 15)

Rule over such a universal empire was assigned, by nature or by God, to the Romans on account of their virtues; this was sanctioned by Christ during his lifetime. The Roman people, with the consent of the pope, transferred it to the Germans, so that the present emperor-elect, Frederick III of Habsburg, possesses

supreme power in temporal matters, committed to [you] from on high . . . so that you may felicitously bring wars to an end, adorn peace and sustain the estate of the commonwealth (*rei publice statum*). For such goals all peoples, all nations and all kings and princes ought with willing hearts to submit themselves to the Empire. (p. 14)

What is new in this defence of the Empire is the self-conscious parallel made with the position of the papacy, especially as supreme appellate court (pp. 14, 17, 21–3). This is reminiscent of Antonio Roselli's massive *Monarchy* (*Monarchia*, 1433). It is partly explained by the fact that the work was composed just when Frederick III, whose service Piccolomini had recently entered, had disowned the Council of Basle and finally made peace with pope Eugenius IV, but when many powerful German princes and the king of France were still refusing to submit to Eugenius. There was a tendency now to regard papacy and Empire no longer as rivals but as potential allies in the restoration of monarchical authority throughout Christendom. This was the serious element in a work otherwise marked by flattery and conceit.

STATE SOVEREIGNTY

The further development of separate states was justified by ideals of patriotism, nationality and independent sovereignty; as well as on grounds of realism ('it is easier to transmit a word than a sword'). The main literary and academic stimulus and justification for concentration of power and the emergence of royal, ducal or civic states came from classical Roman and Greek political thought, especially Cicero and Aristotle. The idea of fatherland (*patria*) was ingrained in medieval culture, and one may assume it was not absent from popular consciousness, as an ideal entity which it was a good, free man's duty to serve and die for. Similarly the idea of *respublica*, the public domain, as an area of social life and activity to which service and sacrifice were due, was kindled among those who read Cicero's *On Duties* and speeches, the Roman poets and historians. This was so in France, Germany and other countries of northern Europe; it received even more emphasis, sometimes verging on the fanatical, among the Italian rhetoricians and humanists. In Italy local civic patriotism developed without the benefit of separate nationhood.

Aristotle's thought was as if anything more specifically orientated towards separate states, the *polis* (literally city-state) being conceived as the preeminent natural habitat for *homo sapiens* since it and it alone could satisfy human needs. The Greek city-states formed a states system of separate political units within an overarching cultural unit comparable to that now emerging in Europe. It was crucial for the whole development of the European concept of 'state' that *polis* or *civitas* was taken to refer not just to city-states but to whatever actual polities there were: kingdoms, principalities, duchies or city-states. From Aquinas onwards *civitas*, *regnum* and *provincia* were commonly treated as belonging to one and the same category. Marsiglio and Ockham suggested that the difference between city-state, duchy and kingdom was mainly one of size (*DP* 1.2.2 and *Dialogue* III.i.2.5,

p. 794, respectively). The more abstract term *respublica* could refer to any political unit.

Ptolemy of Lucca (see below, pp. 122–3), on the other hand, does seem to have applied Aristotle's arguments about the advantages of life in the *polis* specifically to the city-states of his own time, contrasting the city (*civitas*) favourably with the small town or borough (*castrum*) and village (*villa*) on the ground that it contains the many crafts needed for a satisfactory human life and that it 'brings about a certain harmony and gentleness of spirit' (*The Rule of Princes* IV, chs.2–3). He differentiated between a kingdom and a city-state in terms of their constitutions: whereas kingdoms are ruled by royal governments, the 'political principate' or '*politia*', that is, constitutional, elective government according to the laws, 'is especially appropriate for *civitates*, as we see especially in parts of Italy and as it once flourished at Athens'. Such limited government is found in the cities of 'all regions, whether in Germany, Scythia [approximately western Asia] or Gaul' (IV chs. 1–2). Aegidius Romanus (above, p. 51), on the contrary, argued that the advantages ascribed by Aristotle to the city-state were actually more fully attainable in the kingdom with its greater military strength and self-sufficiency. This view was repeated by other neo-Aristotelians.

In Aristotle's *Politics*, as in other classical authors including Cicero and Roman law itself, there was presented as paradigmatic a kind of state in which all legal and governmental powers were exercised at the centre, whether by one ruler, a few or many. There was no place for either local immunities or an overarching empire. Aquinas, incidentally, ignored the question of world government. All the classical authors, and preeminently the ardently republican Cicero, agreed in condemning as conspiratorial the corporatist exercise of partial autonomy by lesser associations.

It is commonly thought and partially true that *national* divisions became sharper during the later Middle Ages. The European peoples had always kept their own languages, laws and customs; and many of them had a distinct consciousness of themselves as political units under their own king, to be governed by their own native traditions.[13] Many people, as individuals and as communities, were aware of national identity and regarded it as a significant social fact about themselves: English, Franks or Frenchmen, Spaniards, Magyars and so on. In the later Middle Ages there were trends towards a more

---

[13] Reynolds, *Kingdoms*, pp. 262–331; Guenée, *States*, pp. 50–64, 216–21; Gaines Post, *Studies in Medieval Life and Thought* (Princeton, N. J.: Princeton University Press, 1964), pp. 434ff.

articulate self-consciousness of nationhood. This might be based upon language; Germans, Italians and Spaniards, despite their lack of political integration, expressed sentiments of nationhood. It might be based upon political factors and hatred of a common foe, as with Scotland under Robert the Bruce. There was no doubt an element of imitation of the relatively successful English and French whose national integration did something to enhance their political potency. Literature became increasingly vernacular as major new works were written in the language of the people. Latin remained a literary language only for a cultured elite; Renaissance humanism itself being largely an Italian phenomenon until the later fifteenth century. In later Gothic more distinctive local and national styles were developed in church architecture. The academic world became less trans-national. New universities founded from the later fourteenth century onwards catered increasingly for students on a local basis.

The church itself began to divide into more distinct national and territorial units, both as regards popular sentiment and for adminis-trative and juridical purposes. The church–state conflicts themselves were conflicts between a supra-national authority and a national dynastic state; victories for the secular power were victories for a less international church order and for national self-consciousness. These debates, in which Roman and Greek ideas were invoked, did as much as anything to assist the formulation of a theory of the independent authority of states and the rejection of universal polity. The period of schism and councils, from 1378 to 1450, saw a great increase in the capacity of states for running their own church affairs and even choosing which pope to adhere to, or whether to adhere to pope or council. The concept of a Gallican church with distinctive traditions emerged. These trends were encouraged by the largely Italian com-position of the papal curia and college of cardinals, and by the papacy being bogged down in Italian affairs. After the return to Rome in 1377, French–Italian rivalry among the cardinals provoked schism; after the reunion of 1417, the pope was invariably Italian.

Several of the emerging states, especially those with a national basis, like France, England and Bohemia, were also developing a sense of separate religious identity. This went furthest in Bohemia when from the 1390s a reform movement gave rise to a fully autonomous evangelical church with a vernacular bible and liturgy (see above pp. 81–2). The development of a sense of nationality was, however, uneven and in many places did not outweigh allegiance based on family, city or dynasty. National sentiment found little support in the ancient authors, except that Italians could look back with pride on the

Roman Republic and Empire; then Italy had been united and dominant. The chief intellectual ally of nationality was history or historical
myth. The English had Arthur, the French Charlemagne and St
Louis, Germans dreamt of a return of the emperor Frederick; all three
had long since invented Trojan origins, as the Florentines claimed
descent from the Etruscans. The ideology of Israel as God's chosen
people, which became a precedent for the nation-state in early
modern times, was seldom invoked in this context; though courtiers
referred back to the Davidic monarchy.

The link between nationhood and statehood was another question.
The prevailing wisdom is that it belongs to a much later period;
medieval Europe being riddled with feudal and dynastic ties, there
was little connection between political allegiance and language or
nationality. Yet some states with an ethnic dimension or basis did
emerge: England, France, Poland, Denmark, Norway, Hungary and
Bohemia (albeit complicated by external dynastic ties). Some rulers
and subjects did claim the right to an independent polity because they
were a separate nation. In early fourteenth-century Scotland there
emerged a consciousness of 'the community of the realm of Scotland'; the *Declaration of Arbroath* (1320) referred to the Scythian
origins of 'the nation of the Scots' and equated political independence
for the Scots with liberty itself:

For as long as there shall but one hundred of us remain alive, we will never
consent to subject ourselves to the dominion of the English ... For it is ...
liberty alone that we fight for, which no honest man will lose but with his
life.[14]

In Italy, it is true, the same ideal of political liberty was championed
by city-states contending with others of the same speech and nation.
Yet here too, as also in Germany, political turbulence was sometimes
blamed by high-minded philosophers on national disunity, as we see
in Dante, Marsiglio and Cusa. Defence of the so-called empire came,
in the course of the fourteenth century, to mean defence of a united
German monarchy governing, principally, German-speaking peoples.

Diversity of laws and customs could be justified in terms of
Roman law itself, since this recognised 'civil' and 'municipal' law as
legitimately varying from one *civitas* or race (*gens*) to another. It was
justified by jurists and philosophers on the ground that 'positive',
'human' law may legitimately vary from place to place, indeed ought

---

[14] Cited by G. W. S. Barrow, *Robert Bruce and the Community of the Realm in Scotland*
(Edinburgh: Edinburgh University Press, 1976), p. 428 (the last phrase is from
Sallust); cf. Reynolds, *Kingdoms*, pp. 274–6.

to, since laws must be suited to their users (see Aquinas, *ST* I/IIae 95.2 *ad* 3; 95.4 *resp.*; 97.2 *resp.*). When people defended a practice in terms of precedent, custom or history, they were defending local, sometimes national norms of behaviour. Such sentiments were not nationalist in an exclusive sense: when Fortescue boasted of England's political and regal constitution, he said that Scotland and 'many other kingdoms have also attained the right to be ruled both politically and regally' (ch. 13: *MPI* p. 329–30).

Philosophers could refer to Aristotle on the 'diversity of climates and languages, different ways of life and different political orders (*politiae*), and the fact that what is virtuous in one people is not virtuous in another' to demonstrate that it is better to have different rulers for different regions rather than one world ruler in temporal matters (John of Paris, ch. 3). Engelbert himself, in the course of his argument for universal empire, described a 'whole nation (*gens tota*)' as 'a community united by language, fatherland, customs and laws' (ch. 12). The peace of a nation or kingdom, he said, is ensured when there exists 'mutually agreed unity of the same fatherland (*patria*), language, customs and laws'; while discord is more likely with foreigners 'who are of a different fatherland, language, customs and laws'. This can be avoided by a peaceful and just disposition, by the inability to make war, or by adequate natural frontiers (ch. 14).

Two French thinkers went further, partly inspired by their opposition to imperial claims. John Buridan, following Aristotle, said that the quality of a state depended upon the temperament (*complexio*) of its people; this in turn is affected, though not determined, 'by the disposition of the place or region'. People in temperate climates, though less subtle than those in hot climates, tend to have the best governments (*Questions* (*Quaestiones in octo libros politicorum Aristotelis*), pp. 377–8). Types of government should vary to fit in with human diversity and changing needs; a world government is, therefore, undesirable (p. 425). Nicole Oresme dismissed the notion that a desire to avoid war might make everyone obey a world sovereign as *une ymagination mathématique*. Political temperament is affected by climate; tyranny cannot last long 'in a temperate region, remote from servile barbarity, where men are free in their social dealings, customs and nature'. Hence

One polity is suitable for one people and another for another, as [Aristotle] says [*Politics* VII.7, 1327b]. For it is appropriate that the positive laws and governments of peoples should differ according to the diversity of their regions, complexions, inclinations and habits. (*Aristotle's 'Politics' (Livre de 'Politiques' d'Aristote)* 7.10, pp. 291b–294a)

The quality of being free and well governed on account of a temperate climate, which Aristotle claimed for the Greeks, was here implicitly claimed for the French. (Aristotle had added that, if the Hellenic race 'could be formed into one state, [it] would be able to rule the world'!) If not an assertion of nationalism in the modern sense, all this supported the claim that different regions and peoples could and perhaps should have their own distinctive political orders.[15]

The concept of sovereignty in the sense of independence from legal constraints by outside powers was asserted in a number of ways. It was conceptually distinct from the claim to jurisdiction or legitimate authority itself, which could go with some subordination to a higher legal power. Words like *dominium* and *jurisdictio* did not necessarily imply sovereignty. But *auctoritas* and *maiestas*, derived from the language of the Roman state, did; it was chiefly by appropriating the terms of Roman dignity for rulers that sovereignty was claimed. Great kings expressed their authority by claiming the title, powers and insignia of *imperium* (empire) itself within their own territories. This was intended to signify that they could act without reference to others, whether inside or outside the realm, and often that they had some right to rule other peoples and lands.

We have seen in chapter 2 how secular rulers warded off papal intervention in what they regarded as their own affairs and how in some cases they asserted some independence from the papacy in church affairs as well. The Roman-law doctrine that temporal sovereignty belonged to the emperor alone, suggesting that, at least, appeals could be made from royal to imperial courts and disputes between kings should be settled by the emperor, was in practice ignored by the major secular powers. But the need for a more precise formulation than existing language provided is suggested by the coining of a precise neologism: the king 'does not recognise a superior at all in temporal matters'. This was stated by pope Innocent III in the famous decretal *Per venerabilem* (1202: *Decretals* 4.17.13), and the term '*princeps* (sovereign prince) in his own kingdom' was applied by French and Sicilian jurists to their own monarchs. It shows how clearly that lawyer-pope thought: for it contradicted imperial claims yet was calculated to attract a secular prince, while the papacy's

---

[15] Writing of the period 900 to 1300, Reynolds says, 'The idea of naturally separate peoples and their inherited right to separate government seems . . . to emerge from a number of works': *Kingdoms*, p. 320.

interests were safeguarded so long as it reserved, implicitly at least, the right to interpret what was 'temporal' (see above, p. 44).

The question of supra-state secular authority was most seriously contested in Italy, where Roman law and the ideas enshrined in it still carried much weight, and where it was complicated by the rival universalist claims of pope and emperor. From the 1330s the German king-emperors abandoned any but a titular role in Italian politics; while the Avignon papacy, weakened by conflict within the papal states, was reduced to a regional power. Even so recognition by or alliance with pope or emperor could still assist a new government. Under these circumstances, Venice, Milan, Florence, Genoa and other city-states and principalities jostled for power in a peninsular states system, developing resident embassies and pitting the power of rhetorical diplomacy against the mercenary sword.

In the Ciceronian and Aristotelian languages of humanists and philosophers, the legal self-sufficiency of the *civitas* required no justification. Jurists, on the other hand, especially those using Roman law, were faced with the problem that their own law envisaged only one sovereign authority, the emperor. Cities and peoples might have certain powers of self-government permitted or delegated to them, but they could not, for example, make laws on their own authority. Jurists responded in two ways. First, they stated that any existing and functioning corporate group (*universitas*) could be said to have legal personality so that it could act as a body through representatives, and certain corporate rights (*iura universitatis*), such as the right to elect officers and to decide by majority vote. Only unjust associations – a category obviously open to wide interpretation – were forbidden. The point was that such groups did not require explicit authorisation by the emperor or other superior. They could be deemed legal, tacitly authorised by the emperor, so long as he had not expressly prohibited them. Alternatively, they were said to be authorised 'by the law itself' if they fell into a category recognised in the *Digest*. All of this could be and was applied both to territorial associations, such as cities, and to personal associations such as guilds and religious orders. Canonists such as Innocent IV were prone to favour guilds, perhaps because they were analogous to ecclesiastical colleges and had a religious aspect. Civic autonomy was a card to play against the emperor. Corporate self-management was thus acquired in a truly 'ascending' way by groups formed spontaneously by their members. This remarkable development in the concept of freedom of association and assembly brought the law into line with the great proliferation of towns and guilds during the expansion of trade and industry.

The status of the city-state as a corporation (*universitas*) entitled it to elect rulers and administer its own internal affairs, but it did not turn it into a sovereign state. The authority to raise taxes, make laws and exercise other sovereign rights was argued at first on the ground that the emperor had tacitly conceded these things to all those cities and peoples who were currently in possession of them. The emperor remained as formal superior with largely ceremonial functions. All this was being claimed by and on behalf of independent communes in Lombardy and Tuscany and later some cities in the Low Countries. German cities, while no less interested in developing the practical machinery of self-government, did not generally press their claims against the emperor, but more often looked to him for support against local lords.

Thus a basis was sought in custom, consent (by both emperor and people) and simple 'fact' as opposed to law. This last point was not unimportant. Innocent III's statement that the king of France 'recognised no superior at all in temporal affairs' had similarly acknowledged existing reality as normative. All this was to imply that political realities had a part to play in the formation of legitimate authority. And it enabled European rulers to continue to make use of Roman law in a very different world.

By the end of the thirteenth century, jurists had accepted the status quo in northern and central Italy: cities may make their own laws, even ones contrary to Roman law provided they are not contrary to natural law, without requiring the consent of the present-day emperor. The pro-imperial jurist Cino da Pistoia (1270–1336), poet and teacher of Bartolus, reported how his teacher, Dino del Mugello (d.1298/1303), held that 'each people has the power of making law, conceded or granted by the prince' (i.e. tacitly recognised by the emperor), and that such an opinion 'is generally accepted by all *doctores*' (on *Digest* 1.3.32, fols. 7v–8r). He himself admitted that the emperor's claim to be 'lord of the world' was true in law but not in fact. Others agreed that this was 'the common view' which 'the whole world observes' (Albericus de Rosate, *On Statutes* (*De statutis*) 1, q.7, n. 1). It was partly upon this that Ockham based his general principle: 'each people and *civitas* can make for itself its own law, which is called civil law (*Digest* 1.1.2). Therefore both a people and a *civitas* can (also) ... elect a head' (McGrade, *Ockham*, p. 105 and n. 73).

Bartolus of Sassoferrato (1314–57: see below, pp. 127–9) was the first jurist to develop all this into a thoroughgoing and consistent theory of state sovereignty. City-states can legislate for themselves and are also 'states' in a fiscal sense: 'in (cities) which, either in law or fact, do not recognise a superior, like the *civitates* of Tuscany, the city itself is the fisc', the imposition of new taxes being 'reserved to the people which in its own city has empire or holds the position of prince'. The point about Bartolus was, first, that he ascribed to the *civitas* not just special privileges but the totality of powers hitherto reserved for the emperor (and certain kings). 'A free people' possesses 'pure and unmixed sovereignty'. A *civitas* 'has as much power in one people as the emperor has in the whole world'. Bartolus' statement that 'the city is sovereign to itself (*civitas sibi princeps*)', 'the people is prince in this city', embodied in bold simplicity both a rationale for existing political realities and a Copernican revolution in public-law jurisprudence (*On Digest* 1.1.9, 4.4.3, 43.6.2, 48.1.7, 50.9.4; *Consilia* 189).

Second, the criterion for entry into the 'sovereign' category was the existing use of powers like legislation, in short recognition by the people and acquiescence by other states. Whether or not this implied that the people in a constitutionalist–democratic sense were the origin of power, it was to some extent accompanied by such a notion in Bartolus himself (below, pp. 127–9).

Bartolus' view became standard juristic teaching. His *civitas sibi princeps* corresponded to the *citta signore* of the Florentine humanists, many of whom trained as jurists. And Bartolus' theory, while specifically designed for Italian city-states like Florence which already had *de facto* sovereignty, was equally applicable to any political community. Thus the emerging states system of Europe was legally baptised. The arrangement of several sovereign states interacting through diplomatic channels was formally legitimised. European law made a non-revolutionary transition from universal dominion to plurality and a formal equality between states. Compared with other civilisations it was a significant achievement.

4

CITY-STATES AND CIVIC
GOVERNMENT

·

We will now look at the structure of authority within political
societies such as city-states, principalities, kingdoms and the church.
To begin with, the *civic* governments of medieval Europe and of
medieval/early Renaisssance Italy, from the twelfth to the fifteenth
centuries, were a phenomenon unique in human history.[1] Towns and
cities developed as centres of local or long-distance trade, artisan
manufacture and administration, which vitally affected their culture,
social structure and political prospects. They were less self-sufficient
than the city-states of ancient Greece, being dependent for food and
raw materials on a countryside which they would have to struggle to
control and whose inhabitants were seldom integrated, socially or
politically, into the citizenry. In the more powerful kingdoms, such
as France and England, they were corporate members of a much
larger commonwealth with special trading privileges, fiscal responsibilities and certain powers of internal self-regulation. In the less
defined, more contested parts of Europe – the Low Countries,
northern and central Italy and the Rhineland corridor extending into
south-western Germany – they entered into more equal relations
with local lords. Some were real city-states ruling their hinterland:
Milan, Venice, Florence, Genoa and, for certain periods and with less
control over their countryside, cities of the Hanseatic League such as
Lübeck and of the Netherlands such as Ghent. The eleventh to the
fifteenth centuries were a golden age of small-scale government and
civic independence.

[1] See bibliography, pp. 202–3, 206.

117

Cities were commonly designated by words indicating community: *commune* in French and Italian, *Gemeinde* in German, *commune*
(again), *communitas* or *universitas civium* or *burgensium* in Latin. Cities
had usually started off being governed by a council chosen by the
body of 'citizens' – hereditary residents qualified by lineage and
wealth, originally a relatively large body but declining rapidly in
proportion to the whole as cities developed and immigrants multi-
plied. Citizenship became oligarchical; some cities, such as Lübeck
and still more Venice, developed stable oligarchical constitutions.
There was conflict, especially in Italy and the Low Countries,
between classes, interest groups and leading families. Successful merchants or craft guilds consolidated their hold on affairs. In Italy
conflict was such that a supreme magistrate (*podesta*) was chosen from
outside, for one year or longer; and sometimes a lifelong or hereditary principate was established, for example at Milan. The later
thirteenth and early fourteenth centuries were a period of constitutional conflict, revolution and experiment. Out of this emerged
either a strengthened oligarchy or a principate, or again, no less often,
a division of power between 'old' and 'new' councils, representing
the old oligarchy and the craft guilds respectively. The struggle went
on until the early fifteenth century. Florence, where all this took place
in the most articulate atmosphere, had a succession of guild uprisings
followed by periods of rearranged government by great families
operating through the major guilds – 'the lords' (*Signoria*).

Political theorists paid relatively little attention to civic government north of the Alps. In Italy it was discussed, as Skinner has
shown, in a variety of languages by theorists of Italian origin who
included some of the foremost political minds of the Middle Ages and
who wrote also about kingdoms, sometimes in the same work or
even sentence. Early Renaissance political thought was mainly about
city-states. First, there was a native language in which was expressed
the idea of the city as a political community: in Latin *civitas*, *cummune*,
universitas civium, *burgensis populus* and in the vernacular *commune*,
Gemeinde and so on. It was to this somewhat abstract and partially
juristic entity that legal and political acts (treaty agreements, municipal laws and so on) tended to be assigned; 'with the consent of the
city', for example.[2] In fourteenth-century constitutional documents,
especially those detailing changes made after conflict or revolution,
for example allocating power between a new and old council, this

---

[2] Otto von Gierke, *Das Deutsche Genossenschaftsrecht* (Berlin, 1881), vol. III,
pp. 192–202, 277–8; Antony Black, *Guilds and Civil Society in European Political
Thought*, pp. 47–9, 68–72.

community was often said to include 'the poor and the rich' side by side. This language was common to all Europe.

The civil-law jurists, especially in Italy, combined it with the language of Roman law to produce a richer and more detailed juristic language. The acts and responsibilities of cities as corporate bodies were defined, and majority voting procedures within the council made clear. As legal corporations, cities could appoint representatives to act on their behalf (*syndici* and so on); it was in their capacity as legal representatives with more or less full powers that the expanding functions and authority of city councils were expressed and justified by jurists.

Some principles underlying city government in the middle of the thirteenth century are suggested by John of Viterbo in his advice to Italian city rulers on how to proceed when faced with a serious decision such as whether to declare war. The *podesta* should first consult the council in the usual way, then a 'fuller council' several times, and after that

> let him make a general assembly of the knights and foot-soldiers of the city and the wise men, captains and consuls of the knights, judges, bankers, merchants and leaders of the craft guilds; so that, when the common will of all (*communi voluntate omnium*) has been thus sought out and agreed, he may be able to proceed the more safely. (ch. 132, p. 270)

The aim seems to have been to make a considered decision with the widest possible support, partly to avoid the *podesta* being blamed for any consequences. Civic language all over Europe refers to a common will of all citizens. What this meant is suggested by the jurists' application to city government of the collegiate principle: when achieving 'common consent' it is not enough to canvas individuals separately in their homes, one must have 'the consent of all at the same time' in an assembly; for 'he who consents in his room could dissent in the chapter'.[3]

Spokesmen for city regimes, whether old or new, oligarchical or guild-democratic, appealed for peace and unity among citizens; still more, they preached brotherhood, friendship and love as the attitudes which citizens should have towards one another. Such values appear to have been native to European civic communities; they were an ethical counterpart to the idea of the city or city-state as a seamless community (*commune, communitas, communio*) which, as a legal corporation, could act as one. These expressions do not of course tell us

---

3 Gierke, *Genossenschaftsrecht*, vol. III, pp. 312–14; P. Gillet, *La Personnalité juridique en droit ecclésiastique* (Malines, 1927), pp. 134–5.

what actually went on. Appeals to 'brotherhood', 'love' and so on were often a response to intense social divisions, arising from kinship, economic class or political faction: the evils to to be avoided were stated as discord, quarrels, strife, violence, ambition, greed. Such an ideology of state unity across divisions of rank corresponded to the Ciceronian ideal of *conspiratio ordinum* (harmony between ranks). It was one of the most pervasive ideas of the late-medieval and early-Renaissance epoch, expressed in a variety of political languages including that of the humanists. It was summed up in the organic concept *concordia* (literally, together-heartedness). For example, the town of Berwick on the Scottish–English border, in 1248–9 and again in 1284, abolished its separate guilds and declared itself a single guild city. The 'many bodies assembled in one place [sc. the guilds]' declared their aim 'to achieve peace and one will and firm and sincere love (*dilectio*) in relation one to another ... with all members having respect to one head', from which they hope will result 'one counsel in good acts, a single firm and friendly society'.[4] At Florence 'brotherhood' was used as an argument for equality of legal status; frescoes at Siena presented charity as a civic virtue.[5] Brunetto Latini wrote that 'the government of cities was based on three pillars: justice, reverence and love' (*Treasury* (*Li livres dou trésor*), p. 392; cf. pp. 211–12). The idea of 'community' as an ethical value was definitely present.

Such ideas were supported, or perhaps inspired, by the full might of the Christian value of love; this had also been present in the earlier 'Peace-of-God' movements which coincided with the development of the first communes and shared with them goals like the elimination of vendetta. The very word *commune* could be associated with the *communio* of Christians in the Eucharist. While expressed in theological language, the universal precept of Christian love (*caritas*) was a convenient moral vehicle for state formation: shared membership of a community and cohabitation in a territory warrants the attitude of love regardless of kinship or social status. As the Dominican friar Ptolemy of Lucca put it, 'Love of country is based on charity as its root (*amor patriae in radice charitatis fundatur* – he brings together classical and Christian idiom) ... love of country will merit a rank of honour above other virtues' (*The Rule of Princes*, III.4). The scholastic theologian Henry of Ghent said that civil communion and society could not exist without

---

[4] Printed in W. Wilda, *Das Gildewesen im Mittelalter* (Halle, 1831; repr. Aalen: Scientia Verlag, 1964), pp. 376ff.

[5] See bibliography, pp. 202–3.

the highest friendship, by which each one is held by the other to be another self, and supreme charity, by which each one loves the other as himself, and the greatest benevolence, by which each one wishes for the other the same as for himself.[6]

This political expression of the theological virtue of charity would be echoed centuries later in Hegel's state ethic. Girolami, also a friar, evoked the community as whole in terms reminiscent of the philosophy of love: since the part is 'more united to the whole than to itself, the citizen must love the city more than himself'. The binding force of any state comes from 'the union or conjunction of hearts, from willing the same thing'; it is natural to love city more than self because the city is greater and more beautiful.[7] Such ideas were commonplace among city chroniclers many of whom were friars or clergy.

The language of Aristotle made an enormous impact on the discussion of city politics. Here was a wealth of concepts forged specifically for city-states, and in addition the doctrine that the city-state was a uniquely natural society, indeed superior in its civilising qualities to any other. Aristotle had gone to great lengths to conceptualise and evaluate different forms of city government, especially oligarchy and democracy, thus providing a ready-made language in which the class and political conflicts of medieval and Renaissance city-states could be discussed.

The first scholastic to comment upon city politics was the Dominican Albert the Great (1206–80), Aquinas' teacher. At Cologne he acted as intermediary between the city and the prince-archbishop; in his writing he referred to 'cities of Lombardy such as Genoa'. Albert used Aristotle's terms 'timocracy' and 'democracy'. Aristotle had used timocracy (literally rule by men of honour) to mean good government by the many and democracy to mean bad government by the many (*Nicomachaean Ethics* VIII.10,1160a–b). Albert changed the meanings of these terms: timocracy, he said, means 'rule by the majority of the rich who have no title to sovereignty except their enormous wealth and treasure', which is not, as might be claimed, that 'polity' or moderate form of government preferred by Aristotle, 'but a kind of corruption'. Democracy, on the other hand, means 'rule for the benefit of the *populares*; and this is not a deviant constitution but polity' (i.e. moderate and good government by the

---

[6] Cited by Georges de Lagarde, *La Naissance de l'esprit laïque*, vol. II, p. 178.

[7] E. L. Minio-Paluello, 'Remigio Girolami's *De Bono Communi*', *Italian Studies* 2 (1956), pp. 56–71 at p. 64; and cited by C. T. Davis, 'An Early Florentine Political Theorist', *Proceedings of the American Philosophical Society* 104 (1960), pp. 668–9.

many). In contemporary terms, Albert thus equated timocracy with rule by merchant oligarchies (sometimes styled *honorabiliores*) and democracy with rule by the broader citizenry, the *popolo*, craft-guilds or rising artisan class. And he made it clear which he preferred: in a democracy, people 'do not defer to princes in matters of justice; natural justice is upheld . . . so that, just as nature made all men equal, so they stand equally in relation to political office' (*Commentary on the Politics*, pp. 238, 344–5, 563; *Commentary on the Sentences*, pp. 807–8). It is the voice of the friar. Aquinas, on the other hand, had little to say about city constitutions.

Aegidius Romanus, in his *The Rule of Princes* (written 1277–9: see above, p. 51), as well as praising monarchy as the best form of government, also legitimised government by 'the many, as the whole people' so long as it aimed at 'the common good of the poor, the middle class and the rich, of all according to their position'. In other words, he was prepared to accommodate civic government, of which he always cited the Italian city-states as the example, by equating rule by the community of citizens, as opposed to rule by either oligarchs or *popolo*, with polity in the Aristotelian sense.

For generally the many as the whole people rule in the cities of Italy. There the consent of the whole people is required for making laws, for electing and correcting rulers. Although a *podesta* or lord who rules the city is always recognised there, the whole people have more power than the lord because it is they who elect him and, if he acts wrongly, correct him. The whole people make the laws which the lord may not transgress. (III.ii. ch. 2, fols. 268v–9r)

This was, clearly, the people in the technical sense, the existing political community; even so, Aegidius' account is stylised. It may also be seen as an example of someone translating native juristic language into Aristotelian without modifying the sense significantly. *The Rule of Princes* was translated into French *c.* 1286 and into several other languages. But although some non-Italian scholastics discussed *civitates* in Aristotelian language, this does not appear to have been of interest to those involved in city politics, least of all in northern and central Europe.

Ptolemy of Lucca (1236–1326), a Dominican who had studied under Aquinas and lived mainly in Italy, wrote much more extensively and enthusiastically about civic government (his political work, called *The Rule of Princes* and originally presented as a continuation of 'Aquinas'' *On Kingship*, was probably written between 1300 and 1305, at a time when both the internal and the external politics of Italian city-states were in turmoil). Ptolemy was unusual among scholastics in coming down strongly in favour of the city-state as the environment uniquely suited to the fullest development of human potentiality. It provides both for men's physical needs through the many crafts, and for their needs as rational beings, the development of understanding and of the virtues of justice and friendship. Here he not only remained true to Aristotle but added his own reflections, as a Christian: city-states fulfil the desire of men 'to communicate their works to the many/society (*multitudini*)', and cause 'a kind of harmony and gentleness of soul' (IV.3).

Ptolemy associated the city-state with the 'political' as opposed to 'royal' type of government (a distinction going back through Aquinas to Aristotle). Political rule is when 'a region, province, city or borough is ruled by one or many *according to its own statutes'*. It means republican government as in ancient Rome before Caesar's tyranny and as found today in the cities of Italy, Germany and other countries (including Russia – *Scythia*). His meaning seems to be that, although political rule may exist in larger states, it is characteristic of city-states – much as Aristotle had said. It is characterised by rulers being elected for a limited term of office, during which they must govern only according to the laws; they are subject to scrutiny when they leave office (II.8, IV.1–2). He preferred short-term office, as under consuls, because then 'honours are distributed to each citizen in turn according to his merits' (IV.3). The emphasis here is on limiting the ruler's power by law; the only reference to communal sovereignty or participation by the *popolo* in government is that the laws are laid down by the *multitudo* (IV.8). All in all, it appears that the chief difference between this and the 'civic humanism' ascribed to Bruni and others writing at Florence in the early fifteenth century, is that this is written in scholastic style using Aristotelian language rather than in the Ciceronian mode.

Of all those influenced by the rediscovery of Aristotle, Marsiglio of Padua was both the most original political theorist, and also the most intimate observer and concerned analyst of Italian civic politics. Still more, he was the one who not only built up the most coherent and subtle political theory, but also, at least in the earlier part of *Defender of the Peace*, stood closest to the actual dynamics of urban life and most faithfully reflected something of the prevailing mentality of city-republics. Although Marsiglio became, especially in the later parts of his work, primarily concerned with the question of civil and ecclesiastical authority in the Empire and kingdoms, there can be no doubt that the *Defender of the Peace* started as a schematic reflection upon the city-states of his native country, an attempt to show how civic peace could be restored by a correct understanding and implementation of the principles of politics (see also above, pp. 58–71). These principles turn out to be based upon the social structures and power relations of cities, and support a return to the supposed original form and ideal of civic government, namely the ultimate sovereignty of the body of citizens as a whole – much as Machiavelli later advocated *ridurre ai principi.*

Marsiglio located ultimate political authority in the entire citizen body conceived as a political corporation (*universitas civium, populus*) or state. He took the key concept *universitas civium* (literally, association of citizens) from the native language of the contemporary communes. His reasons for this were to exclude clerical claims and also to thwart the other major obstacles to republican peace, factionalism and despotism. Remarkably, he initiated discussion of the state by introducing Aristotle's division of the *polis* into its six functional parts (farmers, craftsmen, soldiers, men of wealth, priests, judges: *DP* 1.5; cf. Aristotle, *Politics*, VII.7.4,1328b); thus giving these a prominence in the formation of the state not envisaged by Aristotle or any other theorist. His main purpose was to ensure the subordination of the priestly part to the secular authority of the whole political community; but it also enabled him to draw the sting from social divisions by building them into the constitution of the state. He accepted that city-republics contain two main classes, the wealthy *honorabilitas* and the common people or *vulgus* (*DP* 1.5.1 and 1.13.4); and insisted that these be wholly subject to the government, and that both alike be subsumed into the corporation of citizenry.

His reasons for ascribing authority to the association of citizens included his own insights into the dynamics of human society and the state. It is because men are at heart both irretrievably self-interested and healthily committed to that sufficient life which only a state can provide, that the only fair and effective authority over them can be a body in which all alike participate (*DP* 1.12.5–9). He was careful to state that the chief authority may be either the citizen body itself or its 'preponderant part' (*pars valentior*); or again a person or persons to whom the citizen body or its preponderant part may choose to delegate authority, for a specific period and always with a right of recall. It is, none the less, remarkable how determinedly Marsiglio stuck to the principle of corporate citizen sovereignty in *DP Dictio* I, how scrupulous he was not to allow any exception which could give ground for despotism. When elaborating the principle of 'the people' as the primary legislature, he was careful to insist that 'the preponderant part' could act for them only by the people's 'choice (*electio*) or will expressed by voice in a general assembly of the citizens'; and that any alteration or interpretation of the law could be done only by the authority of this primary legislature (1.12.3). And it is not less remarkable how readily, both in *DP Dictio* II and in the much later *Lesser Defender* (*Defensor Minor*), Marsiglio forsook this original position as his attention shifted to the French monarchy and the Germanic Empire. This has baffled modern interpreters. The reason, as we have seen, can only have been first, that his overriding concern in both instances was the exclusion of clerical power; and, second, that he did not envisage imperial sovereignty as overriding the self-determination of civic communities.

Regarding the procedure for legislation, Marsiglio incorporated aspects of current practice into his scheme. According to a contemporary jurist, the current alternatives were: first, laws may be made 'with the people or corporation of the city assembled in public parliament according to the custom of the city', by majority vote upon a motion put by the ruler: but 'this method is rarely observed'. Second, they may be made by the city council in the presence of the ruler: 'this method is more observed'. Third, they may be made by a panel of experts appointed by the city council: 'this method is more in use' than either of the others (Alberticus de Rosate, *On Statutes* 1.q.4, fol. 2v/a). Marsiglio said that laws are first to be drafted by a select committee of legal experts, delegated by the citizen body; then referred back to the whole association which may add to, subtract from, change or reject them. Any citizen may speak on such an occasion. Laws are finally submitted, for approval or rejection in whole or in part, to a select group, again elected by the whole (this may be the same one as before); alternatively, the whole corporation, or its preponderant part, may do this (1.13.7–8).

Similarly, the executive and judicial authority ('the ruling part: *pars principans*'), which is needed to deal with matters not covered by the laws, to exercise discretion in the application of laws, and to employ armed force against rebels or lawbreakers (1.14.5–8), is always to be elected solely on the authority of the whole people, who may also correct and depose him or them (1.15.2 and 1.18.3). Marsiglio thus incorporated elements of rule by few experts and rule by one; but he clearly ruled out the current options of oligarchy and lordship.

Marsiglio allowed a preponderant part, whose membership was to be determined by 'quality' as well as numbers – implying that it might be a minority – to act in place of the whole; and he accepted the current notion of 'citizen', thus by implication excluding a great number of subjects from the political community (1.12.3). Marsiglio

would probably not have seen a contradiction between these provisions and the sovereignty of 'the community of citizens'; we must
remember how much Rousseau and others have changed the
meaning of 'citizen' and 'people'. Marsiglio may well have seen these
provisions as part of what the authority of the commune meant. He
was also trying to formulate a constitution that would both enshrine
sovereignty of the populus *and* actually work, through being adapt-
able to the wide variety of existing states. On the whole, among
available options in the city-states, Marsiglio chose the more democratic, in the sense of restoring the basic authority of the citizen body
as a united corporation. He certainly did not endorse the option of
transferring power to the *popolo* in the sense of the less well-off,
excluding older families or richer citizens. Marsiglio was not a social
or political revolutionary, only an ecclesiastical one. He wanted
city-republics to stabilise themselves on the basis of their intrinsic and
age-old constitutions clearly understood – and legitimised by philosophy.

When he turned to kingdom and Empire, Marsiglio thought that
the authority of the association of all citizens was sufficiently exercised if it were recognised as the remote origin of all existing civil
authorities, in the sense of the *lex regia* (by which Roman jurists had
legitimised the 'transfer' of power from people to emperor) and of
widespread current views of kingship: it was the whole people which
had originally authorised the present ruling house (or, in Germany,
the electoral princes); their role would only be reactivated if the
polity they had set up fell apart. When thinking in the context of
city-states, Marsiglio seems definitely to have regarded the assembly
of the whole active political community (*universitas civium*) as an
ongoing political authority, meeting periodically to elect rulers for
limited periods, and to sanction legislation. Marsiglio propelled the
concept of the *universitas civium*, derived from communal and juristic
language, into the metaphysical discussion of the state in Aristotelian
language. The solutions he offered were carefully selected from
available options. What was new was the way he tied a fundamental
philosophical argument so closely to a particular theory of the
constitution. But there is no sign that his work influenced, or even
became known in, the milieu for which it was first intended.

The jurists, meanwhile, tended to accept the way in which, in
many city-states, government was exercised variously by a lord or
merchant oligarchy. To say, as most did, that an independent city (or
populus) could legislate implied nothing about the internal distribution of power. Most jurists confined themselves to clarifying

technical points of constitutional procedure; for example, they affirmed the right of a city council, including a small oligarchical council, to act as the authorised representative of the city. The next major theorist of city government was Bartolus of Sassoferrato (1314–57), the greatest civil-law jurist of the Middle Ages. The achievements of this man in his short life were amazing. He studied law under Cino da Pistoia, the leading light of the previous generation, at Perugia, where he later taught the great Baldus and lectured for the last fourteen years of his life. He served in city government at Pisa and elsewhere. His achievement was to develop drastically the application of Roman law to contemporary legal problems and realities, including some constitutional ones. He thus completed the process by which the ancient law of Rome became a living instrument and legal and political language for Europeans, as 'the common law' (*ius commune*) upon which the laws of municipalities and states drew and by which they were sometimes significantly influenced. Later humanists attacked him for his style and misinterpretation of ancient law; this was wholly to misunderstand his purpose (his Latin is accurate, terse and well suited to his task).

Bartolus' constitutional writings were concerned with city-states. They fall into two main categories: his lecture-commentaries on the *Digest* and *Code*, and individual tracts on contemporary topics. Bartolus dealt with constitutional matters mainly in two parts of his commentaries: on *Digest* 1.1.9, where he discussed the procedures for legislation, and on *Codex* 10.32.3, where he discussed procedures for convoking a city council. It will be best to examine his statements closely before attempting an overall view of his opinions. Bartolus, as we have seen (above, pp. 115–16), said that in some states 'the people have full jurisdiction prescriptively or granted by the sovereign [emperor]'. Jurisdiction then lies either in the whole people or in the council. Statutes can be made in the following ways. (1) If senior judges or the lords make them, (1a) it is *humanum* for them to consult the wise, but (1b) they can make them on their own. (2) If they are made by the *populus*, then (2a) the whole people or (2b) the council which represents them should be called, with a two-thirds quorum; then, either (2ai/2bi) they can be asked what they wish to lay down on this matter, or (2aii/2bii) a specific proposal can be put to the people; and (2) if a majority agrees it will be law. Bartolus also said that the council (when unspecified, this refers to any kind of city council), not the magistrates, change laws, and the council elects officials and syndics. Consent of the people to a law (in any of (2) above) requires a public meeting, not private consultations in houses.

Law-making can be delegated to others only by the will of the people (presumably this applies only to (2) above: it would restrain the evolution of lordship out of oligarchy). The general assembly of the people (referred to in (2a) above) is not needed for the election of officials but, in a sovereign state, it elects the council which thereafter 'represents the whole people'. Bartolus also referred to the 'will' or 'mind of the people'.

From all this we can see that Bartolus was trying to straighten out existing procedures. It was not part of his juristic method to start out from or attempt to lay down general principles. On the other hand, where practice and the law left matters unsettled, Bartolus tended to favour consultation of the people. Given the ambiguity in the meaning of *populus*, it is difficult to conclude, as Skinner does, that Bartolus had a 'theory of popular sovereignty' (*Foundations*, vol. 1. pp. 63–5).

Bartolus devoted to these questions a separate tract, *City Government* (*tractatus de regimine civitatum*) written in 1355–7, which was quite widely circulated and may have had some influence on the conduct of government in cities. Here he started with the illuminating comment that jurists needed a theory of government, in the sense of considered opinions about the best form of government, because lords regularly consult them about constitutional reform; but for this they needed to familiarise themselves with Aristotle, and should not as hitherto confine themselves to legal texts. Bartolus said explicitly that what he had in mind was not the superior ideology of Aristotle, because what he had to say was to be found in *Digest* 1.2.2; rather, it was Aristotle's concepts and distinctions, in short his 'language', which Bartolus considered essential (pp. 75–8).

Bartolus said that the best form of government depended on a state's size (compare Rousseau, *Du contrat social*, III.3): for large states monarchy, for medium-sized states government by 'rich and good men', for small states government by the *multitudo* (the many, people, community). Bartolus used throughout the term *civitas*. By large *civitates* he presumably meant provinces or kingdoms; for medium states included Venice, Florence and ancient Rome, while small states included Siena, Pisa and Perugia. Scholars inclined to claim Bartolus for democracy have tended not to point out that these small states are not, according to Bartolus, completely independent, for constitutional reform can only be enacted by the city's superior or lord. It is worth comparing what Bartolus said here with another passage where he classified states according to size (*Consilium* 189), as 'large', 'less large' and 'the smallest', by which he meant small towns and villages subject to a larger city.

There is, however, a sense in which Bartolus did here adumbrate community sovereignty as a general principle for city-states. The 'rich and good men' who rule medium states are in fact, he said, fairly numerous; they form a distinct and stable 'middle class' (*medii*), and the community, being too numerous to be assembled, consents to being governed by them. Government by the *multitudo* in small cities is, he said, what Aristotle called *politeia* and is today called popular government (*regimen ad populum*): 'Jurisdiction belongs to the people or the masses' (*populum, seu multitudinem*), but it excludes 'the lowest people' (*vilissimis*), and it may also exclude the magnates, since, 'as we often observe', these may be 'so powerful that they oppress the rest' (pp. 75–6, 87–90, 93). This is a unique case of a theorist supporting the practice of excluding magnates from office, as some cities did. Bartolus went further: such a democratic constitution is intrinsically good, and, on the authority of the Bible, 'seems to be of God rather than men'. These views of Bartolus were not on the whole adopted by other jurists. His greatest successor, Baldus, who was closely involved in city government at Perugia and spent some time in Florence, emphasised the representative status of city councils in the sense of their authority to act independently of the people as a whole, whose capacities for decision-making he did not rate highly.

BRUNI

The language of the Roman Republic had been present in the Italian and other communes from their beginnings: they elected 'consuls', the city council was a *senatus* and so on. The literary revival of the Italian Renaissance gave this a wholly new dimension; Ciceronian became a new style for civic political discourse. The real innovator was Petrarch, who in his writings and life generated a new model for learning, authorship and the relation between scholar and community. He was 'the famous author sitting at his desk, withdrawn from the world, but conscious of the devoted attention of a million admirers'.[8] With his 'simultaneous affirmation and rejection of civic life', derived from Cicero, Petrarch as an orator loved the *civitas*, but as a philosopher preferred solitude.[9] The impact on political discourse and theory of these changes in the dominant intellectual and spiritual culture, which would eventually affect the whole mentality of the educated and the governing élite throughout Europe, first became

[8] Bolgar, *Classical Heritage*, pp. 247–68 at p. 248.
[9] J. E. Seigel, '"Civic Humanism" or Ciceronian Rhetoric? The Culture of Petrarch and Bruni', *Past and Present* 34 (1966), pp. 3–48 at pp. 36–7.

evident among the Florentines during their conflict with the duke of Milan around 1400, notably in the speeches and writings of Coluccio Salutati (1331–1406) and Leonardo Bruni of Arezzo (1369–1444).

This movement has been described as 'civic humanism', that is, as a direct application of humanist values to social and political life in the context of the city-state: the highest value is individual personality, and this is affirmed through political action, inspired by virtue and aimed at glory, in an independent, self-governing republic, where men can use their talents for the benefit of the whole community. Literary or artistic excellence and political liberty are interdependent. Athens and Rome in its republican bloom, as described by Livy and Cicero, were the models. But the connection between the Renaissance and political thought suggested by the concept 'civic humanism' has been severely challenged. Part of this ideology was 'Ciceronian rhetoric', and there was much continuity between the ideologies of the earlier *commune* and of the Renaissance *respublica*. Monarchy continued to be advocated, by humanists as well as others, during the Renaissance. Humanists were ready to defend a variety of forms of government. Many were far from consistent in their professed political beliefs, developing their views in accordance with the patron they were working for. They were still partly advocates, from the same backgrounds and intellectual stables as the jurists, presenting as best they could a cause they were paid to defend. Bruni himself found nothing incongruous in leaving republican Florence to serve the papal monarchy for ten years, and later dedicated his new Latin translation of Aristotle's *Politics* (1435) to the absolutist pope, Eugenius IV.

The application of Ciceronian ideas to contemporary city-states like Florence gave rise to new attitudes to politics, new emphases and moral priorities but not to identifiably new constitutional ideas. Bruni accepted the existing tradition of the medieval civic commune as a self-governing state (*civitas*) and the age-old communal belief that city rulers should be chosen by their fellow-citizens, govern according to city laws, and seek the consent of the political community for legislation and other major decisions. Inspired by intense admiration for the ancient Roman Republic as portrayed by Livy and Cicero, with its liberty under the law, its constitutional balance between consuls, senate and popular assemblies, and its virile yet generous approach to political conflict, Bruni saw Florence as its moral successor. His adopted country displayed virtues such as prudence, *industria*, liberality, humanity and above all faith and *integritas*. She gave exiles protection, refused to violate treaties for the sake of *utilitas*, and whenever possible composed quarrels 'by words and moral authority' (*auctoritas*) (*Praise of Florence* (*Laudatio Florentinae urbis*), pp. 251–8).

In his *Praise of Florence* (1403–4), his epistolary description of the Florentine constitution for the Emperor-elect Sigismund (1413), and his *Funeral Oration for Nanno Strozzi* (*Oratio in funere Nannis Strozae*) (1428), Bruni described Florence as having a 'popular' constitution, equivalent to what the Greeks called *demokratia*. This means that 'we stand in terror of no one person as lord, nor are we enslaved to the power of a few' (in fact Florence was becoming a relatively stable oligarchy under the developing control of the Medici clan). In his most detailed account of the workings of this constitution (*Praise of Florence*, pp. 258–62), Bruni described how Florence was ruled by a college of nine: two men are chosen from each 'quarter' of the city 'not haphazardly but [they are] long since approved by the judgement of the people' (a gloss for the absence of real elections), and a ninth is added as 'prince of the college' for his outstanding 'virtue and authority'. Sometimes a further twelve join their counsel, and also military leaders, again selected from the quarters. Sometimes the decisions of these three colleges 'are referred to the popular council and the commune. For [the city] has judged that it is consonant with law and reason that what touches many should only be decided by the opinion of many' (p. 260). (Here a traditional constitutional principle, 'Let what touches all be approved by all', originally derived from the *Codex*, was simply touched up in Renaissance prose.) After listing various public officials, Bruni introduced 'the leaders of the patrician parties' whose magistracy 'has the greatest authority in the city'. He was not being untruthful exactly; he was doing his best to describe a mercantile oligarchy as a genuine republic, and in so far as it was not yet a principality there was some validity in this. But it gives support to the view that this should be treated as a literary essay as much as a serious political treatise. And it is not surprising that Bruni barely mentioned popular sovereignty or majority rule; here 'civic humanism' actually retreated from the more democratic theses of earlier writers.

But in fact, to be fair, Bruni's grounds for extolling Florence's constitution and its 'popular' character lay elsewhere: not in the kind of democratic, participatory processes envisaged, on occasion, by Marsiglio and Bartolus, but rather in law and liberty. The constitution praised by Bruni was, in the first place, one in which 'no one man's power has more weight in the city than the laws' (p. 259). In the public sphere, all the magistracies are designed to prevent tyranny: for they are collective institutions with short tenure; and the supreme magistracy belongs 'not to one man but to nine, not for a year but for two months'. They are also limited by each other, Florence being characterised by its variety of magistracies each with its own properly defined role ('distincta officia, distincti magistratus, distincta iudicia [courts of law], distincti ordines [ranks]': p. 259). It is a kind of pluralism. According to Bruni this arrangement produces 'elegantia ... concinnitas [symphony] ... [and] a single harmony out of different notes, most sweet and pleasing to the ear' (pp. 258–9); this was, again, a new way of expressing the age-old ideal of *concordia* (see above, pp. 15, 18). In the private sphere, all citizens have recourse to the courts.

Wherefore no-one here can suffer injury, nor can anyone lose their property except by their own will. The law courts are ever prepared, so are the magistrates; the *curia* is open, so is the supreme court. In this city one is quite free to engage in a suit against persons of any rank ... Nowhere on earth is justice more equal for all. For nowhere is there such liberty, nor is the condition of the greater people made so equal (*exequata conditio*) with that of the lesser. (p. 262)

Here Bruni was putting in his own polished style what John of Viterbo and Brunetto Latini had said a century and a half before, appropriating for 'republican' Florence in contrast with 'despotic' Milan the old ideal of the legal protection and equality afforded by cities in contrast to feudal domains. Indeed he went further, for he endorsed the practice of certain 'popular' regimes by which crimes against the property or persons of ordinary citizens were more harshly punished if committed by nobles or 'the more powerful' (p. 262). This (in modern language) positive discrimination produced, according to Bruni, 'equality'; he identified this as one of the chief virtues of the Florentine constitution. The law and courts redress social imbalances, so that

there arises a certain equality (*equabilitas*) among the different ranks, the greater being defended by their own power, the lesser by the state (*res publica*), and both by the fear of punishment (p. 262)

Our laws strive so far as possible to depress the lofty standing of individual citizens and to bring it down to equality and moderation (*paritatem mediocritatemque*). (Letter of 1413)

Thus Bruni identified as his ideal the 'equal condition for all' which later writers such as Rousseau and de Tocqueville would see as a hallmark of a free and just, or democratic and modern society.

This then was what Bruni generally meant by popular government. And he was one of very few authors who not only legitimised it – as many had done – but actually, in some of his writings, declared it superior to other forms. Here he did put his argument in terms which superficially suggest the superiority of rule by many over rule by one or a few: the last two are based on a fiction because no one man or few men can always be good. 'Therefore the only legitimate form of governing a state which remains is the popular one (*popularis una relinquitur legitima reipublicae gubernandae forma*).' However, he promptly defined what he meant by the popular form as one 'in which there is true liberty, in which all citizens are treated fairly and equally before the law (*aequitas iuris cunctis pariter civibus*), in which people can studiously pursue the virtues without being suspect' (*Funeral Oration*, pp. 230–1). This further claim that this is the *only* legitimate form, unique for the time, must be understood as referring to equal liberty under the law for all; for this could, as Bruni all but said, be achieved without ascribing sovereignty to the whole body of citizens. We are in fact getting rather close to the way many would see western liberal democracy today.

Bruni did indeed further qualify his definition of the constitution of Florence in *On the Constitution of the Florentines* (1439, written in Greek) in response to the restoration and entrenchment of Medici interests after a brief counter-coup in 1433–4. Now he described Florence as having not a popular regime but a mixture of patrician and popular rule inclining more 'towards the *optimates* (patricians) and the wealthier people, though not towards the excessively powerful'; one may interpret this as referring to a mercantile rather than a feudal oligarchy, in which those with economic power control the political system but not the legal system. 'The power of the city is seen to reside not in the multitude but in the patricians and the wealthy: these supply the state with money and employ counsel rather than weapons'.

In the second place, one finds in Bruni and other humanists a much more intense attachment to liberty which, while it had always figured in medieval civic discourse, now came closer to being the preeminent priority in politics. Liberty had been the traditional boast and ideal of Florence and other city republics, in Germany as well as Italy. The new emphasis came from the special value humanists placed upon inward liberty, the liberty to think and write according to one's own *genius*; the human being was eulogised on account of, and sometimes defined in terms of, his unique capacity for self-determination.

Bruni followed Cicero in linking the meaning of 'liberty' closely to the kind of legal equality discussed above: that is, freedom from another person's violent and especially domineering behaviour, freedom from domination by a despot, over-powerful individuals or privileged classes. Freedom for him always included property rights and freedom of person. But for Bruni, just as legality applied to the public as well as the private sphere, so liberty had a political – indeed a civic – meaning as well as a private one. It meant free access to public offices open to all comers by competition.

[At Florence] the hope of attaining honour and raising oneself up is equal for everyone, so long as they make the effort, possess talent (*ingenium*) and have an approved, serious way of life. Our city requires virtue and honesty in a citizen; whoever possesses these is considered sufficiently noble to govern the state. [*Funeral Speech*, pp. 230–1.]

This too was a traditional aspiration of the urban commons and of new men confronting entrenched oligarchies. But Bruni developed it in accordance with the new, distinctively humanist ideology of the culturally self-made man, which fitted in naturally with the life prospects of talented boys from humble origins.[10] Bruni's originality was to apply this to political life as well; although here too he lent on Cicero, the self-styled 'man famous on his own account, descended from no glorious ancestors'. Bruni extolled a social and political system which he saw as enabling and encouraging outstanding individuals to make their mark, fulfil themselves and their talents in public life, the service of the state. He saw the Stoic and humanist goal of self-development as attainable through the active life of politics and government, thus reviving in a strongly individualist spirit the political ethics of Aristotle and Cicero. This emerges as the first explicit statement of the doctrine of incentive, for glory, not profit, in the activity of the republic, not commerce.

It has been implanted in mortals by nature that, when the path to greatness and honours lies open, they more easily lift themselves up; when it is closed, they sit back inert. (Letter of 1413)

It is amazing how this opportunity for attaining honours, this power of achievement, when put before a free people, stirs up the citizens' talents. For when hope of honour is before them, men exert themselves and raise themselves up. (*Funeral Speech*, p. 231)

Bruni then emphasised the openness of the political system, the freedom for individuals to participate in politics and attain high office in the state, rather than the authority of the citizen body. This was

[10] See Lauro Martines, *Power and Imagination*, p. 277.

what he meant when he declared that here at Florence 'in everything liberty and people rule' (*Praise of Florence*, p. 260). 'Popolo e liberta' was a slogan of the Italian communes to which Bruni gave some new meaning, making it refer to people as individuals rather than as a community. In his conception of liberty, private and public run together.

In this way the history and principles of republican Rome, as found in Livy and Cicero, provided a new basis from which to make elected, plural, limited government look attractive. But it would be untrue to say that even in humanist circles monarchy had become less intellectually respectable by the middle of the fifteenth century. Humanists contributed to the endorsement of monarchy that followed the collapse of constitutionalism in the church and the rule of powerful monarchs like Alfonso V of Aragon; after all, as they said, the principate of Augustus had been the golden age of Latin letters.

Changes in political language did not signify changes in the conditions written about. They did not immediately signify changes in ideas about political legitimacy or which form of government is best. Older languages continued to be used alongside new ones. The languages of Roman law, Aristotle and Cicero made it possible to say things in a new way, to distinguish between the community as a random group and as a legal–political whole, to conceptualise oligarchy and democracy, and so on. In fact the old concept *universitas civium* (association of citizens) ran through popular speech, civil jurisprudence and Marsiglio; and this was how some still expressed their ideal in the age of Machiavelli. The one school to whom it was alien was the humanists.

The close of the Middle Ages, and in Italy the deepening of the Renaissance, saw the rise of the Medici in Florence and the decline of civic independence in some places. Cities and city-states soon ceased to be treated as a *genus* apart with any distinctive political role in European society.

$$5$$

KINGSHIP, LAW AND COUNSEL

Kingship was the form of government most generally favoured by medieval Europeans. Not unlike 'democracy' today, it connoted a whole bundle of ideals, and could mean a variety of things. We will consider first the general conception of monarchy, then the problems associated with kingship or monarchy. This will take us through the major constitutional cruxes of later medieval Europe: election against hereditary succession; rebellion and the means of deposing a tyrant; the relationship between king and law; the place of counsel, especially by wise persons, in royal decision-making; and in chapter 6 the role of parliaments, and the concept of representation.[1]

Belief in the rightness of kingship was a deep-seated conviction seldom contested outside the Italian city-republics. The word kingship (*regnum*) was commonly used for one's country or state; king (*rex*) was connected etymologically with right rule (*recte regere*). *Rex* and so on were not merely descriptive but, again like our 'democracy', carried favourable undertones; and were, therefore, sharply distinguished from tyranny. In France, the Hispanic realms, England, Poland, Hungary and elsewhere the title *rex* was an object of respect and awe. Allegiance and obedience to one's king was a serious moral obligation. Apart from ideological reasons for this, developments in royal justice, administration and control in kingdoms such as France and England (two of the evidently most powerful states in Europe) encouraged support for a king as one who stood above the local

[1] See bibliography, pp. 203–4.

136

nobility and even clergy – above faction – who could bring peace to the countryside, impose more impartial justice, and defend the realm against outside attack. Yet the period 1250–1450 witnessed severe crises for all the European monarchies; the secular royal order was faced with opposition from nobles jealous of their traditional status, ecclesiastical dissent in the name of the rival authority of the church, and occasionally the townsmen or commons. The apparently greatest monarchy, Germany, now went into decline; in the Hispanic kingdoms, loyalty to king was balanced by the nobles' and towns' fierce adherence to constitutional legalism; France was temporarily dismembered by the English, and England by her own rival factions. It would at times have been impossible to predict the emergence of unity and absolutism in the former, of Tudor stability let alone constitutional monarchy in the latter. But only in northern and central Italy was kingship itself seriously contested.

Yet what a king could actually do, the extent to which he could govern alone, were entirely debatable; and much debated in words and blood. A king was not necessarily a *monarcha* in the (Aristotelian) sense of one who rules by himself for the public good; few saw him as an absolute ruler who could dispense with law and the advice of his council. The idea of the king as *princeps* in the Roman-law sense, entitled to make laws without consent, was stoutly resisted by most. The view of the Middle Ages as more authoritarian than later times needs to be carefully restated. The theocratic notion, that the king derived his authority from God (*rex dei gratia*), did not mean that royal power was unlimited; unless one also added, as only few did, that the king's power was actually comparable to God's. In the event medieval monarchies evolved either into absolute or into constitutional monarchies. But there was no absolute secular monarchy in this period, perhaps because the necessary means of communication and control were lacking.

Kings derived their authority from God. The metaphor of royalty played a large part in the language of medieval theology. Coronation was viewed as a quasi-sacramental rite; the feast of 'Christ the King' was introduced. Still this did not mean that the royal power was absolute, nor the royal title in any particular case indisputable, though it could be interpreted in that way. And kings were at the same time said to derive their authority from the people – the political community, however structured. This was a mysterious as much as a constitutional belief: as the constitutional monarchist Sir John Fortescue put it, 'from the people there breaks forth a kingdom, which is a mystic body governed by one man as head' (*In Praise of England's*

Laws, ch. 13: *MPI* p. 329). The king–people relationship was a two-way one. Courtly political language, some of it religious or feudal, emphasised its personal character: it is for subjects to exercise faithfulness, obedience, reverence and gratitude (*fides, fidelitas, obedientia, adherentia, reverentia, gratitudo*) and for rulers to show grace, mercy, benevolence and care (*gratia, misericordia, benevolentia, sollicitudo*). The idea of people agreeing together to set up a king was often recited, typically in its Ciceronian form, but seldom pressed to the point of saying a king was contractually obliged to his people. It was sometimes said that the king had contractual obligations to particular persons or corporations – the church or clergy, his barons or 'peers' (*pares*: equals), and incorporated towns; these could form a basis for quasi-legal or military opposition. But to say that royal power came from the people was a way of enhancing rather than limiting it, especially when one interpreted this as meaning that what the king does is done in the name of the people. It did not necessarily mean that the people, or indeed anyone, could control the king's actions or punish his misconduct; although, again, it made such things believable.

As political theory became more explicit, the argument from the inherent social need for law and order, for clear direction and organisation in society as a whole, was developed as a further bedrock of royal authorisation. The need for *unity* was especially appropriate if one wished to argue that human societies are best ruled by a single person. It seemed a simple enough step to go from saying that human societies can only achieve 'the common good', 'felicity', 'prosperity' and the like if some form of government is set up, to saying that these can most effectively, or only effectively, be achieved by the direction of a single will. At the same time, however, once the purposes of monarchy were identified, these could become criteria by which to assess a monarch's performance.

Monarchical doctrine was developed in a variety of genres. Theology provided the idea that all human authority comes ultimately from God, as Christ said to Pilate, and that therefore human authorities as presently constituted should be treated as having divine sanction; St Paul had specifically mentioned 'the king' or Roman emperor. A longstanding Christian tradition stressed the excellence of state authority and the obedience, indeed devotion, due to it: the ruler protects the church, administers justice, is the representative of God on earth, stands in God's place, acts in his name, and his acts must be treated as those of God. This was especially applicable to monarchs because most of this language had originated under the Christianised

Roman Empire. By the same token, the monarch must act like God: he must be perfectly endowed with all the virtues, honest, just, merciful and so on. This was the theme of works written for the instruction and enlightenment of a prince, and especially of a prince-to-be, the *Mirror of the Prince* (*Speculum principis*); much care was given to the upbringing and education of a future king.

Roman law was much more specific about the extent of powers at the disposal of a *princeps* or *imperator*. He is not obliged to follow the laws (*legibus solutus*) and his own decisions have the full force of law (*Digest* 1.3.31); he should, none the less, oblige himself to act according to law (*Codex* 1.14.4). Most influential was the *lex regia* (quoted by Ulpian: *Digest* 1.4.1pr) which stated that the people had conferred all their power, legislative as well as executive, upon the *princeps* or emperor. Medieval civil-law jurists enthusiastically quoted these and other texts in order to establish, against enormous practical odds, the unfettered power of the present-day emperor. But the real importance of these texts in the Middle Ages lay in their application to other rulers. Canon lawyers appropriated them for the pope. Then secular lawyers, working within national or local milieux but using the language of Roman-imperial law, began steadily to apply them to the several existing secular monarchs of Europe, beginning with France and the kingdom of Sicily. This accompanied a wide-ranging adoption of imperial language by kings and dukes, which implied that the powers ascribed to the Roman emperor properly belonged to every ruler *vis à vis* his own subjects (*rex est imperator in regno suo*: see above, p. 113).

None the less, even in this discipline so friendly to monarchy, the contrary case could be put. If the people had conferred all their power upon the sovereign, might they not under certain circumstances be able to take it back? This opened up a long debate on the terms of this mandate.

Aristotle's discussions of the different forms of government gave rise to a new genre of argument. Particularly germane here were Aristotle's distinctions between, first, the 'despotic' rule of master over slaves whether or not for their benefit as well as his, and the 'political' or constitutional rule of free persons over their equals (*Politics* I.7, 1255b and III.6, 1278b–9a). This could hardly assist the case for kingship; Ptolemy of Lucca employed it in stating his preference for constitutional rather than monarchical government (above, pp. 122–3). Second, Aristotle distinguished between rule by one, few and many, either for the common good or for the private good of the ruler or rulers. This gave him three good forms, aimed at the common weal: monarchy, 'aristocracy' (rule by the best) and 'polity' (rule by the many for the common good); and three bad forms, aimed at the selfish good of the ruler: tyranny, oligarchy and democracy (III.7, 1279a–b). These distinctions gave political thought from the later thirteenth century onwards increased clarity and flexibility. A good example of the way theorists adapted Aristotle to their own purposes was Aquinas' restatement of Aristotle's first distinction as one between *royal*, rather than 'despotic', and 'political' rule (*On Politics*, 1.1, n. 13 at p. 6). Aristotle had recognised certain merits in kingship (III.14–16, 1284b–6a), although he did not see it as a form of government likely to be suited to a city-state. But Aquinas' adaptation of Aristotle's terminology enabled both him and others to say that there were two *equally legitimate* types of regime, appropriate for different kinds of state: roughly, monarchical and constitutional. Sir John Fortescue completed both the travesty of Aristotle and the development of constitutional monarchy when he praised as ideal England's combination of political with royal rule.

The main use to which medieval thinkers put Aristotelian language was to discuss the pros and cons of the different governmental forms, usually with a view to determining which was best. We have seen how Albert the Great discussed the democratic and oligarchical elements in contemporary city-states and preferred what he saw as democracy. Few followed him. The great majority of writers who went in for this kind of exercise were in fact convinced supporters of kingship. Some were ready to admit that aristocracy or polity were perfectly legitimate, but insisted that, compared with monarchy, they were defective. The catch was that, if they then declared themselves for 'monarchy' in Aristotle's terms, they were preferring something more absolute than existing medieval regimes, and in most cases (though not in Aegidius' or Buridan's) something more absolute than they actually wished to defend. For 'monarchy' here meant excluding the few and the many from rule; and it was a brave or foolish person who would advise kings to deny the role of council and parliament altogether. Consequently, it was very common for medieval theorists to end up by opting for 'mixed monarchy/government', meaning a mixture of Aristotle's three good forms; this was something that Plutarch and Cicero, but not Aristotle himself, had also praised. This preference for monarchy, almost universal outside the Italian city-states, was counterbalanced by extensive diatribes against tyranny.

The one major political language in which, taken as a whole, kingship was difficult to defend was Ciceronian; for to the Romans kingship traditionally had meant tyranny. Elective monarchy, however, could be supported especially if, as we have just seen, it were mixed monarchy. This did not prevent a flood of humanistic literature from fifteenth-century Italy in praise of particular kings and royal governments; which showed the impurity of their Ciceronian language or, often enough, their willingness – which they shared with many of the Aristotelian genre – to praise existing kingship as if it were elective. The ethos of Rome and the composition of the papal court enabled some Italians to make their own very special contribution to the theory of monarchy as defenders of papal absolutism (see above, pp. 49–52).

The first monarchical treatise in the Aristotelian genre was *On Kingship* (*De regno; ad regem Cypri*, or *De regimine principum*), doubtfully attributed to Aquinas. This original work, a stern but optimistic essay in moral theology, unambiguously preferred monarchy but spent as much time warning against tyranny. It seems to be aimed at the Italian *signori* rather than the northern kings; no mention is made of hereditary succession. The author argued that the social and political needs of humanity, which Aristotle showed require people to live in states, can best be met through monarchy, defined as rule by one over a city or province for the common good (chs. 1–2). Similarly, John of Paris, following 'Aquinas' closely, stated that rule by one is needed to achieve the common good, maintain peace and preserve society from disintegration (ch. 1). 'Aquinas' could not of course use Aristotle to prove this point. Instead he invoked as his principal argument for monarchy modern experience (*experimentum*), that is, the civic discord in the Italian city-states (chs. 2–6); the cosmological argument came much later (ch. 12). Monarchy is best because it is the regime most likely to achieve social peace and unity, the least prone to discord (*dissensio*) (chs. 2, 5). 'Aquinas' did admit that rule by 'the community of citizens ... through annually appointed rulers' had its advantages in the flourishing days of the Roman Republic (ch. 4); but rule by several persons is more likely to lead to dissension and hence to tyranny. The author proceeded to stress very emphatically the dangers of tyranny – oppressive rule by one person for private gain. Kingship differs from tyranny in that the king pursues justice, rules over free subjects and aims at the common good – which is precisely why subjects accept it willingly. If kingship is the best, tyranny is the worst kind of government (ch. 3). Here 'Aquinas' was applying Aristotle's categories to the contemporary world freshly and in a way that clearly showed concern for the Italian cities. The need for civic unity, the dangers of discord, peace as the supreme goal of government were standard themes among supporters of the burgeoning Italian city-lords (*signori*).

In order to show how tyranny is to be avoided, the author argued that a ruling individual could be motivated to rule as a king and not a tyrant by a proper understanding of his own happiness (chs. 6–11). Yoking the Judaeo–Christian beside the Graeco–Roman, he showed by psychological, moral and religious arguments how Christian faith was most likely to inspire true kingship. Tyranny can be avoided by ensuring, first, that a suitable person is chosen – he does not say how – and, second, that the king's power 'is moderated so that it cannot easily decline into tyranny' (ch. 6). But he shrewdly observed that 'a king's duty seems too onerous if it does not bring him any benefit'. Cicero and Aristotle suggest personal glory as the appropriate motive for a prince; 'the best among all earthly things seems to be that a man's virtue should be publicly attested by other men'. But experience shows that people bestow their esteem in unpredictable ways; besides, 'a virtuous and strong spirit despises glory as well as life for the sake of justice'. 'The reward of human glory is, therefore, irrelevant to the duties of a king' (ch. 7). Rather, he should seek his reward from God, who alone can make one happy (ch. 8). The consolation prize is that, since 'the good of society is greater and more divine than the good of the individual', being a good king requires greater virtue than any other human undertaking (*officium*), and will consequently receive an appropriately greater reward in heaven (ch. 9). Indeed a king is also more likely than a tyrant to achieve stable power, wealth, honour and glory on earth – though not because he has aimed at these alone (ch. 11: cf. Matt. 6:33). And, unlike the tyrant, he will acquire the greatest earthly blessing of all, friendship: for this (as Aristotle said) is rooted in what people share in common (*communio*: community in the ethical sense), and subjects will bestow their *love* upon a king who takes care to pursue the common profit (chs. 10–11). This treatise is remarkable for its combination of classical ideas, Ciceronian as well as Aristotelian, with Christian ones, and for its appeal to moral theology as enlightened self-interest.

Aegidius Romanus' *The Rule of Princes*, written 1277–9 and dedicated to his pupil, the future Philip IV of France, was a thoroughly Aristotelian work in the sense that it was written in Aristotelian language and rehearsed Aristotle's general views about the importance of political society for human existence. Aegidius came out even more strongly in favour of rule by one: 'kingship is the best form of sovereignty' (*regnum est optimus principatus*) (ch. 3, fol. 269v). The reasons given are similar to 'Aquinas', but more systematically expounded. Kingship is superior in terms of unity and peace; in political power (*civilis potentia*) since unity confers strength; on naturalistic grounds because this is how other animal societies are organised; and 'from what we see and have learned by experience in the government of [city-] states (*civitates*)'. *Civitates* without kingship suffer from poverty, do not enjoy peace and 'are molested with dissensions and civil wars (*guerrae*)' (ch. 3, fols. 270r–v). Once again, it would appear, it is Italian experience speaking to northern Europe. Aegidius made the same caveats as 'Aquinas' about kingship being distinguished from tyranny by the king's ruling over willing, freely obeying subjects and in the interests of the whole people, and about the king's need to be absolutely just and subject to the moral code of nature. But by kingship Aegidius clearly did mean hereditary power unlimited by legal constraints; even consultation is only morally obligatory, and the king may dispense from the law when equity and circumstances require it. What Aegidius offered the King of France was not merely a preference for monarchy over aristocracy and democracy; it was absolute monarchy. He later defended the papal monarchy against Philip, but this did not prevent him subsequently re-entering Philip's service. *The Rule of Princes* was the most widely read treatise of its kind.

A much less favourable view of kingship was taken by the Dominican, Ptolemy of Lucca. In principle he preferred 'political' rather than royal (or, as he sometimes called it, despotic) rule (*The Rule of Princes* II.8; III.3, 14–17), with rulers having short terms of office prescribed by constitutional laws which also delimit their powers (it is worth comparing this with the constitution of the Dominican order), and being subject to scrutiny after office to see whether they have judged in accordance with the laws. This was the form of government proposed by the prophet Samuel and enjoyed by the Romans under the Republic before Caesar's despotic tyranny (IV chs. 1–2). And it was the kind known to the human race before the Fall of Man introduced servitude. But royal rule may be more appropriate in particular circumstances. Since the Fall brought sin, human beings stand in greater need of discipline. Second, peoples vary in temperament according to the stars and latitudes in which they live; political rule is especially suitable for self-confident people like the Italians, disdainful of alien decision-making, and in their courageous libertarianism unwilling to bow the neck to kings. Third, while political rule suits city-states, royal rule is better suited to larger states (II chs. 8–9; III chs. 9–11; IV ch. 2). This demonstrates the diversity of viewpoints that could be arrived at within an Aristotelian framework.

The theory of *absolute* monarchy derived partly from ideas associated with the Roman principate and empire (above, p. 139), and partly from ideas associated with the papacy. Monarchy in general benefited from the prestigious image established by the contemporary empire and papacy. As a monarchy, the papacy was in several ways unique (see above, pp. 42–4). Popes claimed that their powers rested on the explicit commission of St Peter by Christ as ruler of the Christian church (Matt. 16:18); the bishop of Rome inherited the Petrine powers. This had been developed into the theory of the vicariate of Christ: popes stood in the place of Christ on earth. Their powers were absolute in the precise sense that no-one could validly appeal from papal jurisdiction, while anyone anywhere may lodge an appeal with the pope; he had wide legislative powers and a vast range of executive powers including taxation and appointments. On the other hand, the papacy was elective. Statements of papal absolutism were current from the later thirteenth century, deriving from canon and ultimately Roman-imperial constitutional language. For example,

> He is the successor of Peter and the vicar of Christ, playing on earth the part not of a mere man but of the true God ... He rules, disposes and judges all things as he pleases ... For the pope has the fullness of power (*plenitudo potestatis*) ... In all things and through all things, he can do and say whatever he pleases, taking away from anyone he wishes their right; for no-one can say to him, Why do this? ... For with him will stands in the place of reason, and what he decides has the force of law (Guilelmus Durandus the Elder, cited by Wilks, *Sovereignty*, p. 151).

What 'the pope alone' could do was clearly spelled out by one canonist after another: all may appeal to him, none from him, he may make church laws, appoint and depose bishops, and raise church taxes. The papacy provided a sacred language and living exemplar of centralised jurisdiction and relatively efficient administration (see also below, pp. 184–5).

Absolutist doctrine was further boosted as the doctrine of monotheism began to be used as the systematic organising principle around which to structure a comprehensive theory of the universe and life in general, in response to the intellectual challenges of pagan Aristotelianism, Averroism and Manichaeanism, and as part of a broader endeavour to achieve a coherent, stable and just Christian society. Monarchical writing, papal and royal, now developed a complete cosmology; the monarchical principle runs right through the universe. The language of Christian Neoplatonism, as developed by the sixth-century Greek mystical theologian Pseudo-Denis, fused with

Aristotelian cosmology and science. The result was a cosmic and political ideal at once monist and hierarchical: all beings depend on their one source, the multiplicity of spiritual and material creation returns ultimately to God (*reductio ad unum*); yet each subordinate species and being has its own proper place. It was a view perfectly if idiosyncratically expressed by Nicholas of Cusa (see below, pp. 179–83). This ideological movement presented an almost opposite picture to the quasi-Marxist cliché that medieval thought reflected in its celestial hierarchy the feudal hierarchy on earth. For the whole point was not hierarchy (except in the literal sense of holy rule) but the subordination of others to the supreme One. The crucial analogy now drawn between the monarch – in church or state – and God himself gave a model of the omnipotent and omnicompetent sovereign convenient for centralising, anti-baronial, bureaucratic kingship. It is true that radical inequalities in society, between noble, burgher, peasant and so on, were at the same time justified in the light of this cosmic system. Radical differences between human classes were justified by reference to gradations inherent in the universe itself. But above all it was a means by which the theory of absolute monarchy was expounded, long before it came to be practised except in the church.

A clear early example of this argument is found in Aquinas, whose analogies between the *universitas* of human society and the *universitas* of the cosmos offer striking clues to his theology (see *ST* Ia/IIae 90). Having stated that 'the whole community of the universe (*communitas universi*) is governed by divine reason' (*ST* Ia/IIae 91.1 *resp.*), he proceeded to give the clearest possible monist argument for rule by one, but in a theological rather than a political context: the analogy between society and the world was used to demonstrate the oneness of *God*.

The purpose of the governor of a society is unity or peace. But the cause of unity must in itself be singular; for it is clear that a number of persons could not bring unity and harmony to a plurality unless they were in some way unified. Yet that which is one *in itself* can be a better and more effective cause of unity than can many individuals even if united together. A society, therefore, is better governed by one than by several. (*ST* I.103.3 *resp.*)

Arguing that the principles of unity and monarchy were found throughout nature and human society, later medieval writers became profligate in their use of sociological and sociobiological analogies. Bees and sheep, fathers and generals were pressed into service. A fine example, for its literary flourish and factual inaccuracy, comes from Engelbert of Admont (see above, pp. 93–6), writing in a German-imperial, monastic milieu. His description of the origin of kingship subtly wove together Plato, Cicero and observation of animal behaviour. Throughout nature we find that 'the lower (*inferiores*) are of necessity ruled by the higher (*superiores*)'; this is especially so amongst the gregarious, as opposed to the more savage, animal species:

as in flocks of sheep and goats, cattle and horses, poultry and bees. In each species the better are put in front of and in command of the inferior, the stronger are put over the weaker, the more industrious over the simpler, the older over the younger; and finally one from the whole flock is put in front of and in command of all, as being greater, stronger and more industrious than all the rest; so that the lesser, simpler and weaker may be ruled or even saved by the greater, stronger and more industrious … We find the same in wild animals and birds: a herd of deer has one guardian and leader; so too among wild goats and chamois, and among storks and cranes; in the forests and savannah the lion is king of beasts, and in the air the eagle is king of birds. (ch. 1)

So it is among humans; reason imitates nature and puts the greater in charge of the lesser. Hence 'men stronger in intellect and reason are by nature lords of others' (see Aristotle, *Politics* I.5, 1254a–b). Cicero (*On Duties* II.12.41) informs us that primitive men, acting on natural instinct and reason, set one man stronger in intellect over themselves and obeyed him 'through a pact and bond of subjection'; again, kingdoms were originally set up 'to organise and consolidate peace and justice among inhabitants'. When kings lost their original virtue, kingship declined into tyranny. This led to 'the oppression of neighbours, the tearing-up of boundaries, discord among citizens and against kings themselves, and finally the oppression of the lesser by the greater' (chs. 2, 4, 19). Kingship and tyranny thus played a part in this view of the origins of inequality.

Powerful ideological currents ensured that the language of the prince as lord, father, shepherd, prelate (*praelatus*: set in charge), and of the people as underlings, subjects, servants, children, sheep was available for secular use.

ELECTION AND HEREDITY

Theorists discussed the legitimacy and relative merits of election and hereditary succession. The latter was the norm in France, England and most kingdoms and principalities. The German king-emperors were elected from dynastic houses. In Italy great lords such as the

Visconti established new dynasties, but the myth of popular choice remained. It was also preserved in royal coronation rites. When the French Capetian dynasty died out in 1328, the Valois succeeded. In the church, election was the norm, although the pope claimed a general right of appointment. The popes themselves were elected by the college of cardinals.

Opinion among theorists was divided. Aegidius Romanus, writing *c.* 1277–85, addressed the question systematically and with great insight, rehearsing arguments that would dominate discussion in the future (*The Rules of Princes*, book III, part ii, ch. 5). His conclusion in favour of hereditary succession was not unlike Dr Johnson's defence of free will: all argument is against it, all experience for it. The people, he said (contrary to Marsiglio), are as it were naturally inclined to obey the sons of kings voluntarily; those who are catapulted into power are more prone to bad behaviour than those who have grown up accustomed to it; the fact that his sons will succeed will make a king more solicitous for his kingdom. In order to avoid the kind of disputes that dog electoral succession, not only the family but the individual who will succeed must be stipulated (e.g. male primogeniture).

Aquinas, on the other hand, described the 'democratic' element in an ideal mixed constitution as meaning that 'the princes can be elected from among ordinary people (*popularibus*), and the election of the princes belongs to the people' (*ST* 1a/11ae 105.1 *resp.*). This was 'instituted by divine law': he cited Deut. 1:13, 15 and Exod. 18:21 (which refer to the choice of tribal leaders and judges). Bartolus similarly asserted that 'government by election is more divine than by succession' on the basis of Deut. 17.14–15 (which refers to the possibility of the Israelites appointing 'a king of Yahweh's choosing') and of canon law.

Marsiglio again treated the question systematically (*DP* 1.9.5–9 and 1.1.16). There are different kinds of elective monarchy: people may elect a ruler for a fixed period, say one or two years, for his lifetime, or with his posterity (as the founder of hereditary dynasty). Marsiglio definitely preferred election to hereditary succession, on the grounds that subjection through election is more voluntary and elected rulers govern constitutionally and for the common good. Compared with election of a monarch with his posterity, individual election ensures that a prince rules in his own right; this makes him 'more like the prince of the universe' (*DP* 1.16.24). Oresme (writing in the 1370s), while generally under Marsiglio's influence, as a loyal supporter of the Valois against English claims, preferred *election de lignage* 'made by the better part of the community expressly, or by tacit consent, or by custom' (p. 109). Nicholas of Cusa, writing on the German Empire in the 1430s and also under Marsilian influence, said that the best form of monarchical sovereignty is that in which the monarch is elected 'without his successors' (*CC* III *Pref.*, pp. 321–2). In all these contexts, the electors in question were 'the better/greater part' of the community, that is, the senior nobility or electoral princes. One has the impression that the main stimuli behind the case for election were ecclesiastical doctrine and Italian communal practice.

RESISTANCE

Given the near ubiquity of kingship, it is not surprising that much attention was given to the definition of, and remedies against, tyranny. Armed opposition to kings was not infrequent, usually by groups of nobility, on grounds of illegitimate title or consistently bad government. In England during the 1260s and in France during the 1350s, there were attempts to compel kings to accept control by council or the Estates, who should appoint royal ministers (the English baronial rebellion of the 1260s was led by Simon de Montfort who had read Bishop Grosseteste's *On Tyranny*). On the other hand, Edward II of England was deposed, killed and replaced by Edward III in 1327; and Richard II was deposed and replaced by Henry IV in 1399. In both cases the barons sought 'to prove that the people as a whole had co-operated in, agreed to and acclaimed the depositions' (*CHMPT* p. 517). In Germany kings were deposed by the electoral princes in the cases of Adolf of Nassau in 1298 and Wenceslas in 1400 (from 1314 to *c*. 1340 Ludwig of Bavaria was opposed on grounds of a disputed election). These and other attempts to resist or overthrow 'tyrants' did not weaken loyalty to kingship in principle.

The idea of personal 'self-help' against a king's injustice, the so-called Germanic right of resistance, had faded into the background. Tyrannicide was advocated by few; no doubt experience in both the northern kingdoms and the Italian communes warned people that the likely consequences were civil disorder and war.

Until the early fourteenth century the role of papacy and Empire remained relevant to discussions of what to do about a bad ruler. The anonymous *Quaestio* written in Paris in 1302 during the Philip–Boniface dispute (see above, p. 49) proposed an indirect or 'incidental' power for the pope over a bad king in the sense that, if a king committed an ecclesiatical crime such as heresy, the pope 'can absolve his vassals, or rather declare them absolved, from their oath of fidelity'. John of Paris said that in such a case the pope could excommunicate anyone who obeyed the king, 'and so the people would depose [the king], and the pope would do so *per accidens*' (*CHMPT*, pp. 407–8). Those who held that the emperor had to be confirmed in office by the pope generally held that the pope could depose the emperor 'for just cause'. Dante saw the *emperor* as the scourge of tyrants.

Theologians insisted, at the least, on the right and duty to resist immoral commands. The development of more effective legal systems and in some cases of a kind of rule of law reduced the perceived need for extra-legal forms of redress. But all this did not remove the understanding that a ruler claiming to be king might in fact be a usurper or tyrant, and there remained a widespread conviction that in that case the gloves were off. The alternative strategies, so far as political theory was concerned, were either to stress the need to educate the future monarch so well that sanctions would not be required; or to say that it was God's will that subjects should always obey, or refrain from actively resisting, a sovereign ruler, however bad. This divine-right view was first put forward on behalf of the papacy, and began to be accepted for secular rulers towards the end of the Middle Ages.

The first problem was to identify the tyrant. Unless one were prepared to say either that tyrants should be tolerated or that some agency had legal authority to act against a tyrant, this was an exercise in winning hearts and minds. Typical complaints against a tyrant were that he broke laws through personal immorality or arbitrary acts of government, disregarded justice, contravened or failed to uphold personal and property rights, neglected to take the advice of his barons (usually cloaked as 'wise men'). Thereby he forfeited the (feudal) allegiance of his vassals and subjects, and the consent of the political community. Theorists summed all this up by distinguishing kingship from tyranny in terms of, first, whether someone governed according to the laws and, second, whether they ruled for their own private good or the good of the whole society. Even the monarchist Buridan said that, at least in a 'constitutional state' (*politia*), a law-breaking prince should be 'punished or deposed'; otherwise 'it would destroy the whole community' (III, q. 12). Tyranny was a distortion of reality, and as in nature *nullum violentum perpetuum*.

Looking at the question in more detail, Aquinas in his first treatment of the subject said that government (*praelatio*) could 'not be of God' either by defective title or by defective use.[2] While personal unworthiness alone does not disqualify a ruler, if power has been acquired through violence, bribery 'or other illicit means', then 'one can shake off such lordship when opportunity arises, unless it happens that he subsequently becomes a true lord either through the consent of the subjects or the authority of a superior'. Defective use, on the other hand, is when a ruler commands something contrary to virtue; then, like the martyrs of old, the subject 'is not only not bound to obey, but is also bound not to obey'. Alternatively, a ruler may exceed his competence, for example when 'a lord demands taxes which his servant is not bound to give'; then 'the subject is *obliged* neither to obey nor to disobey' (*Commentary on the Sentences*, II, d.44.2.2 *resp.*). Aquinas also remarked that he who liberates his country by killing a tyrant who has usurped power against the subjects' will, and when there is no recourse to a superior, is rewarded. It is noticeable that throughout this, his most 'revolutionary' passage, Aquinas did not once mention a king; it was easier to say all this about a lesser ruler.

In his theological compendium (*Summa Theologiae*), Aquinas stated that the sin of sedition consisted not in overthrowing a tyrant but in being a tyrant; unless more harm would result from the attempted overthrow than from the tyranny itself, in which case such action would be sinful (*ST* IIa/IIae 42.2.*ad* 3). This passage reads more like a moral condemnation of tyranny than a sanction for deposition. But he did establish the principle of prudential calculation.

The discussion in *On Kingship* (attributed to Aquinas) tells a different story. In the first instance, tyranny should be endured as long as possible because of the immense dangers in taking action: if rebellion fails, the tyrant will be incensed, if it succeeds the people are liable to fall into severe disagreement about the constitution and become divided into factions (*partes*). If the tyranny becomes unbearable, some say one should kill the tyrant, exposing oneself to death for the liberation of one's people; but that is not the teaching of the New Testament, which commends rather the patience of the innocent sufferer (1 Peter 2:20). There are, on the other hand, three possible solutions. The first two involve action not by an individual but 'by public authority'. First, if the community is one that has the right to appoint its own king, it is permissible for them to depose him, or to restrict his power; for here it is not they but he who acts

---

[2] Compare Bartolus' *Tractatus de tyranno*; C. N. S. Woolf, *Bartolus of Sassoferrato – His Position in the History of Medieval Political Thought* (Cambridge: Cambridge University Press, 1913), pp. 163–74.

'faithlessly' by deserting the royal *officium* (office and duty) and so breaking his agreement (*pactum*) with his subjects. Second, if the community is one in which the king is appointed by a superior, then they should seek remedy from him. Third, if there is no human recourse – that is, presumablly, in most kingdoms – the people should turn to God, 'king of all', for a miraculous or providential release; and abstain from those sins which, in the nature of the case, were the ultimate cause of the tyranny. This was a clear statement of the doctrine of non-resistance (ch. 6).

Sometimes the moral right of redress against bad government was given a quasi-judicial form so as not to require recourse to violence. England's Magna Carta (1215) had stated that, if the king did not observe the agreements safeguarding the peace and liberties of his subjects, a committee of twenty-five barons could 'with the community of the whole land, distrain and distress [the King] in all possible ways, namely, by seizing our castles, lands, possessions ... until redress has been obtained as they deem fit, saving harmless our own person' (clause 61, cited by Kern, *Kingship and Law*, p. 128). In the Italian city-republics the political community, usually acting through the city council, had an acknowledged power to 'scrutinise' the conduct of leading officials or the chief judge (*podesta*) when he left office. Marsiglio, generalising from this, stated that the community of citizens is empowered to correct, and if necessary to depose, the ruler 'if it shall be necessary for the common benefit' (*DP* 1.15.2; cf. 1.18).

Constitutional remedies against abuses of monarchical authority were developed most articulately by churchmen, canon-lawyers and theologians concerned to combat the excesses of the papacy. In the process, they sometimes reinterpreted secular norms: Gerson quoted in support of the council's right to judge the pope a dubious analogy with France 'where the king has instituted Parlement by which he does not refuse to be judged' (*MPI* p. 417). During the later fourteenth and fifteenth centuries many came to the view that bad popes could be tried before a general council and in the last resort deposed by it. Some said this could be done only if the pope were a heretic, others that he could also be judged for lesser crimes, even for failure to carry out reforms. Some said that in such cases the council itself deposed the pope, others that it merely declared him deposed. Some said that in such cases the pope deposed himself or (as even the absolutist Torquemada was prepared to admit) 'falls from the papacy by the very law' or 'by the very fact (*ipso iure/facto*)' of his crime. This was an attempt to preserve the principle of monarchical sovereignty;

since it was not said who should declare the pope deposed – certainly not a council! – these statements may be regarded as little more than juristic formulae. But they showed the general concern that remedies should exist in a monarchical system.

KING AND LAW

The relationship between king and law was perhaps the greatest crux in constitutional theory and practice. It went to the heart of the problem of sovereignty. It was momentous precisely because, in both theory and practice, king and law depended on each other. The primary function of a king was to obtain justice for his subjects, and this he could only do through the impartial procedure known as law. On the other hand, no amount of laws would safeguard a subject's rights without courts and powers capable of enforcing them. A king functioned as, among other things, representative of God and therefore of justice itself. Certain laws were authoritative not on account of the person who had made them but because they were the law from time immemorial. Hence for a king to disregard laws, or to be seen to contravene them, posed a conundrum which for a long time statesmen and theorists found baffling.

All this was acutely felt by those involved in the politics of Magna Carta, and again by the English baronial and parliamentary movement of 1258–65; a large body of opinion wished to retain royal authority while at the same time restraining it, safeguarding due process of law, placing royal government under the law as (in 'Bracton's' words) a bridle upon the monarch.

It was generally agreed that every king had a supreme *moral* obligation to obey laws of the land in so far as they applied to himself and to his actions as ruler. In the language of Roman law, the king was subject to the laws' moral force (*vis directiva*) but not to their coercive force (*vis coactiva*) (see *Codex* 1.14.4). Second, it was generally agreed that the king could depart from the letter of the law for either of two reasons. The supreme appellate court sitting under the king could interpret the existing laws to the extent of setting aside their rigour in particular cases. This was justified by analogy with divine mercy or on the basis of natural law, those general principles which are supposed to inform positive law. In the language of Roman Stoicism, this meant the king exercising the virtues of gentleness (*mansuetudo*) and *humanitas*. It was more elaborately defended on the basis of Aristotle's argument in *Nichomachaean Ethics* v.10, where he explained how on occasion justice was better served by adhering to the general principles of fairness (*epieikeia, aequitas,* equity) rather than the written law as it stood. A prince might also, on rare occasions, act outside the law in cases of 'urgent need' or 'evident utility', especially in defence of the realm. As the ancient Romans said, 'Let the salvation of the people be the supreme law' (*salus populi suprema lex esto*).

None of this touched the problem of what to do when a king was believed to be breaking the law unjustly and without cause. *On The Laws and Customs of England* (chiefly composed in the 1220s and 1230s and formerly ascribed to Henry de Bracton) at first stated the matter in such a way as to suggest an embarrassed uncertainty or ambivalence felt, it would seem, by someone working within the confines of Roman, and for that matter English, law:

> The king must not be under man but under God and under the law, because law makes the king. Let him therefore bestow upon the law what the law bestows upon him, namely rule and power, for there is no *rex* [king] where will rules rather than *lex* [law]. (vol. II, p. 33)

By 'law makes the king' (based on *Codex* 1.14.4), 'Bracton' presumably meant that an individual becomes king when he assumes office in a lawful manner. In defending a case, the author goes on, the king cannot issue a writ against himself and so he must be approached by petition 'that he correct and amend his act', or else be left to the vengeance of God. Additions to the text go much further and give a clear picture of an intended constitution, of the kind aimed at by the barons under Simon de Montfort.

> The king has a superior, namely God. Also the law by which he is made king. Also his *curia* [court], namely the earls and barons, because if he is without bridle, that is without law, they ought to put the bridle on him. That is why the earls are called the partners (*socii*) of the king; he who has a partner has a master. (vol. II, p. 110)

This author clearly thought that, to put the king under the law, it was necessary to put him under a tribunal.

Another way of stating the problem was to use theological language and distinguish between the 'absolute' and the 'ordinary' power of a ruler. This distinction originated out of discussion about how God, who has unlimited power, could choose to operate within the laws of nature ordained by himself. It was used by Hostiensis and Aegidius as a means of understanding the pope's prerogative powers: as a rule the pope operates under the church's positive law, but he may on occasion act outside it, for example in dispensing from vows;

although, Aegidius added, it is in the interests of the stability of his own laws that he govern by them. This was a way of saying that the pope normally should, and does, govern in accordance with canon law, but that he can, on very special occasions, act against or outside it.

It is interesting to see how the introduction of Aristotle changed the language in which the discussion was put and the problem conceived, but not, to begin with at least, the substance of what was said; and how the greater clarity made possible by Aristotle's language did, in all probability, make it much easier for certain more definite positions eventually to be stated. Briefly, in a careful discussion of the relation between rulers and the laws, and especially between a king and the law (*Politics* III.14–17), Aristotle said that in a 'political' (i.e. constitutional, civic) regime, it is more accurate to say that the laws rule ('are dominant'), rather than particular individuals, since they stipulate the procedures by which individuals obtain offices. But in an absolute kingship, one individual has the power to override the laws, and, if he is sufficiently virtuous and does so for the right reasons, this may be justifiable. Amongst writers using Aristotle, discussion centred upon whether the 'political' or the 'regal' mode of government was preferable, which meant whether it was 'better to be ruled by the best man or by the best laws'.

Judging by what theorists now said, it is possible that Aristotle's more precise definitions helped to polarise and perhaps clarify opinion, making theorists opt either for 'regal' or for 'political' rule. Aegidius stated an unequivocal preference for regal over political regimes; it is preferable to be ruled by the best man than the best laws. But this view was not widespread. Even the monarchist Buridan, while admitting that it would be better in principle to be ruled by a good prince, concluded with a rare dash of common sense that 'in modern times it is simply better for a state to be ruled by a good law without a prince than by any prince without law' (*Questions*, III.4, pp. 120–2).

Ptolemy of Lucca followed Aristotelian doctrine more closely, while also interpreting it to suit the medieval world generally and the civic world of Italy in particular. He identified 'political' rule, which on the whole he preferred to royal rule, as meaning rule in accordance with the laws, in particular the constitutional laws which define and delimit a ruler's powers; it is also especially appropriate for, and commonly found in, city-states all over the world, and especially in Italy (II. ch. 8; IV chs. 1–2; cf. above, p. 123).

The most celebrated medieval statement on this subject came from

Sir John Fortescue (*c*. 1394–*c*. 1476; Chief Justice of the King's Bench, 1442). Writing in the 1460s during his exile in France due to his support for the Lancastrian claims to the English throne, he too used Aristotelian language, this time to distinguish between the 'regal lordship' of the French monarchy and the 'political and regal lordship' enjoyed by England (*In Praise of England's Laws*, ch. 11; *The Law of Nature* (*De natura legis naturae*), book 1, chs. 16, 24). This extraordinary combination of concepts which in Aristotle and earlier medieval writers had been treated as opposites, was designed precisely as a means of describing the specific constitutional balance, which he regards as the best available, of the English constitution. It was a restatement of the traditional view that the king must rule within the law, except on special occasions when justice or higher utility require extra-legal action. It justified both the rule of law and the royal prerogative. But Fortescue, like Cusa some years previously on the subject of the German monarchy (*CC* III, ch. 12, p. 375), linked the constitutional rule of law with the legislative supremacy of the parliament. In England, writes Fortescue, on the one hand 'the judges of the realm are all bound by their oaths not to render judgements against the laws of the land even if they receive commands of the prince to the contrary'; on the other hand, the king may and should exercise the powers of discretion (*epieikeia*), dispensation and emergency action – in other words, prerogative.

One may note a contrast here with the properly feudal language of constitutionalism in Aragon, which left no scope for prerogative and was perhaps less flexible and open to development. Laws are oaths or pacts, which the king at his coronation swears to uphold; they have the binding force of civil contracts (*pactionatae leges et inviolabiles contractus*: Marongiu, *Medieval Parliaments*, p. 161). Fortescue's language subjected the prince to law but did not so explicitly subject him to the nobility or towns, the usual beneficiaries of such contractual doctrine.

As the statements of Cusa and Fortescue suggest, the relation of king to law was closely connected to the relation of king to parliament. But, although the weight of opinion was that rule by laws was preferable to rule by men, there was no consensus on how to deal with a monarch who acted illegally. Medieval theory and practice could, and did, develop in different directions. Of critical importance here was the concept of the Crown as an entity distinct from the king (see below, pp. 189–90).

COUNSEL AND WISDOM

The taking of counsel, or consultation of the wise and virtuous, was subscribed to by practically all writers of all schools in later medieval and early Renaissance thought. In monarchical states, it meant that the king ought to take advice regularly from certain people; the same was said of the pope. The constitutional question was whether this was more than a moral obligation, whether something could be done if he refused advice. In city republics, 'the wise' were assigned a somewhat different role as expert legal advisers, distinct from any question of wider representation. Aristocracy proper, on the other hand, in the sense of actual government by the wise and virtuous few, was not widely advocated.

The argument for counsel or wisdom in government could be employed on behalf of several practical programmes. It could be employed on behalf of the supposedly traditional role of the baronage, or certain select barons, as the 'natural counsellors' of the king, a hereditary aristocracy; or, alternatively, on behalf of experts, men trained in law, theology or the liberal arts, a meritocracy (*sapientes*, *savi*, *prud'hommes*). These two were liable to conflict: barons frequently objected to royal use of 'new men', who in turn proclaimed the rights of merit against the accident of birth.

'Bracton' said that the magnates constituted a superior court and could restrain the king if he refused the restraint of law, and he suggested that royal acts may be subjected to correction by 'the corporation of the realm and his baronage in the court of the king himself' (vol. II, p. 110). The conflict between Henry III of England and the barons was partly about whether the barons could impose advisers and ministers on the king; this they tried to do, in the form of a committee of twenty-four, twelve chosen by the king and twelve by the barons acting 'on behalf of the community'. Edward I asserted that he was bound by oath to act on matters touching the Crown only 'with the consent of the prelates and magnates'. Walter Burley, who was at times close to the government of Edward III, said in his *Commentary on Aristotle's Politics* (*c.* 1340) that a king together with his magnates and wise experts can do all that the king can do alone, and even more. Nicole Oresme, friend and adviser to Charles V of France from 1364 to 1380, stated that a king must rule in collaboration with magnates and men of prudence as his counsellors (pp. 329–30); and Philippe de Mezières, tutor to the future Charles VI, insisted that the king's council should always be attended by 'a person of secular status with a good grounding in the laws of God and in the civil and moral laws' (pp. 332–7). In the church, the same claim was put forward on behalf of the college of cardinals, especially in virtue of their position as electors of the pope: the pope was obliged to consult them 'on difficult questions'; this ought to be legally enforceable.[3]

On the other hand, schoolmen, educated clergy and humanists argued that a ruler should employ counsellors whose wisdom and virtue were empirically verified; 'true nobility' being contrasted with mere nobility of birth or the sword. Scholars often argued that counsel should be the prerogative of genuine *doctores*, as opposed to those who had acquired a degree by purchase, bribe or privilege. The theoretical case for good counsel and government in consultation with the wise was especially strong in the church, the most Platonic of polities in which authority was supposed to mean possession of the truth. The two keys symbolising St Peter's authority stood, it was said, for knowledge and power, which must always go together; during the Council of Basle it was argued that, since bishops were no longer chosen for their intellectual and moral qualities, genuine *doctores* should have some role in religious decision-making.

The political interests supporting consultation thus ranged from aristocratic traditionalism to reformers with their own view of the public good. The cultural and intellectual pressure came from every point of the compass. Judges, as men selected for their learning, experience and moral virtue, were supposed to exercise discretion when written laws did not cover a particular case, and equity when their strict application would be manifestly unfair. In the frequent attempts at legal and constitutional reform undertaken in Italian and other cities and city republics, the advice of qualified jurists was generally sought. Theologians, canon lawyers and churchmen believed that secular government had recognised, rational purposes, about the nature and means of attaining which they themselves were uniquely qualified to advise. The case for giving the wise an important place in government was virtually unanswerable, given the belief in rationality endemic in European culture, or at least the literate culture which produced political theory. This belief stemmed from Platonism, Stoicism and their Christianised variations which came to dominate the mental perspectives of late Rome, Byzantium and the early and high Middle Ages in the West. It was the way to keep the

[3] F. M. Powicke, *The Thirteenth Century*, 2nd edn (Oxford: Oxford University Press, 1962), pp. 130–1, 522; G. W. S. Barrow, *Feudal Britain* (London; Edward Arnold, 1956), pp. 269–78), *CHMPT*, pp. 500–1, 549–51; Brian Tierney, *Foundations of the Conciliar Theory* (Cambridge: Cambridge University Press, 1955), pp. 180–91.

myth of the monarch as the seat of wisdom, as he who 'has all the laws in his breast', in touch with reality. Both the Biblical and the Platonic concepts of 'wisdom' connoted moral excellence as well. Aristotle hardened this by introducing the concept of practical wisdom (*phronesis*) as a distinct quality and practice, at once a skill and a virtue, which medieval thinkers translated as *prudentia politica*. His concept of politics (in the sense of civic social life) as a distinct area of human understanding (translated as *politica scientia*) combined the humane and almost saintly person's grasp of the true ends of life with empirical and practical expertise of the kind conveyed in *Politics* III–VI. In general, the proposition that those few who possess true wisdom ought to instruct and guide the hand upon the tiller of the state was virtually unquestioned. One may hazard that it was unchallengeable until Rousseau, in his protest against Enlightenment rationality, placed instinct above book learning and the philosophy of the philosophers.

The prospects for this kind of thinking were enchanced by the institutionalisation of learning in the disciplines expounded, developed and transmitted by the universities. These not only provided a supply of trained minds for princely and papal service; their status as quasi-autonomous corporations (*universitates*) ensured that the education of European *literati* – it would be an exaggeration to call them Platonic 'guardians' though they aspired to that role – took place in a milieu with an element of independence from the political and ecclesiastical authorities. *Studium* was conceptualised as the third branch of Christian society, beside *ecclesia* (church) and *regnum* (kingdom). Universities encouraged the idea – as was in their corporate interest – that problems are soluble by effort, study and enquiry, and that the best way to judge a difficult question is to discuss it. Belief in public debate amongst intellectuals could easily be translated into the assumption that difficult political problems are best solved by a group of wise men, a *concilium*. It was in this context that freedom of speech came to be advocated, when for example a pope or king bribed or threatened *doctores* with confiscation of goods and imprisonment.[4] (No-one however, with the possible exception of Marsiglio, went to the point of thinking that institutions could be re-designed from first principles by architectonic reasoners.)

Adoption of Aristotle's language increased the opportunities for expressing such ideas and getting them accepted, in more ways than

---

[4] Marsiglio, *DP* II.21.15; Ockham, *Imperial and Papal Power*, ch. 15 (cf. McGrade, *Ockham*, p. 71); and Juan de Segovia, the conciliarist, in Antony Black, *Council and Commune*, pp. 155–6.

one. Aristotle himself preferred, if only as a higher ideal unlikely to be achieved, government by 'the best men' in the sense of those who excel in intellectual and moral virtues. Aquinas defended the view that rank (*ordo*) exists among humans with another of Aristotle's statements, that intellectual excellence confers a natural right to be master over those natural slaves who are physically strong but less intelligent (*Against the Pagans* (*Summa contra Gentiles*) III.81; cf. Aristotle, *Politics* I.2, 1252a–b). Engelbert of Admont also applied this to the relationship between rulers and ruled; intellect entitles persons to rule, and kings were originally chosen for their mental powers (ch. 1, p. 754 and ch. 2, p. 755; cf. ch. 3, p. 755, line 5 and ch. 5, p. 756, line 6). The dedicated monarchist, Aegidius Romanus, gave convincing testimony to sapientialism: in his argument that rule by one is better than rule by a few or many, after refuting the argument based on the superior (because collective) wisdom of a few *or* many, he nevertheless concluded that a monarch 'ought to associate with himself wise men . . . and virtuous men . . . and thus he will become one man with many eyes, many hands and many feet' (III. part 2, ch. 4, fol. 272r; based on Aristotle, *Politics* III.16 1287b). A monarchical regime will become perverted, aiming at the ruler's private good, only if 'the whole council and all the wise men' become perverted; but if a monarch 'despises counsel and dismisses the society of the wise', then you will have tyranny, the worst form of government. This was tantamount to saying that the probity and indeed legitimacy of kingship depends upon consultation of the wise – a remarkable statement from an otherwise pure monarchist.

Marsiglio, as one might expect, revolutionised the topic. Against the argument that the few wise are entitled to govern (supported by a Vulgate mistranslation of Eccles. 1:15 to the effect that 'infinite is the number of fools'), he brought to bear, first, Aristotle's argument (*Politics* III.11) that the collective reasoning of a large number of oridinary, not very wise individuals adds up to a greater degree of enlightenment and a sounder judgement than the reasoning of the few with more wisdom *per capita*. Then Marsiglio added his own view – and it was eventually to become an almost characteristically modern-European view: anyone of unimpaired judgement, that is, the great majority of citizens, has the desire for self-preservation and a decent life, and, along with this, sufficient good sense to know good from bad political decisions (*DP* I.13, esp. 3–4, pp. 56–7). It is helpful to have laws and civic arrangements first sifted and discussed by prudent experts, designated by the ruling group or elected by all citizens; but their recommendations only become law when they have been put for approval or rejection to 'the assembled community of citizens, so that, if any citizen thinks that anything should be added, modified, changed or completely thrown out, he is able to say so; in this way the law will be more usefully drawn up' (*DP* 1.13.8, p. 60). Marsiglio thus reduced the gulf between the better and less informed from one of 'wisdom' to one of expertise. It is not, as Platonists would have it, that a select few are morally and intellectually superior to other citizens by nature or education, only that some are 'more learned and more experienced' than others. It is no longer a moral gulf; the few act only as legal and constitutional advisers. The ordinary citizen may not be capable of expounding a new law, but he is capable of judging the soundness of proposals that are put to him (see *DP* III.3, p. 56). The concept of wisdom was democratised as common sense.

Ockham insisted that on theological questions the opinions of the learned were to be preferred to the opinions of those in authority; and his Christian faith led him further to assert that ordinary, simple people were just as capable as anyone else of holding correct theological views and making sound moral judgements (McGrade, *Ockham*, pp. 55–61). In this way Ockham arrived at a view very different to Marsiglio's: he rejected the superior wisdom and moral authority of the majority. But he too democratised the authority of the mind, in an individualist sense.

The sapiential idea was again prominent in the thinking of supporters of councils against the papacy in the early fifteenth century. At the Council of Basle the idea of the *studium* as a third branch of authority in Christendom was partially institutionalised through voting procedures and more or less officially expressed (1439): universities have an official role to play in the authoritative formulation of Christian doctrine since it is there, rather than among the episcopate, that nowadays you will find men learned 'in the science of faith'. The idea of wisdom, and indeed justice, as the product of a *group* was formulated in a new way by Juan de Segovia, a prominent theorist at the Council: informed debate gives rise to better understanding and better decisions. This was not so much in line with the Aristotelian notion of the superior collective wisdom of the many, for the groups Segovia had in mind were relatively small (the Council and its committees); rather, it was based on the didactic and investigative traditions of the European universities. For a sound decision concerning the public good to be reached, each person must 'hear the other and his deliberation'. What happens is not merely that a greater number of people are more likely to reach a good majority decision; rather, each individual's own insight is sharpened. There is a universal law of nature that the powers of individuals are increased when exercised in unison, as in 'common discussion and conference'. Here the age-old idea of counsel became a theory of kowledge, and also of interpersonal intellectual relationships (Black, *Council*, pp. 156–9).

Both Segovia and his more famous contemporary, Nicholas of Cusa (see below, pp. 178–83) formulated general theories of political authority in church and state, based upon a revision of the classical sapientialism of Plato and Aristotle in the light of Christian faith and the ideas of Marsiglio. According to Cusa (writing on the Empire in 1433), political authority is based upon the superior wisdom of some and the foolishness of others; but none the less, or rather for that very reason, this entails 'voluntary subordination' because each party recognises its rightful position. Right authority rests upon inner relationships between persons ('not nature but folly makes a slave, not manumission but discipline makes a free man'). To take account of the role of the German princes and nobility, Cusa here modified Marsiglio's authority of all citizens into the authority of 'all or at least the wise and the heroic' (*CC* III. *Preface*, pp. 314–16). Segovia expressed a similar view, first for the church and then for all states, based upon his own theological insight into 'faith' as a category of true knowledge. This rests not on personal expertise nor on blind trust but rather upon a capacity in individuals to distinguish between trustworthy and untrustworthy argument, and trustworthy or untrustworthy claimants to intellectual or political *auctoritas*. He called this *credulitas*, the quality of being trusting. All society, he argued, rests upon people adopting an attitude towards one another of faith, 'belief in things not seen' – or not evidently proved. By this he meant that you trust the other person without being able to check up on everything he says (Black, *Council*, pp. 167–8, 176–83, 191–2). Thus the personal aspect of the religious concept of faith led to the authority of the wise and popular consent being seen as interdependent. In general, wise counsellors, whether noble or learned, were regarded as embodying a greater degree of community consent than the king acting alone.

6

PARLIAMENTARY REPRESENTATION

Parliaments developed in the thirteenth and fourteenth centuries, in some cases earlier, and became a familiar part of the political process in most European states. The later fifteenth century saw a decline in the use and power of the Estates in France, England and elsewhere, but an increased use of them in some German principalities. This wave-like pattern created an illusion that medieval government was more autocratic, and that constitutional government developed later, than was in fact the case. There was considerable continuity between medieval parliamentary traditions and the emergence of modern representative government.[1]

This is the less surprising because what parliaments were, what they stood for and were conceived to be, and the roles they undertook, sprang from roots deep in the political cultures of the European lands. The primary function of parliament was usually to grant the ruler a tax for specific purposes, often war. Such purposes were presented as, and generally considered to be, for the benefit of the realm as a whole. The 'talking' or negotiating aspect of parliament concerned the fixing of a rate of taxation acceptable to both sides. In England parliament had a supreme judicial role which gave it added importance.

The reasons why parliaments were called by kings for such purposes and played the role they did lie in the social structure of medieval Europe, in the way power and wealth were distributed.

[1] See bibliography, pp. 203–4.

Parliaments became important because they were the means by which kings were able to gain entitlement to income from their subjects, both their major vassals and others, over and above what they could acquire through applications of existing feudal contracts and rights. In this respect parliaments depended upon a relatively decentralised control over the material bases of power. By the later thirteenth century the barons were by no means the only people in a position to bargain. The characteristic form taken by medieval parliaments of three 'Estates' (*status*) – clergy, barons, commons or *communia* (towns) – reflected the diversity of sources of income. Clergy as landowners were expected to contribute a share. The Third Estate consisted in most countries of the towns, the wealth of whose citizens came principally from commerce and manufacture. In England, the shires were incorporated beside the towns; non-baronial landowners (knights, gentry) were expected to contribute, thus initiating a direct link between the royal government and a widening band of subjects in the towns and countryside.

Part of the *raison e'être* of the Estates or parliament rested upon the idea of the *communitas regni* that a given realm, such as England or Scotland, was what we would call a political unit, with common interests and a common duty of allegiance and participation. Every man was expected in time of need to contribute what was required for the welfare of that community: money, arms, a horse, his person. The means by which this political community found practical coherence depended largely upon the property relations between king, barons, gentry and so on. This was what made parliaments necessary and effective. It is reflected in the native language for parliamentary phenomena. That 'many' should be consulted about legislation and war was a commonplace in northern and southern Europe. Kings are called upon, and agree, to recognise the rights and liberties of persons and groups, especially towns, in return for a tax. The reciprocity of the relationship between the king and others is stressed, and forms a basis for action against the king if he is thought to have used the money for illicit (private) ends, or incompetently; hence attempts by barons and parliaments to have a say in the appointment of royal ministers. Here the language of the common good was of critical importance.

Practical needs alone do not create the political institutions needed to handle them. Parliaments depended for their success, development and credibility upon specific procedures and specific modes of political thought. These amounted to what we now call representation. The whole point – some would say the political genius of

Europe[2] – was the capability of a group of persons physically assembled at a royal court such as the palace of Westminster to act effectively and legitimately in the name of a vast kingdom. We must now consider how this came about.

First, there was the fundamental point that agreements entered into were binding: what people said they would contribute, they must; what the king said he would perform, he must. This contractual component in parliamentary arrangements, which became most prominent in Catalonia and Aragon, developed out of what we may justly call the feudal ethos. But, if this worked for bishops and nobles who were present in person, what of those communities whose members were present only by representation, in the person of their proctor (*procurator*)? Such people had to be given, by the groups they represented, 'full power', that is, the right to bind their community to pay whatever tax emerged out of negotiations between the king and the Estates; although electors often tried to impose conditions and limits on what they would agree to, so that the proctor or member of parliament might have to refer back to his constituents.[3]

This was one process by which large kingdoms were bound together into political units that could speak and act consensually with one voice – into modern states, if we like. It explains in part that tremendous expansion of 'intensive' political power, of the capacity to call upon the heartfelt allegiance of large groups of individuals, which seems to differentiate modern European-type states from more fragile structures where authority rests on intermediary magnates or patron–client relationships. Of course a king could and did claim to represent the realm, but his position alone, as king *solus*, was that much weaker simply because, and in so far as, others did not feel morally or legally – constitutionally, we would say – obliged to go along with him. In most of medieval Europe they would not go along with a king acting alone on the crucial issue of taxation on account of the prevailing system of property rights; these rested upon the feudal agreement and were therefore adjustable only by the mutual consent of the parties concerned. Given this, king and parliament needed each other. 'Feudalism' did indeed place limits on royal power and the way round this limitation was for representative assemblies to act alongside the king. The collaborative nature of the enterprise was shown by the use of parliaments in times of national crisis. Again, a kingdom's cohesion depended in part upon the willingness of towns and districts to be represented by such means,

[2] James Madison, *The Federalist*, no. 14.
[3] *CHMPT*, pp. 554ff.; Post, *Studies*, pp. 91–162.

which in turn required a certain cohesion within these lesser units. In all of this there is evident contrast with non-European societies.

Both the techniques of representation and the very idea of assemblies as the legitimate arena for collective decisions, owed a great deal to the church. Ecclesiastical bodies, such as monasteries, developed the practice of empowering one of their number to represent them in negotiations with outside bodies. The inclusion of proctors of collegiate churches in medieval general councils provides an analogy with parliaments. Councils of bishops had often been the instrument for church government, and legislation, in Visigothic Spain for example. It may be here that we find the origin of the idea of representation, for it was taught and widely believed, in the words of St Cyprian (a third-century bishop of Carthage) that 'the church is in the bishop, the bishop in the church': that is, in extra-diocesan dealings the bishop stands for the church and what he does binds his flock, but he is also expected in some way to reflect his flock, if only so that he may carry them with him. Here representation was no mere legal mandate, but rested on a whole metaphysic in which prelates were spiritually identified with their flocks.

This metaphysic could be developed in a monarchical direction, as when some argued that the pope represented the whole church so closely that he was empowered to act in its name and with its authority without consultation. Similarly a king could claim that he represented his realm. But this was not an image that met the reality of medieval kingdoms, at least in respect of taxation. The organic analogy (see above, pp. 15–18), with the king as head ruling in co-operation with other members, rank upon rank, expressed the situation more aptly. Precedents provided by church councils suggested, again, that groups were represented by individuals who then consulted together as a group. The metaphysic of representation also suggested that a prelate or prince, being identified with his flock, is obliged to attend to their interests. This was related to the concept of governmental authority as service, which derived from Matt. 20:25–7; the ruler as *minister* entered the theological language of medieval politics. Medieval parliamentary representation came to a climax in church politics with the conciliar movement of the early fifteenth century, the failure of which coincided with a decline in representative assemblies generally. Thus representation involved legal techniques and moral beliefs which make it less of a coincidence that it evolved in a Christian society.

The parliamentary process was expressed and justified in a variety of political languages. The language of local (or national) customary law was used: it seemed reasonable that arrangements sanctioned by custom should only be changed by the same means by which custom was held to have been established, namely the consent of the users and of those to whom the laws applied, as 'Bracton' argued (*On the Laws and Customs of England*, vol. II, pp. 19–22: in *MPI* pp. 39–41). The language of Roman jurisprudence was introduced, often through the mediation of canon law, to explain what was happening in this un-Roman context. For example, Roman law happened to state that, in matters concerning a guardian and a ward, all beneficiaries of the will must be consulted: 'what touches all should be approved by all' (*quod omnes tangit ab omnibus approbetur*: *Codex* 5.59.5.2). This was in fact the commonest justification for parliaments and was used both by kings and Estates, to express both the duty and the right to consultation. It was cited, with no reference to its original context, to show that matters concerning 'all' members of a kingdom should be decided only with their approval, that is through parliament.[4]

Next, canon law provided that disputed elections should be decided by 'the greater and wiser part' (*maior et sanior pars*) or a corporation or electoral college; and parliament – or sometimes the king's own council – was said to constitute the greater and wiser part of a kingdom. Majority voting, when the optimum of unanimity could not be achieved, was introduced, partly on the model of ecclesiastical procedures derived from the early church and the Roman law on municipalities. Parliament itself came to be seen as a corporate body (*universitas regni*) so that the procedures and rights of corporations under 'common law' (that is, Roman law as currently interpreted) should be available to it. Parliament stands in the place of the whole, partly because it is composed of wise and virtuous persons who are select members of the community; and partly because those present have been expressly chosen by those not present, as in the case of towns which send corporate representatives (*procuratores, syndici*). There is, therefore, a strong presumption that parliament acts as the people as a whole would wish.

When parliament was described as *universitas regni* – the kingdom as a whole acting as a corporation – this implied that it embodied the consent, tacit or express, of all members. Yet on the whole it cannot be said that parliamentary theory kept abreast of practice. The chief

[4] Post, *Studies* pp. 163–240; J. A. Maravall, *Estudio de Historia del Pensiamento Español, Edad Media*, 1st series (Madrid, 1966), pp. 159–76; Bruno Paradisi, 'Il Pensiero Politico dei Giuristi Medievali', in Luigi Firpo (ed.), *Storia delle Idee Politiche, Economiche e Sociali* (Turin: Unione Tipografico-Editrice Torinese, 1973), pp. 336–42.

authoritative sources behind republican and democratic theory, Aristotle and Cicero, had nothing to say about representation as it was now developing. Something could have been made out of the notion that the ideal form of government is a *mixture* of the three good types, in which one king, the wise few and the many or the people each have a part, providing moderation, balance and stability (see Cicero, *Republic*, I.xxix.45 and I.xlv.69). But Aquinas' statement that 'the best constitution is one well mixed out of kingship, in which one is in charge, aristocracy, in which many rule on account of their virtue, and democracy, that is the power of the people, in so far as the rulers (*principes*) are elected by and from the people' (*ST* Ia/IIae 105.1 *resp*; cf. 95.4 *resp*.) makes no explicit reference to parliaments, of which Aquinas may have been barely aware.

The first systematic statement came from Nicole Oresme in a discussion of Aristotle. In a *democratie*, the popular multitude holds sovereignty. In a polity (*commune policie*) or an aristocracy, it is not the popular multitude but 'the multitude and universal congregation of all the princes or officials and of the principal citizens' which 'has sovereign lordship and [can ensure] the correction or alternation of the particular princes and officials', and determines major questions such as legislation and constitutional reform. The example he gave was the general assembly of the masters of Paris University. Also, in a *policie royal* (that is, a limited, constitutional monarchy)

on occasion (*par aventure*) it is expedient that such a reasonable multitude or part of it has this power ... since this whole multitude, of which the king and his familiar council are a small part, knows better how to consider and direct all that is good for the commonwealth (*la chose publique*). And also, that which all do and approve is more firm and stable, more acceptable and agreeable to the community, and gives less occasion for murmurings or rebellion.

This clearly referred to the Estates even though Oresme did not support the extreme demands made by them during 1355–8. This suggests that, once one conceded that a regime was monarchical, it was possible to use Aristotelian language in a quasi-parliamentarist way to indicate a manner of ruling that it was advisable and expedient for a king to adopt, but not one that could be enforced against his will. The influence of Marsiglio, towards whom Oresme was generally sympathetic, was not significant here.

On the other hand, a somewhat different picture emerged when Oresme considered the *means of assembling* the multitude. This may be done (1) by a law stating when the Estates must be assembled, (2) by stating the questions which can only be resolved by the Estates, or (3) by a prince or official who decides when it is expedient to call the Estates. In support of the first two possibilities, which alone would give the Estates a real share in sovereignty, Oresme cited the ancient practices of church councils (6.12.2, pp. 274–5).[5]

The only other important secular theorist was Sir John Fortescue. His reflections on parliament were couched in a combination of feudal, Aristotelian and theological language. The fundamental point was that 'the kings of England do not establish laws nor impose taxes on their subjects without the consent of the three Estates'. This, combined with government according to the laws (see above, p. 155), made England a lordship at once '*political* – that is, regulated by the control of the many' and '*royal*, since the subjects themselves cannot establish laws without the royal authority' (my italics) (*The Law of Nature*, part 1, ch. 16 and *In Praise of England's Laws*, ch. 9: *MPI* pp. 259–60, 327). Laws can be made only 'with the consent of the whole realm', 'by the prudence of three hundred select men'; and their defects 'can be reformed immediately with the consent of the Commons and Lords of the realm, with which they were first made' (*In Praise of England's Laws*, ch. 18: *MPI* p. 87). This resembled what Oresme had said, but Fortescue's argument – and the position of the English parliament – were immeasurably strengthened by the control of taxation, which by Fortescue's day the French Estates General had lost.

And indeed Fortescue was the first to emphasise this point in such a way as to link parliament firmly to *property*. The king's obligation to get parliamentary consent for taxation meant that the English people 'freely enjoys its property under the rule of the laws which it desires, and is not despoiled by its king nor by anyone else'.

Wherefore every inhabitant of his kingdom uses at his own pleasure the fruits which his land yields to him, and which his herds produce, and all the gains which accrue to him from his own labour or that of another, on land or sea; and if he suffers injury or robbery he receives the amends due to him thence; whence the inhabitants of that country are rich in land, and have abundance of gold and silver and all the necessities of life. (*In Praise of England's Laws*, chs. 9, 36: trans. E. Lewis, *MPI*, pp. 327 and 136)

---

[5] Mario Grignaschi, 'Nicole Oresme et son commentaire à la "Politique" d'Aristote', in *Album Cam*, 1, *Studies Presented to the International Committee for the History of Representative and Parliamentary Institutions*, 23 (Louvain, 1960), pp. 119–20; *CHMPT*, pp. 565–6.

This was the point which John Locke, possibly assisted by his reading of John of Paris,[6] developed. The kind of feudal property arrangements native to England made parliamentary control of the material levers of government possible. Fortescue also employed the organic analogy, borrowing the theological term 'mystical body' as an expression for the whole kingdom *qua* coordinated structure, and with the specific meaning that power is shared between the king (head) and other organs: 'the intention of the people' (heart) and the laws (nerves) (*In Praise of England's Laws*, ch. 13: *MPI* p. 329). All this backed up his contention that the consent of parliament was equivalent to the consent of the whole realm.

THE CONCILIAR MOVEMENT

The poverty of theory about secular parliaments contrasts with the wealth of ideas about the representative and constitutional role of councils in the late medieval church. This was no accident. The idea and practice of representation, if not born in the Christian church, was made a regular, inherent and sanctified part of it as of no other organisation. From the early church, councils had been essential to Christianity as the only way in which, given the structure of the church with its far-flung units and their bishops, decisions deemed necessary to religion could be credibly and effectively arrived at. Bishops from Gaul to Mesopotamia attended to determine what the apostolic tradition, transmitted to the bishops, really was; their decisions were deemed to have at least the tacit consent of the faithful because congregations were spiritually identified with their leaders. Both universal ('general') and local ('particular') councils were an especially regular feature of the medieval church. The papacy used councils as kings used parliaments, to put across, get consent to and give effect to new measures. Local councils sometimes corresponded to the boundaries of a kingdom. In the church–state conflicts from the middle of the thirteenth century onwards (see above, pp. 48–56), secular rulers like Philip the Fair and Ludwig the Bavarian, in controversy with the papacy, appealed from the pope to the higher ecclesiastical authority of a general council. This action was defended by systematic theories of councils as the means by which Christ intended the church to be governed. It is here that we must look for a further development of the *theory* of 'parliamentary' representation.

[6] Janet Coleman, '*Dominium* in Thirteenth- and Fourteenth-Century Political Thought and its Seventeenth-Century Heirs: John of Paris and John Locke', *Political Studies* 33 (1985), pp. 73–100.

The events of the conciliar epoch clearly suggest its significance for the history of constitutionalism. Opposition between conciliar and papal authority was brought to a climax by the great schism between rival popes from 1378 to 1417. In the conciliar movement beginning in the 1380s, a wide spectrum of church leaders, secular rulers and theologians sought to resolve the constitutional crisis by means of a general council which should have authority to appoint a true pope. As the dispute dragged on, the papacy's moral standing slumped further; and the notion of the papacy as an absolute monarchy seemed to make negotiation and compromise more difficult. This helped to bring into new focus longstanding and increasingly widespread criticism of abuses of church authority and clerical immorality. It focussed responsibility for misgovernment on the papacy itself and encouraged the belief that reform of the 'head' could only be achieved by a general council.

The council which met at Constance in 1414 under the leadership of the emperor-elect Sigismund of Luxemburg and the pastoral theologian Jean Gerson, chancellor of Paris University, deposed two popes while a third resigned, and elected Martin V. These actions were justified by the decree *Haec sancta* (1415) which declared that a council was superior to a pope in matters of faith, unity and reform. The decree *Frequens* (1417) stated that henceforth councils must be summoned at regular and previously agreed times. Both decrees were part of an attempt to ensure that from now on councils, beside the pope, would play a leading role in the government of the church; some saw them as giving councils actual *supremacy* over popes.

When another council met at Basle in 1431, Sigismund and the German princes saw it, in addition, as a forum for negotiations with the Hussites (see above, pp. 103–4). Consequently, when Eugenius tried to dissolve the council as soon as it met, he found himself opposed by a powerful secular lobby as well as by an increasingly determined body of church reformers and conciliarists. The council re-issued the decrees *Haec sancta* and *Frequens*, added new decrees explicitly asserting a council's right to determine its own dissolution (1432–3) and, in the face of Eugenius' opposition, took over the central machinery of church government, setting up its own appellate courts and raising taxes. The majority at Basle saw their task as resolving the major problems facing Christendom and putting church government on a right course for the future. For a while the council acted like a constituent assembly of Christendom, passing decrees on elections, taxation, local synods and clerical conduct. It hammered out an agreement with the moderate Hussites, later repudiated by Eugenius; and in 1435 helped reconcile Burgundy with France, thus vitally changing the balance of power in Europe. But divisions arose over the scope and financial implications of reforms, and Eugenius succeeded in persuading a large body of senior clergy to attend a rival council at Florence (1437–8). With many states moving into neutrality, the supporters of conciliar sovereignty found their ranks suddenly thinned, reduced mainly to devotees from the universities and clergy of middle rank. In 1439 Basle declared the supremacy of council over pope to be an 'article of faith' and deposed Eugenius for, among other things, rejecting it. Time and the assiduous diplomacy of Rome told against the council; by the late 1440s most powers were signing fresh concordats with the papacy. This had been the most far-reaching attempt by any representative assembly to establish a regime that was recognisably non-monarchical and parliamentarian.

Such was the background to a movement of ideas which went far beyond anything conceived by secular parliamentarians and laid a basis for future theories of representative parliamentary government. As with such later movements, there were moderate and radical versions of conciliarism. Some said only that a pope must get the consent of a council for certain acts, such as definition of doctrine and major legislation. Theologians and canon-lawyers could claim support for this in church tradition: councils could only be convoked and dissolved by the pope, but it was still held that a pope could not act alone. Here the pope-in-council resembled the king-in-parliament.

Radical conciliarists, on the other hand, held that, in a dispute between council and pope, the council was in the last resort superior. This view drew on religious tradition at lower levels of church government, in dioceses and cathedral chapters, monasteries and religious orders, where considerable powers were vested in the assembled community of clergy. There was subtle interplay here between secular practice and ecclesiastical theory. What the conciliarists attempted had been attempted before in a secular context, as some conciliarists were aware. But there was, as we have seen, no theory of secular parliamentarism. This was what the conciliarists provided.

Conciliar doctrine as it developed from the 1380s owed its inspiration to two main sources. In the first place, Jean Gerson (1363–1429), a spiritual leader of his generation, reinterpreted *theology* to prove that God intended his church to be governed by councils; Christ transmitted his supreme authority to the church as a community, not as an individual, and therefore general councils represent Christ. Here theorists drew on the whole communitarian culture of Europe including the lawyers' theory of corporations.

Second, there was the intellectual legacy of Marsiglio and Ockham, regarded as heterodox but still influential. Marsiglio, in his determination to eradicate clerical power (see above, pp. 58–71), had argued that, even in the sphere of religious legislation on doctrine, ritual and church organisation, final authority lay not with the papacy but with a general council. This was to be convoked by 'the faithful human legislator who knows no superior', that is the emperor and the other public authorities to whom in Christian countries the people have given coercive authority. Members of the council were to be selected by the 'human legislators' from each region of the church, so that it would indeed represent 'the association of the faithful (*universitas fidelium*)'. Its decisions were enforceable only by the supreme human legislator (*DP* II.20).

Ockham discussed how a general council should be convened, how its members were to be chosen, and by what means and in what sense it 'represents' the whole body of the faithful. A general council is 'an assembly (*congregatio*) of certain persons who represent (*vicem gerant*) the whole of Christendom'. Originally the church was so small that all its members could meet together.

> But the universal church is of no less power or authority when it cannot assemble together because of its great numbers, than when it could do so. Therefore, whatever the universal church could do through itself (*per se*) if it assembled together, it can do through certain men selected (*electos*) from different parts of the church.

As for how they are selected,

> It would be reasonable for some person or persons to be sent from every parish or every community which can easily come together, to an episcopal council or to the parliament of a king, prince or other public power; which would choose certain persons to be sent to the general council. (*Dialogue* 1.6.84 and III (i) 3.13)

Here then was a clear statement of representation by some kind of election; Ockham was probably drawing on English parliamentary practice.

Yet, quite unlike other conciliarists, Ockham denied that a council was a final authority on religious questions. For him every clause of the church's constitution was riddled with exceptions (see above, pp. 00–00). Ultimate authority lay only with whoever was actually right in a particular instance; and, while there was some presumption in favour of the learned, this might by any baptised individual. Thus Ockham granted that a council could override and depose an erring pope, and vice versa. He could say with bland irony that 'all Catholics tacitly or expressly consent and as it were grant authority to those going to the council when they proceed in a canonical, Catholic and correct way' (*Dialogue* III(i) 3.13): a council's decisions are tantamount to decisions by the universal church itself. *But* this is always on the understanding that such decisions are in reality correct. To become binding, conciliar decisions have to be approved by the faithful at large (the process of 'reception'). The more a doctrinal pronounce-ment or other decision becomes accepted, the more authority it has. But, on Ockham's terms, would it ever become unquestionable? Yet, even though Ockham himself undermined his own theory of repre-sentation by insisting on this individualist process of reception, it was possible to extract from his writings a clearer explanation of how representation worked than one could find anywhere else.

The conciliarists were very selective in what they took from Marsiglio and Ockham; but all in all they had a clearly defined constititional programme based on intellectual conviction. The church, they argued, whenever faced with a serious emergency, has the right to assemble itself; that is, a general council can meet spontaneously without papal convocation. This right derives, first, from the New Testament; second from the common-law rights of corporations (such as chapters and universities) and of free associ-ations (such as cities); and third from a 'common law of nature' which enables any organism under threat to 'assemble all its members' (Gerson in *MPI* p. 403; Black, *Council*, p. 20). The council is itself a self-governing corporation, and as such can determine when and where it should meet and who should be admitted to membership; it cannot be dissolved except by its own consent. The authority of a council overrides that of the pope on all matters of fundamental principle, such as the definition of faith. It can depose a pope if he persistently errs in serious matters, that is, doctrine (if he is a heretic), unity (if he is schismatic), and – implied by Gerson, strongly asserted by the Basle conciliarists – general conduct (if he rejects reform).

This raised the issue of the relation of council as legislature to pope as executive. Conciliarists, worried as they were that, once a council was dissolved, the pope might simply carry on as before, persuaded the Council of Constance, as we have seen, to decree stated intervals at which future councils should meet. The Council of Basle went further and claimed power to suspend a pope pending his trial for alleged misconduct. The council meanwhile could take over the pope's judicial and executive functions, make appointments to church benefices, raise church taxes and so on. The conciliarists of Basle thus ascribed, in effect, unlimited sovereignty to the council; the pope was an accountable *executor*, 'the church's first minister (*primus minister*)'.

If we compare this programme with secular parliamentary constitutionalism, there are some notable similarities with what was attempted by the English barons in the 1260s, the French Estates General in 1355–8, and on certain occasions by the Cortes of Aragon and of Castile. On the other hand, the council never came near to establishing in practice the claim to authorise taxation. Yet the arguments advanced to defend the sovereignty of the council went far further towards defining the relationship between the church at large and the council itself, in other words towards developing a theory of representation. Conciliarism was stronger on theory but weaker in practice than its secular counterparts.

To support this programme, a many-faceted theory of representation was worked out. In the first place, the conciliarists formulated a strong conception of the church-at-large as a whole, a single unit, a legally endowed corporation with inherent rights, a 'body'. For this they drew on the language of theology, liturgy and piety, on the theory of corporations developed by jurists, especially canon-lawyers, and on the organic analogy of the theologians. This last was as we have seen (above, pp. 15–18) a commonplace of medieval and Renaissance thought. But it was especially powerful in the case of the church, indeed had partly originated there: Christians had from the start defined the church as 'the body of Christ'; that is to say, as the real presence of the God-man on earth. This was central to Christian theology. Some conciliarists also said that the church is a real essence in a Platonic sense underlying and living through the many Christian individuals. The point of all this was to suggest that the church as a whole could act as one in exactly the same sort of way as an animal, human being or again a small corporation. Therefore, whenever a council is needed, it can assemble spontaneously, and thereafter act in the name of the church itself.

Alternatively, the church can be conceived in two ways, 'dispersed through the world' or 'assembled in one place': but these are but two modes of being of the same entity, so that what is ascribed to the one belongs also to the other. Some went yet further and claimed that the council, so far from operating at one remove from the actual church-at-large (as Ockham would have it) with a diminished or dependent authority, increased and brought to fruition powers that were only latent in the dispersed church. Conciliar representation was thus based opon a heightened conception of the political community of the church as a real, invisible object (Black, *Council*, pp. 20–4, 138, 141). Church theorists developed the notion of a political community, including its ruler, as a collective entity which can most adequately express itself in a representative assembly. This combination of representation and collectivism derived from the jurists' theory of corporations which distinguished between the competence of officials and of the corporation as a whole and sometimes subordinated the former to the latter, and from the idea of society as a 'mystical body'. And indeed conciliarists themselves occasionally applied these notions to parliaments. Gerson spoke of the French Estates General as 'the mystical body of the realm'.[7] Cusa said of the emperor, 'he is called a public and common person and father of each . . .; while he acknowledges himself the creature of all those subject to him collectively (*omnium collective*), he is the father of each' (*CC*, III.4, p. 348). On the other hand, the adage that the prince is 'greater than each, less than all (*maior singulis, universis minor*)' (see Aristotle, *Politics* III.15,1286b) was only applied to king and parliament in the later sixteenth century.

The council also represented the church because it looked like it; it was itself a community and its members were drawn from all (well, almost all) walks of ecclesiastical life. This was stated by Conrad of Gelnhausen, writing about 1380:

A general council is the assembly . . . of many or several persons, representing or acting on behalf of the various ranks, orders and sexes, duly summoned to attend or send proctors, and of persons of greater weight and ability from the whole of Christendom, to work for the good of the universal church. (After Ockham)[8]

In this sense it was said that the council represents the church *virtualiter*: it represents all the power (*virtutes*) and ministries of the church, its wisdom, virtue and other essential qualities.

Lastly, councils represented the church in a more elective sense: just as a person or corporation may choose a proctor or agent to act on their behalf in a law court, so too (as Ockham had said) parishes and colleges may choose representatives to attend a council. The council of Basle did in fact include a number of representatives elected by monasteries, chapters and in a few cases towns, to attend the

[7] E. H. Kantorowicz, *The King's Two Bodies: A Study in Medieval Political Theology* (Princeton, NJ: Princeton University, 1957), pp. 218–30.

[8] *Epistola Concordiae*, ed. E. Martène and U. Durand, *Veterum Scriptorum Amplissima Collectio*, vol. II (Paris, 1723), 1200–26 at 1217; also F. Bliemetzrieder (ed.), *Literarische Polemik zur Beginnung der grossen abendländischen Schismas* (Vienna, 1909), pp. 111–40.

council on their behalf. But these were only a small proportion of the council; many middle- and lower-rank clergy participated, but as individuals. It was nevertheless seen as highly significant that these were given the same voting power as bishops and princes' representatives. (Here indeed was a representative body which anticipated a famous development of the French Revolution of 1789 by abolishing separate 'Estates' within itself!) This caused resentment. In any case, conciliarists did not emphasise this elective aspect very much. On the other hand, considering that in secular parliaments there was a whole 'Third Estate' of those elected by towns (and in England shires), it is interesting that it took churchmen to elaborate this point at all.

One reason why conciliarism developed such an articulate theory and parliamentarism did not was that leading lights of the international intellectual community, as well as hosts of lesser academics, jurists and *literati*, were, or felt, called upon to contribute their opinions. Nothing better illustrates the way in which separate 'languages' could be employed for the same cause. Some were theologians, some canon-lawyers, some teachers of liberal arts. They combined arguments from different intellectual disciplines, arguing sometimes in juristic terms, using the theory of corporations, sometimes in political terms, using Aristotle's *Politics* and contemporary institutions, sometimes in philosophical terms, drawing upon the 'realist' or Neoplatonic rather than the nominalist tradition since this suited their case. Renaissance humanism was represented and precedents were sought in contemporary city-states. Most of all they argued in theological terms, using Scripture, especially the New Testament, the early church fathers and the pronouncements of earlier councils.

Theology provided the language of the people of God (*populus dei*), and of the council as a religious community bound together by fraternal love, the legitimate successor of the band of the first apostles. Ultimate authority in the Christian dispensation, it was argued, can only belong to a *community*. Juan de Segovia, in particular, in his doctrinal speeches to the Council, diplomatic orations and rambling reflections buried in his history of the Council of Basle (written during 1440–53 and probably hardly read till today), expounded Christian love as the principle that should underlie decision-making in the church and on religious questions: all members of the council should love one another, find out the special problems of different parts of the world, and so arrive at a consensus which will at once be mutually agreed and divinely inspired (Black, *Council*, pp. 135–59). The council being a fraternal institution, a representative miniature of the Christian community, membership confers on all who are admitted the same share of the collective authority, regardless of their ecclesiastical rank – this in defence of the council's controversial egalitarian voting procedures. For Segovia the council became a sacramental sign of the real qualities inhering in the Christian community; it embodies and brings to be the community it represents. God can be truly present only in a loving community; and the very fact of community means that God is present. The pope and all rulers should conduct themselves as the humble servants of those they govern, in accordance with Christ's principle, 'anyone who wants to be great among you must be your servant' (Matt. 20:25–7).

Many conciliarists, and Segovia in particular, believed, like certain later Protestant constitutionalists, that spirituality and public law, rather than either rendering the other superfluous, must be made to complement one another. The theological criteria for church government were to be given teeth by procedures for dealing with delinquent prelates, especially the pope. These procedures were defended in the languages of corporation theory, the *respublica* (approximately, Ciceronian) and mixed monarchy, a synthesis of Aristotle's categories of monarchy, aristocracy and polity-democracy.

Argument from history, which arose out of the argument from tradition, was given new prominence. The records of church history were scoured for evidence in favour of conciliar supremacy; a good, old constitution was discovered in the ecumenical councils of the late Graeco-Roman age. Some went further and adopted a truly historicist argument that the church's constitution had evolved like a living organism, passing developmentally from one form to another.

Juristic argument was used by Cardinal Zabarella (d. 1417) to say that, as in any corporation, fullness of power lies in the community (the council) and in the pope as head in such a way that the council can correct the pope when he errs. Civic republican arguments were used to make the same point: power lies fundamentally and inalienably with the whole community; they delegate it to a ruler (the pope) who must, therefore, remain accountable.

Juan de Segovia (1393–1458) who after 1437 emerged as the chief theorist of the Council of Basle, merged juristic and republican languages to produce something new. Any ruler, not only in the church, stands in the same relation as the governing head (*rector*) to a corporation (*universitas*), meaning that in the last resort the assembled citizens can overturn his judgement: this in order to justify the Council's definition of conciliar supremacy, rejected by Eugenius IV. Segovia explained this by saying that the ruler represents the community as its agent – the proctorial notion of representation – so that his acts can be countermanded by the community itself, if it so chooses, acting as its own principal. He rammed this home by saying that the ruler is a 'public person' (*persona publica*) only so long as he is understood to be pursuing the public good (*bonum publicum*). Then the public authority of the ruler is a valid and necessary constitutional fiction. But if the people (*multitudo*) declare the public good to be other than what the 'president' says it is, they must have their way; for his authority depends upon his views being 'presumed' to be the 'will of all' (*intentio omnium*). If they are shown not to be, his authority lapses (*Amplification*, pp. 720–1).

Analogies were made with contemporary *kingdoms*: the church has a mixed constitution, which is the best of all, combining kingship in the pope, aristocracy in the cardinals and timocracy or polity (the good form of democracy) in the council. The mixed constitution was at last made to work for the parliamentarist cause. Some went further and suggested that a council's deposition of a bad pope was analogous to the deposition of bad kings by 'the whole kingdom'. There were indeed such secular precedents (see above, p. 148), but secular statesmen tended to brush them under the carpet. Ecclesiastical conciliarism provided a general theory of constitutions for use by aspiring parliamentarians. Defenders of papal monarchy tried to exploit this as an argument why all secular princes should support the papacy to avoid subversion. When some Protestant groups espoused secular constitutionalism, they could look back, if with mixed feelings, on conciliarism as the closest historical precedent for what they were trying to do.

NICHOLAS OF CUSA

Nicholas of Cusa (1401–64) combined canon law, Neoplatonic philosophy and argument from history to produce a unique political theory in support of conciliarism. Cusa trained as a canon-lawyer and became famous as a Neoplatonic philosopher and theologian. He wrote his chief political work, *Catholic Concordance*, in 1432–3 while at the Council of Basle on behalf of Ulrich von Manderscheid, a candidate for the prince-archbishopric of Trier whose election by the local chapter had been quashed by Eugenius IV. In seeking to demonstrate the truth of conciliar authority and the justice of the stand taken by Basle – and by Ulrich – Cusa combined the languages of church jurisprudence, theology, church history and Neoplatonism so as to develop at once a constitutional theology of the church and a general theory of politics.

The result was something quite original. Cusa was thinking things through as he went along and his mind kept branching out on new tracks. While engaged on this work, he read Marsiglio's *Defender of the Peace*: and by the end of book 2 he is saying that Christ gave the clergy no coercive power and the pope has no more authority than other bishops (II. 34). In his most 'democratic' passages (II.14, III.4), he launched into Stoic natural theology, which had recently been given a radical social meaning by the Hussites (whose leaders Cusa met at Basle). Even so, the work began and in its main thrust remained a systematic application to the constitution of Christendom as a whole of traditional church-law principles of consent and election (in, for example, the law governing chapters with which Cusa was at this time personally concerned). And he remained a strong supporter of the church hierarchy and the secular hierarchy, in particular the German Empire. When the Council split in 1437, Cusa sided with the papacy. Thereafter he became an ideologist of papal monarchy, and viewed Basle as an unrepresentative rabble. It says a lot about his theoretical approach that such a change involved only minor adjustments to his stated philosophy of organisations.

Cusa's move away from conciliar supremacy coincided with his development as a philosopher. His *Learned Ignorance* (*De docta ignorantia*), composed in the mid 1430s, was based on the *via negativa* of mystical theology – that the most we know about God is what we do not know – and the mathematical notion of infinity, an ultimate known to exist but unknowable in itself. Yet the finite shares in the infinite in the same way that the world is related to God. The world and our knowledge of it operate according to the 'coincidence of opposites' or, dialectic. For Cusa, in Gilson's words, 'the whole universe is in everything in a contracted way'; the infinite is 'the ineffable coincidence of the maximum and the minimum'. He later expressed the relation of pope to church-at-large in the same way: authority (*plenitudo potestatis*) is 'contracted' in the one and 'expanded' in the other.[9] He was one of those philosophers whose analysis of things is partly poetic, allowing words to acquire their own momentum of possible double-meanings. When reading Cusa it also helps if one bears in mind that he was a philosopher to whom commonplace realities, including the way the church's constitution operates in practice, sometimes appeared as a sub-problem.

[9] *Deutsche Reichstagsakten*, Historische Kommission bei der Bayerischen Akademie der Wissenschaften (Munich–Stuttgart–Göttingen, 1857–1935), vol. XVI, pp. 421–3; Paul Sigmund, *Nicholas of Cusa and Medieval Political Thought* (Harvard University

This mentality appears already in *Catholic Concordance*. Cusa here reached out towards a mystical underlying essence of the church which would indicate the distribution of authority within it. His conception of Christendom as an articulated whole with clerical and lay branches was typically medieval and Germanic: book I is about the whole church, book II about the priesthood and church councils, book III about the empire and its reform (see also above, pp. 104–6). Cusa remained a lifelong advocate of reform; after 1450 he undertook an important though unsuccessful mission to promote reform of the clergy in Germany. The idea of *reformatio* – the assimilation of existing practice to the ideal essence – was indeed part of Cusa's Neoplatonic approach to institutions since it spanned the gulf between the ideal archetypes of church or empire and the lamentable facts. In the *Catholic Concordance*, he tried to arrive at precise conclusions about the lawful powers of institutions. He based these on a formidable and original analysis of the church's law and history – indeed, we may say, of its *Rechtsgeschichte*. This led him to a set of relations between church, council and papacy remarkably close to something that the early church or Eastern Orthodoxy might recognise. Cusa's awareness of the traditional authority of the five ancient patriarchates, four of which were in the East, made him especially sympathetic to Eugenius' attempt to reunite the Latin and Greek churches at the Council of Florence.

Cusa's basic idea was that 'concord' confers authority. Concord means consent, but Cusa uses this word deliberately because he is thinking not in purely legalistic terms, but in terms of spiritual reality as well. Concord cannot be measured solely by numbers, it requires also 'liberty, and oneness of heart' (*unanimitas*). This led him to the concrete point that freedom of speech is essential in a council (II.3–4). Again, representation was central to Cusa's philosophy of organisations. Like Hegel's *Vorstellung*, it is a principle of knowledge and of the relation of things to each other as well as a constitutional idea. Cusa's notion that all beings somehow contain one another 'by contraction' made it possible for him to envisage one or several human persons 'representing' – standing in the place of – other persons in all kinds of ways. In *Catholic Concordance* book I, he said that God, as supreme hierarch, 'comprehends in himself inferior beings *representative*' (I.6); and that when Christ gave authority to Peter this was because Peter 'figured and represented' the whole church (I.11,14). This he interpreted as meaning that the powers given to Peter and claimed by the popes were in the final analysis given to the church as a whole.

In the *Catholic Concordance* Cusa developed his notion of representation in a rather democratic direction, by linking it to concord. It is a general principle that the greater the agreement to a proposal, the more reason there is to think it correct and divinely inspired. But Cusa, rather than following Ockham by embracing the laity or even following many at Basle by embracing all members of the clergy in this *concordantia*, interpreted it, rather, in the spirit of the great ecumenical councils of the fourth to the seventh centuries. His first conclusion, tentative enough, was that the judgement of a united council, convoked (as history tells us it should be) by the consent of the five patriarchs through the emperor, is 'safer and more infallible' than the judgement of the pope alone; but the safest judgement is when council and pope are in unison (II.7). Here Cusa followed tradition and remained close to canon law.

Cusa appeared to draw more radical conclusions from the idea of consent. Here too he started out from a canon-law position. Consent is required for any valid legislation because laws have to be 'received' by those to whom they are to apply. But a council, because it represents those for whom it legislates, can legislate on its own authority (II.9). At this point, Cusa quite suddenly, it seems, started talking about the concord (or agreement) of subjects (*concordantia subiectionalis*) in much broader, less juristic terms, as the preeminent basis for legitimate authority (II.12–15). For

The binding power of all laws consists in concord and in tacit or express consent, which [comes] from custom or from the say of those who by some sort of delegation or presidency have others in their power. (II.15, p. 166)

This led him to the fundamental doctrine of the whole work, namely that sovereignty comes at once from God and from the people (II.13): this was a typical application of the coincidence of opposites, which may perhaps be compared here with Hegel's dialectic. Cusa deduced the 'democratic' argument from existing church law and natural theology. For both teach us that every human decree is based on and must be compatible with natural justice. But natural justice is ascertained by human reason so that every man is able to make a judgement about it. Cusa now leaps to a much more sweeping statement:

Therefore, since all are free by nature, all government (*principatus*), whether it consists in written law or lives in the prince, through whose government subjects are restrained from evil deeds and their liberty is regulated towards good by fear of punishments, exists solely by the concord and consent of subjects (*est a sola concordantia et consensu subiectivo*). For if all men are equally powerful and free by nature, the true and valid (*ordinata*) power of one common and equally powerful man naturally cannot be constituted except by the choice (*electione*) and consent of the rest. (II.14, p. 162)

Here the idea of a shared human nature and reason *is* used to give an apparently democratic view, so that Cusa does make the move sometimes falsely attributed to Aquinas and others. The striking similarity to John Locke is due, I think, to the common theological background.

The constitutional conclusions which Cusa drew from this were selectively radical. First, the authority of a council is superior to that of a pope; second, all clergy ought to be appointed by those subject to them. Cusa's view of the priesthood demonstrates more clearly than anything else his idea of coincidence and co-operation between God and the people: the clergy derive their power from the people below them and from God above them. He put this in psychological language. The clergy are the church's 'soul': just as the human soul derives its motor and sensory powers from matter and its rational power from God,

So the priesthood takes from the *people* of the faithful below it that governing, moving, living, sensory power (*praesidentialem motivam, vegetitivam et sensitivam potestatem*) – a power which proceeds from the subjects as from its 'potency' or 'matter', through voluntary subordination; and from God through the sacraments it takes the power of the rational soul, which comes from above; so that thus, by the supernal power and through the mediation of the power derived and granted [by the people], [the priesthood] is enabled in sweet harmony (*concordantia*) to pour into the body of the subjects those things which lead to perfect and saving union with Christ, the head. (II.9, p. 204)

But Cusa went on dramatically to suggest the same pattern for the state:

And beautiful is this reflection (*speculatio*), that all powers, both spiritual and also temporal or bodily, lie hidden in potency within the people; although for the presidential power to be constituted in full reality (*in actu*), there must also come together from above [sc. from God] the formative ray, which constitutes this [power] in being, since 'all power is from above'. (II.19, p. 205)

When discussing the Empire and secular government in greater detail in book III, Cusa repeated the view that the principle of election is based on both divine and natural law: it is found in Scripture and church tradition, and is also the normal means whereby rational beings exercise authority over one another. Thus the electoral princes of Germany 'hold their power in its root from the common consent of all, who by natural right were entitled to set up for themselves an emperor' (III.4, p. 348 and *Preface*, pp. 314, 317–18, 321). And the Imperial Diet or Reichstag, in which 'the whole Empire is assembled in one representative unit (*in uno compendio representativo*)' (III.25, p. 422), mirrors the general council of the church. But taken in context this is virtual representation with a vengeance; despite the quasi-Hussite language Cusa used in II.14, there is no hint that today this means anything more than tacit consent. And in his later writings Cusa did indeed use representation and consent in a monarchical sense. He now stated that the church as a whole could be represented as properly by the pope, in whom it is 'contracted', as by a council, in which the church is 'expanded'. The church could even be 'represented' by the princes, whose support therefore strengthens Eugenius' claims. This importation of the loose secular notion of tacit consent into the church shocked and infuriated Cusa's erstwhile conciliarist colleagues.

It is difficult to know what to make of this work as a whole, both because Cusa was obviously changing his mind as he wrote it, and because the more radical-sounding passages are eventually glossed over by his making tacit consent equivalent to express consent or actual election. The one idea that seems to emerge with some consistency from this self-contradictory essay is that legitimate governmental authority, whether in the church or in the state, comes into being through the people's own personal recognition of the superior wisdom of those who rule over them; through their consciously willing to be ruled by the wise and virtuous. This is only explicitly stated in the context of secular authority (III. *Preface*, p. 314). This coincided with what other conciliarists thought about the nature of authority in the church (see above, p. 160–1): the common man, though he himself does not have the capacity to be an authority, is able to discriminate between trustworthy and untrustworthy authorities. Cusa's Christian Platonism adapted the Platonic notion of philosopher-rulers in much the same way that Christian faith claimed to offer the fullness of philosophical enlightenment to the ordinary believer. People like Cusa and Segovia applied to all forms of social and political authority the criteria they found in the New Testament and extrapolated from Christian tradition. In this respect and in their general spirit they were forerunners of Erasmus.

ABSOLUTE MONARCHY

The defeat of the conciliar movement coincided with new developments towards absolute monarchy in several states, notably Aragon, Castile, France and parts of Germany. It marked the beginning of an alliance between throne and altar. In the middle of the fifteenth century the theory of the papacy as a monarchy took its final form in such a way as to give an initial boost to a theory of absolute monarchy for all kings and princes, which could justify their abandoning the constraints of law, counsel and parliament, and finally tilted the medieval mix of king and people away from any 'democratic' interpretation. This new ideological movement drew strength from the restoration of papal authority in the church after the crises of 1378–1450. During the 1430s and 1440s, a new generation of papal monarchists, their arguments sharpened by combat with constitutionalism in the church, advanced an ambitious theory of monarchy as the necessary underpinning of any social order. The Castilian Cardinal Juan de Torquemada (or Turrecremata: uncle to a famous inquisitor) now systematised ideas developed in the age of Philip the Fair and Ludwig of Bavaria. This, combined with concessions to royal demands on church revenues and appointments, enabled the new papalists to suggest an alliance and fellowship of crowned heads.

Monarchial sovereignty (*principatus*) is the best, indeed the only correct, form of government for *any* state. This was stated as a general truth; they argued from cosmic principles to human polity, and from human polity to the church, so that what was claimed for the pope was claimed for all kings. As Torquemada put it:

In *every state*, the power of jurisdiction devolves upon every person in the state from the monarch or prince of that state. This is clear from the opinion of [Pseudo-Denis], who teaches, both on the ecclesiastical and the heavenly hierarchy, that illumination flows to all persons of the hierarchy from the hierarch [sc. God] himself (*Summary on the Church*, c. 1450, book II, ch. 55, fols. 171r–2r)

Above all, the avenue of opposition through a representative assembly was rigorously ruled out. The claims that notables or parliament may overturn royal decrees, that one may appeal from the prince, that a monarch may be corrected or deposed, were systematically refuted. Plurality of rulers leads to discord; monarchy alone can produce social order and political stability. The public safety and common welfare can most effectively be promoted through rule by one individual. The principle of centralisation was clearly stated:

In every order, when the whole power of inferiors depends on and originates from the power of the superior, the power of the superior can extend itself over all those things over which the power of the inferiors can extend itself. Any king in his realm can perform without intermediary whatever the inferior powers can perform, even without their having been requested. (*Summary on the Church*, II, ch. 65, fol. 188v)

It was by this route that the medieval theory of monarchy, which could and usually did include limits on royal power, was transmuted into a theory of absolute monarchy. It was now unambiguously asserted of princes that they owed their position directly to God himself with no human intermediary. As Antonio Roselli put it in his *Monarchy* (*c.* 1433), again basing his argument for the pope on the presumed nature of all political authority, '[The pope] holds power from himself and directly from God . . . by his own right and no-one else's; this is because he holds it according to the law by which (power) is principally founded and rooted in the person of the prince . . . jurisdiction is principally in him through himself' (pp. 278–9). This was close to the central doctrine of the divine right of kings: the monarch is self-substantive because personally empowered by God and therefore cannot be accountable to any mortal.

7

THE STATE

Can we, in this period, detect the emergence of 'the modern state'? There has been some dispute about whether we can properly speak of 'the state' itself before 1450 or even 1600. The answers to such questions depend upon how one defines the terms. Here we are concerned with the *idea* of the state.[1] For our purposes the following definitions are relevant: (1) an order of power distinct from other orders (military, religious, economic and so on), which we call political; (2) authority exercised over a defined territory and all its inhabitants; (3) the monopoly of the legitimate use of physical coercion (as Weber put it); (4) legitimacy derived from inside the political community, not delegated by an external authority; (5) a body or authority with some moral (as opposed to merely repressive) functions, such as the imposition of law and order, the defence of justice and rights, promotion of a common welfare; (6) 'an apparatus of power whose existence remains independent of those who may happen to have control of it at any given time', which Skinner calls 'a recognisably modern conception of the state'.[2]

We have seen that the idea of the state in most of these senses was present or developing in this period. Words specifically referring to political sovereignty included *principatus*, *auctoritas* or *potestas suprema*,

---

[1] See bibliography, pp. 206–7.

[2] Quentin Skinner, 'The State', in Terence Ball, J. Farr and R. L. Hanson (eds.), *Political Innovation and Conceptual Change* (Cambridge: Cambridge University Press, 1989), pp. 90–131 at p. 102; and *Foundations*, vol. II: *The Reformation*, pp. 349–58.

maiestas, superioritas, plenitudo potestatis (or *plena potestas*). Regarding
(1), the authority to make and enforce laws was conceptually distinct
from military and economic power; and during this period the
distinction between secular and ecclesiastical authority was fully
worked out (chapter 2). Regarding (2), the ruler or rulers were seen as
acting in the name of and on behalf of the entire political community
or 'people' of a territory (chapter 1). Regarding (4), rulers' legitimacy
seldom depended upon pope or emperor (chapters 2 and 3); power
came from God by a direct delegation to the political community in
question. Regarding (5), all rulers and political communities were
thought to have been established precisely, indeed primarily, for
moral purposes (chapter 1). The terms *bonum commune, utilitas publica*
and *status regni* were used to identify the sphere of collective human
need within which political authority was required to act. They also
provided an important criterion for distinguishing between the use
and abuse of authority. *Jurisdictio* signified the ability to make law by
defending justice. The *monopoly* of coercion (3), however, is problematic. Coercion was still exercised legitimately by others than the
central authority and its agencies, for example by feudal lords and
semi-autonomous towns. We note that, when the church required
physical force to implement its judgements, it looked to the secular
authorities because priests themselves were not supposed to shed
blood (except when bishop or pope was at the same time territorial
lord). The idea that the sovereign alone can make law and that all may
appeal to him was spreading. In saying all this I am not of course suggesting that concepts of the state were non-existent before 1250; and it
remains true that political authority became *more* distinct from religious authority and so on after *c.*1550, and still more so after *c.*1650.

Regarding (6), Skinner has argued that this concept of the state
finally developed only in the early seventeenth century. Hobbes and
natural-law theorists of absolutism needed a locus of authority identifiable neither with the whims of individual princes nor with the
people; it was, therefore, no accident that the new term 'state' became
current in this period. It is true that previously no single word corresponded exactly to our term 'state'. *Status regis/civitatis/ecclesiae* referred to the 'estate' or 'good estate' of king, city or church, their standing in relation to others. But to argue that the *idea* was not present
because no single word corresponded to it is surely to press the connection between language and thought too far. It is abundantly clear
that the meaning of 'state' was fully conveyed by a range of terms.[3]

---

[3] Argued by Guenée, *States*, pp. 4–6, and Reynolds, *Kingdoms*, pp. 323–4.

For we have seen how the political community was conceived precisely as an impersonal, incorporeal entity – *universitas, civitas, regnum* – whose existence was expressly independent of whoever belonged to it at a particular time. 'The association does not die' (*universitas non moritur*): this arose out of the lawyers' practical need to establish the continuity of corporate rights and obligations. The conceptual sphere of social entities was a necessary invention: even when all inhabitants die and are succeeded by new ones, the community remains the same. Again, numerous words expressed political authority in the abstract: in addition to those already noted, *auctoritas* or *potestas publica/secularis/temporalis/civilis*; *dominium, praelatio, maioritas, gubernaculum, vis coactiva* and so on. *Respublica* (*la chose publique*, commonwealth) suggested a public domain with its own claims. So did *officium* (German *Amt*: literally, duty), especially in cities and in the context of economic management. Medieval authors did conceive public power as a distinct category of human relationships.

The most important distinction that was made in the period from 1250–1450 was between this 'secular power' and the religious authority of the church. From the early fourteenth century onwards, a widening circle of the governing and educated élites expressed a consciousness of secular power as separate in origin, purpose, scope and legitimation from the church; this was true even of those who still maintained that spiritual authority was in some ultimate sense superior. Drawing on Aristotle and Cicero, people spoke of *vita civilis* (or *politica*), *societas civilis, potestas civilis*, and *humanitas*.

If we compare European with other civilisations, this period appears as the decisive moment, and the separation of church and secular power may appear as the decisive issue, in the development of the state idea. Here it was that Europe became differentiated from its East-Christian cousins and the world of Islam, not to mention other civilisations. It was of crucial importance that Aristotle was received in the West in a manner and to a degree to which he was not received in Islam. This in turn was symptomatic of a different attitude towards truth, even amongst the orthodox: while the ultimate truth was securely held to be as the church said it was, this could none the less be grasped not only – not so much, Aquinas would say – by unquestioning obedience or mystical intuition as by disputation in which opposing views were presented and refuted – or, rather, transcended. Much was owed to the Abelardian enterprise: *dubitando veritatem percipimus* (it is by doubting that we perceive the truth). The secular state was able to gain a secure place in the western mind partly because areas of law and government were left vacant by religious authority. Scripture and tradition explicitly stated that the message of Christ was not concerned with 'worldly' issues; 'spiritual persons' should not concern themselves with mundane matters, especially when physical force was involved. Beyond this, Christianity rejected the idea of ritual religious 'law' governing human conduct and social relationships yet at the same time made these the object of intense moral concern. A society claiming to be Christian could, therefore, envisage legitimate changes and varieties in institutions and practices.

This secular state power found expression in the practice and ideology of sovereignty as a norm within states and between states. The withering-away of papacy and Empire coincided with the strengthening hold of kings over barons, bishops and towns. In the rise and rise of monarchical theory from the 1420s onwards, part of the initiative came from the religious concerns of the papacy itself; sovereignty on the papal model was offered to all kings. The power of a large territorial population was seen as concentrated in a single office and person.

That there existed an explicit idea of the state as 'an apparatus of power whose existence remains independent of those who may happen to control it at any given time' is further suggested by the use of the term 'crown' (*corona*). This was a way of depersonalising royal authority. Similarly, the ruler as a 'public person' distinct from himself in his private capacities was familiar to some from Cicero and current in canon and civil law. The concept and imagery of the Crown achieved currency not only amongst theoreticians but amongst statesmen and to some extent the public at large. 'The Crown' and other symbols of royal or high office were part of public symbolic imagery and life. As an official part of royal language, this referred to the continuity of public authority ('the king is dead: long live the king'). It was a way of handling the problems of a king who was under age, captured by the enemy or incapacitated: the properly royal powers could still be exercised, the people still be cowed with the awe of the true king, because his public *persona* was really there. What happened was that others, usually a council of senior barons and advisers, acted in his name. This also helped to support the view that the rights of the Crown (of England and so on) were whole and inalienable. Lands or rights wrongfully alienated, usurped by others or conquered by an alien power had eventually to be vindicated.

By thus locating power in an idealised object, a distinction was made between person and office so that the royal authority was not implicated in the errors or weaknesses of a king. It suggested a conceptual solution to the problem of king and law (see above, pp. 152–5): the Crown, but not the king in person, is above the law. The Crown was a metaphor for sovereignty without personal irresponsibility. It could even embrace others than the king, as when a fourteenth-century English bishop said: 'The substance of the nature of the crown is found chiefly in the person of the king as head and the peers as members . . . and especially of the prelates' (*CHMPT* p. 500). The implication of all this was that the individual person of the king was an essential part of proceedings, and his consent was always conclusive; but it was not simply a matter of an individual human being deliberating and commanding. All this shows that the idea of the state was no mere afterthought in the Middle Ages; it was woven into the fabric of political sentiment.

Such a way of thinking came easily to a culture so laden with symbolism and allegory. Loyalty to an abstract entity was not unthinkable to people brought up on Platonic realism. But the chief source probably lay in church doctrine. The sacraments of the church were actually believed to perform what they signified. And Catholic Christians were accustomed to distinguish between person and office in the traditional doctrine of apostolic succession: 'the seat does not die' (*sedes non moritur*), that is the powers of the *sedes* (episcopal see, seat, throne) are transmitted intact from one tenant to the next. This was clearly conveyed by Gerson:

> The church community can be said to be composed of two-fold elements: some are transitory, some permanent and, so to speak, essential. The former are the mortal individuals themselves, constituted in a variety of ranks; the others are the ranks of the dignities and administrative functions themselves (*gradus dignitatum et administrationum*). For example, the pope and the papacy, the bishop and the see, and so forth; the pope is transitory, the papacy stable. (*Proposal for the English*, p. 132; *Ecclesiastical Power*, p. 222)

This concept of an objective and abiding impersonal office recurred in the theory that the pope stands in the place of Christ as his *vicarius* (place-holder). Persons in authority were understood to be 'playing the role' (*vicem gerit*) of Christ or the church. The same was claimed for secular power when kings were said to represent God and play his part on earth.

While Crown implied a king, the parallel language of *status* could, as Skinner observes, do for a republic; as indeed could *dignitas* or *officium*. While the language of *principatus*, from which the notion of sovereignty as embracing the judicial, legislative and executive spheres largely derived, originally implied one ruler, Oresme offered another view: 'by "the prince", Aristotle often means not only the sovereign ruler but generally any public position or authority or any honourable office which has regard to the whole community, or any member thereof'. This is because the state requires not only the distributive justice of the prince but also the commutative justice carried out by judges, and acts of expediency which are the domain of counsellors (*Aristotle's 'Politics'*, III.I.I). Both Gerson and Oresme, then, expressed the notion of the state precisely as an impersonal hierarchy of offices.

CONCLUSION

Even though the era of Machiavelli and Luther saw dramatic changes in political thought, there was more continuity than the 'medieval'– 'modern' contrast usually suggests. It is true that one may detect a 'waning' of the Middle Ages. After about 1450 church authority seemed more manifestly not what it claimed to be, representative of Christ. Juristic theory provided faint and ambiguous answers to constitutional questions. Scholasticism tended to avoid painful detail, while its most original exponents, Marsiglio and Ockham, had been largely dismissed as heterodox. Humanist rhetoric wafted over the world of power and faction. The new paradigms of Machiavelli and Luther were to carry conviction because they were closer to people's actual experiences.

Yet some of the main configurations of political thought in modern Europe were laid down before 1450: the authority of the state and its separation from the church, the rule of law, the legitimacy of lesser associations; absolute monarchy, popular consent, parliamentary representation. Justice, liberty, peace, the common good remained dominant social norms. Similarly, there was underlying continuity in the evolution of territorial states, legal systems, monarchies and, in some cases, parliaments. The truly epochal shifts in European political thought occurred in the eleventh and eighteenth centuries: in between was essentially a single epoch. This can be seen most clearly in political languages. The older ones remained alive and served as vehicles for new ideas. Theological language underwent a traumatic rebirth in Reformation and Counter-Reformation. Scholastic language reaped its final harvest in Vitoria, Hooker and Suarez and was still alive in Locke. Juristic language – well, there were Grotius and Hobbes, but actually no theorist could avoid it, for out of it was minted the staple currency of political speech: sovereignty, contract, natural law, rights, trust. As for Ciceronian, it is still with us.

SELECT BIBLIOGRAPHY

———— · ————

The bibliography is divided into the following sections:
1 Original texts and studies
    Selections of original texts in translation
    Authors: original texts and studies
2 Further reading
    General
    Historical background
    Aristotle
    Church and State
    City-states and civic government
    Florence
    International relations and state sovereignty
    The jurists
    Kingship, law and representation
    Liberty and the individual
    Natural law
    The political community
    The Renaissance
    The state
3 Works of reference

ORIGINAL TEXTS AND STUDIES

Selections of original texts in translation

Lerner, Ralph and Mahdi, Muhsin. *Medieval Political Philosophy: a Sourcebook* (New York: Collier-Macmillan, 1963). Also contains Islamic and Judaic texts.

Lewis, Ewart. *Medieval Political Ideas (MPI)* 2 vols. (London: Routledge and Kegan Paul, 1954). A wide range of major and minor authors, arranged by topics, with extensive commentaries and notes.

Nederman, Cary and Forhan, Kate. *Medieval Political Theory, 1100–1400: Readings in the Secular Tradition* (London: Routledge, forthcoming 1992).

Spinka, M., ed. *Advocates of Reform from Wyclif to Erasmus* (Library of Christian Classics, 14) (London: SCM 1953).

Tierney, Brian. *The Crisis of Church and State 1050–1300* (Englewood Cliffs, N.J.: Prentice-Hall, 1964). Useful on papacy and empire and the Philip–Boniface dispute.

Authors: original texts and studies

ADMONT (or Volkersdorf), ENGELBERT OF. *De ortu et fine Romani imperii (The Rise and Conclusion of the Roman Empire)*, in M. Goldast (ed.), *Politica Imperialia* (Frankfurt, 1614), pp. 754–73 (part in *MPI* pp. 473–84).

On Admont, see:

LTK, vol. III, pp. 876–7.

Posch, A. *Die staats- und kirchenpolitische Tätigkeit Engelberts von Admont* (Paderborn: F. Schöningh, 1920).

Schmidinger, H. 'Romana Regia Potestas'. *Staats- und Reichsgedanken bei Engelbert von Admont und Enea Silvio Piccolomini* (Vorträge der Aeneas-Silvius-Stiftung an der Universität Basel, 13) (Basle, 1978).

AEGIDIUS ROMANUS (Giles of Rome, Egidio Romano/Colonna). *De ecclesiastica potestate (Ecclesiastical Power)*, ed. R. Scholz (Aalen: Scientia Verlag, 1961). Trans. R. W. Dyson (Woodbridge-Dover, N. H.: Beydell Press, 1986).

De regimine principum (The Rule of Princes) (Rome, 1607).

Molenaer, S. P. (ed.). 'Li livres du gouvernement des rois': A Thirteenth-century Version of Egidio Colonna's 'De regimine principum' (New York: Columbia University Press, 1899; repr. 1966).

On Aegidius, see:

Scholz, R. *Publizistik zur Zeit Philipps des Schönen und Bonifaz VIII* (Stuttgart: F. Enke, 1903).

AQUINAS, THOMAS

Selections

Bigongiari, D. (ed.). *The Political Writings of St Thomas Aquinas* (New York: Hafner, 1966).

d'Entrèves, A. Passerin, (ed.). *Aquinas: Selected Political Writings*, trans. J. G. Dawson (Oxford: Basil Blackwell, 1954). Latin and English; includes *On Kingship* and parts of commentaries on *Ethics* and *Politics*; exceptionally useful.

Sigmund, Paul (ed. and trans.). *St Thomas Aquinas on Politics and Ethics* (New York: Norton, 1988). Also contains a wide selection of interpretations.

Works

Summa theologiae (*ST*), ed. Thomas Gilby and T. C. O'Brien, 61 vols. (Cambridge and London: Blackfriars and Eyre and Spottiswoode, and New York: McGraw Hill, 1964–80), esp. vol. XXVIII: *Law and Political Theory* (1a/11ae 90–97), trans. Thomas Gilby (1966). Latin and English.

De regno (or *De regimine principum*) *ad regem Cypri* (attributed) (*On Kingship*), ed. R. M. Spiazzi, *Aquinas, Opuscula philosophica* (Turin: Marietti, 1954); Latin and English in d'Entrèves, *Aquinas: Selected Political Writings* (see above); trans. G. B. Phelan, rev. I. T. Eschmann (Toronto: Pontifical Institute of Medieval Studies, 1949).

For other works, see *CHMPT*, p. 747.

On Aquinas, see:

Eschmann, I. T. 'Studies on the Notion of Society in St Thomas Aquinas', *Medieval Studies* 8 (1946), pp. 1–42. On group personality and corporate delict.

Gilby, Thomas. *Principality and Polity: Aquinas and the Rise of State theory in the West* (London: Longmans, 1958); also published as *The Political Thought of Thomas Aquinas* (Chicago: Chicago University Press, 1958). Heavily interpretative from a neo-Thomist viewpoint; stimulating.

McInerny, Ralph. *St Thomas Aquinas* (Notre Dame, Ind.: Notre Dame Press, 1982).

Weisheipl, James A. *Friar Thomas de Aquino* (New York: Doubleday, 1974). The best biography in English.

BARTOLUS OF SASSOFERRATO. His commentaries on the *Digest* and *Codex* were printed at Turin, 1577 and Basle in 1588–9; his *Consilia* at Turin, 1577.

Tractatus de regimine civitatum (*City Government*), ed. Diego Quaglioni, *Pensiero Politico* 9 (1976), pp. 70–93.

Tractatus de tyrannia (*Tyranny*), ed. Diego Quaglioni, *Pensiero Politico* 10 (1977), pp. 268–84; partly trans. E. Emerton, *Humanism and Tyranny* (Cambridge, Mass.: Harvard University Press, 1925), pp. 126–54. Also in Diego Quaglioni, *Politica e Diritto nel Trecento Italiano: il 'De tyranno' di Bartolo da Sassoferrato (1314–1357), con l'edizione critica dei trattati 'De Guelphis et Gebellinis', 'De regimine civitatum' e 'De tyranno'* (Florence: Il Pensiero Politico, Biblioteca, 1983).

On Bartolus, see:

Calasso, F. *Medio Evo del Diritto*, vol. 1 (Milan: Giuffré, 1954), pp. 573ff.

Ercole, F. *Da Bartolo all' Althusio: Saggi sulla Storia del Diritto Pubblico del Rinascimento Italiano* (Florence: Vellecchi, 1932).

Woolf, C. N. S. *Bartolus of Sassoferrato – his Position in the History of Medieval Political Thought* (Cambridge: Cambridge University Press, 1913). Still an extraordinarily useful work with long quotations from the original.

BEBENBERG (or Bamberg), LUPOLD VON. *De iuribus regni et imperii* (*The Rights of Kingdom and Empire*), in S. Schard (ed.), *Syntagma tractatuum de imperiali jurisdictione* (Augsburg, 1609), pp. 167–208; also in S. Schard (ed.), *De jurisdictione, auctoritate et praeeminentia imperiali ac potestate ecclesiastica* (Basle, 1566), pp. 328–409. Extracts in *MPI* pp. 310–3, 500–2.

On Bebenberg, see:
Barisch, G. 'Zum Verhältnis von politischer Praxis, Theorie und Politik', *Bericht des Historischen Vereins Bamberg* 113 (1977), pp. 219–433.
LTK, vol. VI, p. 1218.

BRACTON, HENRY DE (attributed). *De legibus et consuetudinibus Angliae* (*On the Laws and Customs of England*), ed. George E. Woodbine, rev. and trans. Samuel E. Thorne, 4 vols. (Cambridge, Mass.: Harvard University Press, 1968–77); parts in *MPI* pp. 39–41, 279–84.

BRUNI, LEONARDO, of AREZZO (Aretinus). *Laudatio Florentinae urbis* (Praise of Florence) (1403–4), ed. Hans Baron, *From Petrarch to Leonardo Bruni* (Chicago: Chicago University Press, 1968), pp. 232–63.
    Letter to emperor-elect Sigismund (1413), ed. Hans Baron as *Epistolary Description of the Florentine Constitution*, in Hans Baron, *Humanistic and Political Literature in Florence and Venice* (Cambridge, Mass.: Harvard University Press, 1955), ch. 8.
    Oratio in funere Nannis Strozze (*Funeral Oration for Nanno Strozzi*) (1428) in S. Baluze (ed.), *Miscellanea*, vol. III (Paris, 1680), pp. 226–48.
    Περὶ τῆς πολιτείας τῶν Φλωρεντίνων (*On the Constitution of the Florentines*) (1439), Latin version in G. C. Galletti, *Philippi Villani Liber de Civitatis Florentiae Famosis Civibus* (Florence, 1847), pp. 94–6.

On Bruni, see the works by Skinner and Baron under 'The Renaissance' and 'Florence' respectively, below.

BURIDAN, JOHN. *Quaestiones in octo libros Politicorum Aristotelis* (*Questions on the Politics of Aristotle*) (Oxford, 1640).

On Buridan, see:
Grignaschi, M. 'Un commentaire nominaliste de la Politique d'Aristote: Jean Buridan', Commission Internationale pour l'Histoire des Assemblées d'États: Anciens Pays et Assemblées d'États 19 (1960), pp. 125–42.
The political thought of this author would repay further research: see Gilson, Étienne, *History of Christian Philosophy in the Middle Ages*, pp. 794–5n.

CUSA (Cues/Kues), NICHOLAS OF. *De concordantia catholica* (*CC: Catholic Concordance*), ed. G. Kallen in *Nicolai Cusani Opera Omnia*, vol. XIV (Hamburg: Felix Meiner, 1959–65).

On Cusa, see:
LTK vol. VII, pp. 988–91.

Sigmund, Paul. *Nicholas of Cusa and Medieval Political Thought* (Cambridge, Mass.: Harvard University Press, 1963).

DANTE ALIGHIERI. *De monarchia* (*On Monarchy*), ed. P. G. Ricci (Milan: Mondadori, 1965). Trans. Donald Nicholl, *Monarchy* (London: Weidenfeld and Nicolson, 1954); parts trans. in Lerner and Mahdi, *Medieval Political Philosophy* (see p. 193), pp. 418–38.
    Dantis Alighierii Epistolae (*Letters*), ed. P. Toynbee (Oxford: Oxford University Press, 1966).
    Monarchy and *Letters* are also conveniently found in *Le Opere di Dante*, ed. E. Moore, rev. P. Toynbee, 4th edn (Oxford: Oxford University Press, 1924).
    Convivio in *Le Opere di Dante*, ed. Moore, pp. 235–338.

On Dante, see:
d'Entrèves, A. Passerin, *Dante as a Political Thinker* (Oxford: Clarendon Press, 1952).
Limentani, U. 'Dante's Political Thought', in U. Limentani (ed.), *The Mind of Dante* (Cambridge: Cambridge University Press, 1965), pp. 113–37.
Löwe, H. 'Dante und das Kaisertum', *Historische Zeitschrift* 190 (1960), pp. 517–52 (p. 519n. for full literature).
Reeves, Marjorie, 'Marsiglio of Padua and Dante Alighieri', in B. Smalley (ed.), *Trends in Medieval Political Thought*, pp. 86–92.

FORTESCUE, SIR JOHN. *De laudibus legum Angliae* (*In Praise of England's Laws*). ed. S. B. Chrimes (Cambridge: Cambridge University Press, 1949). Extract in Lerner and Mahdi, *Medieval Political Philosophy*; extracts from this and other works in *MPI* pp. 85–7, 134–6, 325–30.

On Fortescue, see:
Chrimes, S. B. *English Constitutional Ideas in the Fifteenth Century* (Cambridge: Cambridge University Press, 1936).
Burns, J. H. 'Fortescue and the Political Theory of *dominium*', *Historical Journal* 28 (1985), 777–97.

GERSON, JOHN. *De auctoritate concilii* (*The Council's Authority*) (1408), in P. Glorieux (ed.), *Jean Gerson, Oeuvres Complètes*, vol. VI: *L'Oeuvre Ecclésiologique* (R. Tournai: Desclée-de Brouwer, 1965), pp. 114–23.
    Propositio facta coram Anglicis (*Statement to the English*) (1409), *Oeuvres*, vol. VI, pp. 125–35.
    Tractatus de unitate ecclesiae (*Church Unity*) (1409), *Oeuvres*, vol. VI, pp. 136–45; trans. J. K. Cameron in Matthew Spinka (ed.), *Advocates of Reform*, pp. 140–8.
    De potestate ecclesiastica (*Ecclesiastical Power*), *Oeuvres*, vol. VI, pp. 210–50.

On Gerson, see:

LTK, vol. v, pp.1036–7.

Morrall, John, *Gerson and the Great Schism* (Manchester: Manchester University Press, 1960).

Pascoe, L. B. *Jean Gerson: Principles of Church Reform* (Leiden: E. J. Brill, 1973).

GIROLAMI REMIGIO DE'. *De bono pacis (The Good of Peace)*, ed. C. T. Davis in *Studi Danteschi* 36 (1959), pp. 123–36.

MARSIGLIO (or Marsilius) OF PADUA. *Defensor Pacis (DP) (The Defender of Peace)*, ed. C. W. Previté-Orton (Cambridge: Cambridge University Press, 1928), and ed. R. Scholz (Hanover: Monumenta Germaniae Historica, Fontes Iuris Germanici Antiqui, 7, 1932–3). Trans. Alan Gewirth, *Marsilius of Padua: The Defender of the Peace*, vol. II (London: Macmillan, 1956).

Defensor Minor (The Lesser Defender) (written 1324 or 1339–40) and *De translatione imperii (The Transference of the Empire)*, in C. Jeudy and J. Quillet (eds.), *Marsile de Padoue, Oeuvres Mineurs* (Paris: Éditions du C.N.R.S., 1979).

On Marsiglio, see:

Gewirth, Alan. *Marsilius of Padua: The Defender of the Peace*, vol. I (London: Macmillan, 1951). Thorough and stimulating but greatly exaggerates the modern-democratic element in Marsiglio.

Quillet, Jeannine. *La philosophie politique de Marsile de Padoue* (Paris: J. Vrin, 1970). By far the best study.

Wilks, Michael. 'Corporation and Representation in the *Defensor Pacis*', *Studia Gratiana* 15 (1972), pp. 253–92.

MÉZIÈRES, PHILIPPE DE. *Le Songe du Vieil Pélerin (Somnium Viridarii)*, ed. G. W. Coopland, 2 vols. (Cambridge: Cambridge University Press, 1969).

OCKHAM (or Occam), WILLIAM OF. *Dialogus (Dialogue)*, in M. Goldast (ed.), *Monarchia*, vol. II (Frankfurt, 1614), pp. 392–957. Parts trans. in *MPI* pp. 80–5, 300–8, 398–402, 495–500; and in Lerner and Mahdi, *Medieval Political Philosophy*, pp. 492–506.

Breviloquium de principatu tyrannico (Tyrannical Rule), ed. R. Scholz, *Wilhelm von Ockham als politischer Denker* (Leipzig: Schriften des Reichsinstituts für ältere deutsche Geschichtskunde, 8, 1944; repr. 1952).

De imperatorum et pontificum potestate (Imperial and Papal Power), ed. C. K. Brampton (Oxford: Clarendon Press, 1927). Parts trans. in *MPI* pp. 606–15.

Octo quaestiones de potestate papae (Eight Questions on Papal Power), ed. H. S. Offler in *Guillelmi de Ockham Opera Politica*, vol. I, 2nd edn (Manchester: Manchester University Press, 1974), pp. 1–277.

Opus nonaginta dierum (Ninety Days' Work), eds. H. S. Offler and J. G. Sikes in *Opera Politica*, vol. I, 2nd edn., pp. 287–368 and vol. II (1963); parts trans. in *MPI* pp. 118–20.

On Ockham, see:
Baudry, L. *Guillaume d'Occam: se vie, ses oeuvres, ses idées sociales et politiques* (Paris: J. Vrin, 1949).
Lagarde, G. de. *La Naissance de l'esprit laïque au déclin du moyen âge*, vol. VI: *L'Ockhamisme: la morale et le droit* (Louvain and Paris: Nauwelaerts, 1970).
McGrade, A. S. *The Political Thought of William of Ockham: Personal and Institutional Principles* (Cambridge: Cambridge University Press, 1974). An excellent and lucid exposition, the best available for beginners.
Miethke, Jürgen. *Ockhams Weg zur Sozialphilosophie* (Berlin: Gruyter, 1969).
Tierney, Brian. *Origins of Papal Infallibility* (see below, p. 201), pp. 205ff. Succinct on Ockham's church theories.

ORESME, NICOLE. *Le Livre de 'Politiques' d'Aristote (Aristotle's Politics)*, ed. A. D. Menut, Transactions of the American Philosophical Society, 1970.

On Oresme, see:
Babbit, Susan, M. *Oresme's 'Livre de Politiques' and the France of Charles V*, Transactions of the American Philosophical Society, 75, i (Philadelphia: The American Philosophical Society, 1985).
Grignaschi, M. 'Nicolas Oresme et son commentaire à la "Politique" d'Aristote', *Album Helen Maud Cam*, I: Studies presented to the International Commission for the History of Representative and Parliamentary Institutions, vol. XXIII (Louvain, 1960), pp. 95–154.

PARIS, JOHN, (Quidort) OF. *De potestate regia et papali (Royal and Papal Power)*, ed. J. Leclerq in *Jean de Paris* (Paris: J. Vrin, 1942), pp. 173–260; and F. Bleienstein (Stuttgart: Klett, 1969). Trans. J. A. Watt, *On Royal and Papal Power* (Toronto: Pontifical Institute of Medieval Studies, 1971); part in Lerner and Mahdi, *Medieval Political Philosophy*, pp. 402–17.

On Paris, see:
Coleman, Janet, '*Dominium* in Thirteenth- and Fourteenth-Century Political Thought and its Seventeenth-Century Heirs', *Political Studies* 33(1985), pp. 73–100.
Tierney, Brian. *Foundations of the Conciliar Theory* (Cambridge: Cambridge University Press, 1955), pp. 157–78.

PICCOLOMINI, AENEAS SILVIUS (pope Pius II). *De ortu et auctoritate Romani imperii (Origin and Authority of the Roman Empire)*, in Rudolph Wolkan (ed.), *Der Briefwechsel des Eneas Silvius Piccolomini*, part 2: *Briefe als Priester und als Bischof von Trient (Fontes Rerum Austriacarum*, part 2: *Diplomataria et Acta*, vol. 67) (Vienna: Holder, 1912), pp. 6–24; and in Schard, *De Jurisdictione*, pp. 314–28 (parts in *MPI* pp. 320–5, 502–5).

On Piccolomini, see:
Toews, T. B. 'Dream and Reality in the Imperial Ideology of Pope Pius II', *Medievalia et Humanistica* 16(1964), pp. 77–93.
Widmer, B. *Enea Silvio Piccolomini in der sittlichen und politischen Entscheidung* (Basle: Schwabe, 1963).

PTOLEMY OF LUCCA. *De regimine principum* (*The Rule of Princes*), books 2–4 (*c.* 1301–3) (previously attributed to Aquinas), ed. J. Perrier: *Thomas Aquinas, Opera Omnia necnon Minora*, vol. I (Paris: P. Lethielleux, 1949), pp. 270–426.

QUAESTIO IN UTRAMQUE PARTEM (*Two Sides of the Question*: Anon.). Ed. G. Vinay in 'Egidio Romana e la considetta *Quaestio in utramque partem*', *Bulletino dell' Istituto Storico Italiano* 53(1939), pp. 43–136. See ch. 2, n.5.
Roselli, Antonio de. *Monarchia*, ed. M. Goldast, *Monarchia*, vol. II (Hanover, 1612), pp. 252–556.

ROSELLI, ANTONIO DE. *Monarchia*, ed. M. Goldast, vol. I (Hanover, 1612), pp. 252–556.

SEGOVIA, JUAN DE. *Amplification* (of speech given at Mainz in 1441; written after 1450), *Monumenta Conciliorum Generalium Seculi XV*, eds. F. Palacky, E. Birk and C. Stehlin, vol. III (Basle, 1935), pp. 695–946.

On Segovia, see:
Black, Antony. *Council and Commune* (London: Burns and Oates, 1979).

TORQUEMADA (or Turrecremata) JUAN DE. *Summa de ecclesia* (*Compendium on the Church*) (Venice, 1565); parts in Black, *Monarchy*, pp. 162ff.; parts trans. in *MPI* pp. 239–40, 422–9.
   Commentarium super toto Decreto (*Commentary on the Decretum*) (Venice, 1578).

On Torquenda, see:
Black, Antony. *Monarchy and Community* (Cambridge: Cambridge University Press 1970).
Izbicki, T. M. *Cardinal Johannes Turrecremata and the Defense of the Institutional Church* (Washington, D.C., 1981).

VITERBO, JAMES OF (Jacopo Cappucci). *De regimine christiano* (*Christian Government*), ed. H.-X. Arquillière, *Le plus ancien traité de l'Église: Jacques de Viterbe, 'De regimine christiano' (1301–2)* (Paris: Gabriel Beauchesne, 1926); extracts trans. in *MPI* pp. 182–4, 227–32, 580–5.

VITERBO, JOHN OF. *Liber de regimine civitatum* (*The Government of Cities*), ed. C. Salvemini in A Gaudentius (ed.), *Bibliotheca Juridica Medii Aevi*, vol. III (Bologna, 1901), pp. 217–80.

WYCLIF, JOHN. *Tractatus de civili dominio* (*Civil Dominion*), ed. R. Lane Poole (London: Wyclif Society, 1885).

Tractatus de officio regis (*The Office of the King*), eds. A. W. Pollard and C. Sayle (London: Wyclif Society, 1887).

De dominio divino libri tres (*On God's Dominion*), ed. R. Lane Poole (London: Wyclif Society, 1890).

On Wyclif, see:

Kaminsky, H. 'Wyclifism as Ideology of Revolution', *Church History* 32 (1963), pp. 57–74.

2 FURTHER READING

General

The Cambridge History of Medieval Political Thought, ed. J. H. Burns (Cambridge: Cambridge University Press, 1988), ch. 5. Probably the most useful work of reference today, but with serious omissions, e.g. on the Empire.

Carlyle, R. W. and A. J. *A History of Medieval Political Theory in the West*, 6 vols. (London: William Blackwood and Sons, 1903–36). Still useful as a work of reference although very out of date; exaggerates constitutionalism and popular sovereignty; *schöngeistig*.

Gierke, Otto von. *Das deutsche Genossenschaftsrecht*, vol. III: *Die Staats- und Korporationslehre des Altertums und des Mittelalters und ihre Aufnahme in Deutschland* (Berlin, 1881; repr. Graz: Akademische Druck- u. Verlagsanstalt, 1954) (*The German Law of Fellowship*, vol. III: *The Doctrine of State and Corporate Association in Antiquity and the Middle Ages and its Reception in Germany*); ch. 11 on 'the publicists', i.e. mainstream political theorists such as Marsiglio and Cusa, trans. F. W. Maitland as *Political Theories of the Middle Age* (Cambridge: Cambridge University Press, 1990; repr. 1990). Hard going and heavily interpretative; not for beginners.

Lagarde, Georges de. *La Naissance de l'Esprit Laïque au Déclin du Moyen Âge*, 6 vols., 2nd edn (Paris: Presses Universitaires de France, 1948), 3rd edn., 6 vols. in 5 (Louvain: Edition E. Nauwelaerts and Paris: Béatrice Nauwelaerts, 1956–70). On the social and political doctrines of the scholastics, focussing upon the transformation of a theocentric, clerical into an atomistic, secular view of politics; vol. II is especially useful on lessknown scholastics, and vol. VI on Ockham.

McIlwain, C. H. *The Growth of Political Thought in the West from the Greeks to the End of the Middle Ages* (New York: Macmillan, 1932), chs. 6–7.

Maravall, J. A. *Estudios de Historia del Pensiamento Español, Edad Media*, 1st series (Madrid, 1966).

Rosenthal, Erwin I. J. *Political Thought in Medieval Islam: An Introductory Outline* (Cambridge: Cambridge University Press, 1958).

Storia delle Idee Politiche, Economiche e Sociali, ed. Luigi Firpo, vol. II: *Ebraismo e Cristianesimo. Il Medioevo* (Turin: Unione Tipografico-Editrice Torinese, 1973).

Trends in Medieval Political Thought, ed. Beryl Smalley (Oxford: Basil Blackwell, 1965). Short essays, scholarly, useful for beginners.

Ullmann, Walter. *Law and Politics in the Middle Ages: An Introduction to the Sources of Medieval Political Ideas* (Cambridge: Cambridge University Press, 1975). Helpful and extensive, avoids the tendentiousness of Ullmann's other works.

Historical background

Barraclough, Geoffrey. *The Origins of Modern Germany*, 2nd rev. edn (Oxford: Basil Blackwell, 1988).

Genet, Jean-Philippe. *Le Monde au Moyen Âge* (Paris: Hachette, 1991), part III: 'L'Europe entre états et empire'.

Guenée, Bernard. *States and Rulers in Later Medieval Europe*, trans. J. Vale (Oxford: Basil Blackwell, 1985; French edn 1971). Convenient yet original summaries of disputed topics; full bibliography.

Holmes, G. *Europe: Hierarchy and Revolt. 1320–1450* (Brighton: Harvester, 1975).

Mundy, John H. *Europe in the High Middle Ages, 1150–1309* (London: Longman, 1973).

Rapp, Francis. *L'Église et la vie réligieuse en occident à la fin du Moyen Age*, Nouvelle Clio, 25 (Paris: Presses Universitaires de France, 1971).

Southern, R. W. *Western Society and the Church in the Middle Ages* (Harmondsworth: Penguin, 1970).

Aristotle (see pp. 9–12, 20–1, 45–6, 78)

Latin translations of The Politics
Aristotelis politicorum libri octo, cum vetusta translatione Guilelmi de Moerbeka, ed. F. Susemihl (Leipzig: Teubner, 1872).

Aristotelis politicorum libri octo, trans. Leonardus Aretinus (Venice, 1568).

Studies
Dunbabin, Jean, 'The Reception and Interpretation of Aristotle's *Politics*', in *Cambridge History of Later Medieval Philosophy*, ed. N. Kretzmann and others (Cambridge: Cambridge University Press, 1982), pp. 723–37.

Nederman, Cary. 'Nature, Sin and the Origins of Society: The Ciceronian Tradition in Medieval Political Thought', *Journal of the History of Ideas* 49 (1988), pp. 3–26. Argues for continuity of ideas on the natural origin of political society due to Ciceronian influence; there was no 'Aristotelian revolution' in political thought.

Renna, Thomas. 'Aristotle and the French Monachy', *Viator* 9 (1978), pp. 309–24. Argues that people used Aristotle eclectically to justify many different views. See also the sterling article by Alan Gewirth,

'Philosophy and Political Thought in the Fourteenth Century', in F. Utley (ed.), *The Forward Movement of the Fourteenth Century* (Columbus, Ohio: Ohio State University Press, 1961), pp. 125–64.

Church and state (see chapter 2)

Bertrams, W. *Der neuzeitliche Staatsgedanke und die Konkordate des ausgehenden Mittelalters*, Analecta Gregoriana 30 (Rome, 1950). On new developments in the early and mid fifteenth century.

Martin, Victor. *Les Origins du Gallicanisme*, 2 vols. (Paris: Bloud and Gay, 1939).

Rivière, J. *Le Problème de l'église et de l'état au temps de Philippe le Bel* (Louvain–Paris: Spicilegium Sacrum Lovaniense, 1926).

Scholz, R. *Die Publizistik zur Zeit Philipps des schönen und Bonifaz VIII* (Stuttgart: F. Enke, 1903).

Spinka, M. *John Hus' Concept of the Church* (Princeton, N.J.: Princeton University Press, 1966).

Tierney, Brian. *Origins of Papal Infallibility: A Study on the Concepts of Infallibility, Sovereignty and Tradition in the Middle Ages* (Leiden: E. J. Brill, 1972).

Ullmann, Walter. *Medieval Papalism: The Political Theories of the Medieval Canonists* (London: Methuen, 1949).

Watt, John A. *The Theory of Papal Monarchy in the Thirteenth Century: The Contribution of the Canonists* (London: Burns and Oates, 1965).

Werminghoff, A. *Nationalkirchlirche Bestrebungen im deutschen Mittelalter* (Stuttgart: F. Enke, 1910).

Wilks, Michael. *The Problem of Sovereignty in the Later Middle Ages: The Papal Monarchy with Augustinus Triumphus and the Publicists* (Cambridge: Cambridge University Press, 1963). A difficult but profound book.

City–states and civic government (see chapter 4)

Blickle, Peter. *Deutsche Untertanen: ein Widerspruch* (Munich: C. H. Beck, 1981). Emphasises the role and importance of communal self-government in town and village.

Planitz, H. *Die deutsche Stadt im Mittelalter* (Graz–Cologne: Böhlau, 1954).

Waley, Daniel. *The Italian City-Republics* (London: Weidenfeld and Nicolson, 1969).

Florence (see chapter 4)

Baron, Hans. *The Crisis of the Early Italian Renaissance: Civic Humanism and Republican Liberty in an Age of Classicism and Tyranny*, rev. edn (Princeton, N.J.: Princeton University Press, 1966). Statement of 'civic humanism'.

M. B. Becker, *Florence in Transition*, vol. I: *The Decline of the Medieval Commune* (Baltimore, Md.: Johns Hopkins University Press, 1967).

Brucker, Gene. *The Civic World of Early Renaissance Florence* (Princeton, N.J.: Princeton University Press, 1977).

Holmes, G. 'The Emergence of an Urban Ideology at Florence, *c.* 1250–1400', *Transactions of the Royal Historical Society*, 5th series, 23 (1973), pp. 111–34.

Najemy, John. *Corporatism and Consensus in Florentine Electoral Politics, 1280–1400* (Chapel Hill, N.C.: University of North Carolina Press, 1982).

Rubinstein, Nikolai. 'Florentine Constitutionalism and Medici Ascendancy', in N. Rubinstein (ed.), *Florentine Studies* (London: Faber and Faber, 1968), pp. 442–62.

International relations and state sovereignty (see chapter 3)

Abu-Lughod, Janet L. *Before European Hegemony: The World System A.D. 1250–1350* (Oxford: Oxford University Press, 1989).

Baethgen, Friedrich. 'Zur Geschichte der Weltherrschaftsidee im späteren Mittelalter', *Festschrift P. E. Schramm*, vol. I (Wiesbaden, 1964), pp. 189–203.

Hay, Denys. *Europe: The Emergence of an Idea* (Edinburgh: Edinburgh University Press, 1957).

Kohn, Hans. *The Idea of Nationalism: A Study in its Origins and Background* (New York: Collier, 1944), chs 3–4.

Southern, R. W. *Western Views of Islam in the Middle Ages* (Cambridge, Mass.: Harvard University Press, 1962).

The jurists (see pp. 8–9)

Calasso, F. *Medio Evo de Diritto*, vol. I: *Le Fonti* (Milan: Giuffré, 1954).

Canning, Joseph. *The Political Thought of Baldus de Ubaldis* (Cambridge: Cambridge University Press, 1987).

Gierke, Otto von. *Das deutsche Genossenschaftsrecht*, vol. III, (Berlin 1881, repr. Graz: Akademische Druck- u. Verlagsanstalt, 1954), chs 8–10. Still useful.

Paradisi, Bruno. 'Il Pensiero Politico dei Giuristi Medievali', in Luigi Firpo (ed.), *Storia*, vol. II, pp. 211–366.

Kingship, law and representation (see chapters 5 and 6)

Barrow, G. W. S. *Feudal Britain: The Completion of the Medieval Kingdoms 1066–1314* (London: Edward Arnold, 1956), pp. 269ff.

Berges, W. *Die Fürstenspiegel des hohen und späten Mittelalters* (Leipzig: Hiersemann, 1938).

Black, Antony. *Monarchy and Community: Political Ideas in the Later Conciliar Controversy* (Cambridge: Cambridge University Press, 1970).

Council and Commune: The Conciliar Movement and the Fifteenth-Century Heritage (London: Burns and Oates and Shepherdston, MD.: Patmos Press, 1979).

Bloch, Marc. *The Royal Touch: Sacred Monarchy and Scrofula in England and France*, trans. J. E. Anderson (London: Routledge and Kegan Paul, 1973; French edn., 1924).

Carsten, F. L. *Princes and Parliaments in Germany from the Fifteenth to the Eighteenth Century* (Oxford: Oxford University Press, 1959).

Chrimes, S. B. *English Constitutional Ideas in the Fifteenth Century* (Cambridge: Cambridge University Press, 1936).

Eckermann, Karla. *Studien zur Geschichte des monarchischen Gedankens im 15. Jahrhundert* (Berlin: Rothschild, 1933).

Kern, Fritz. *Kingship and Law in the Middle Ages*, trans. S. B. Chrimes (Oxford: Basil Blackwell, 1968).

McIlwain, C. H. *Constitutionalism, Ancient and Modern*, rev. edn (Ithaca, N.Y.: Cornell University Press, 1947), ch. 4.

Marongiu, Antonio. *Medieval Parliaments: A Comparative Study*, trans. S. J. Woolf (London: Eyre and Spottiswoode, 1968; Italian edn 1949).

Oakley, F. 'On the Road from Constance to 1688', *Journal of British Studies* 1 (1962), pp. 1–32.

Pitkin, Hannah. *The Concept of Representation* (Berkeley, Calif.: University of California Press, 1967).

Post, Gaines. *Studies in Medieval Legal Thought: Public Law and the State, 1100–1322* (Princeton, N.J.: Princeton University Press, 1964).

Powicke, F. M. *The Thirteenth Century* (Oxford History of England), 2nd edn (Oxford: Oxford University Press, 1962).

Rueger, Z. 'Gerson, the Conciliar Movement and the Right of Resistance', *Journal of the History of Ideas* 25 (1964), pp. 467–80.

Schramm, Percy. *Der König von Frankreich: das Wesen der Monarchie von 9. zum 16. Jahrhundert. Ein Kapitel aus der Geschichte des abendländischen Staates*, 2 vols. (Weimar: H. Böhlaus, 1960).

Tierney, Brian. *Foundations of the Conciliar Theory: The Contribution of the Medieval Canonists from Gratian to the Great Schism* (Cambridge: Cambridge University Press, 1955).

Religion, Law and the Growth of Constitutional Thought (1150–1650) (Cambridge: Cambridge University Press, 1982).

Walther, H. G. *Imperiales Königtum, Konziliarismus und Volkssouveranität. Studien zu den Grenzen des mittelalterlichen Souveranitätsgedanken* (Munich: Wilhelm Fink, 1976).

Liberty and the individual (see pp. 28–33)

Grundmann, H. 'Freiheit als religiöses, politisches und persönliches Postulat im Mittelalter', *Historische Zeitschrift* 183 (1957), pp. 23–53.

Harding, A. 'Political Liberty in the Middle Ages', *Speculum* 55 (1980), pp. 423–43.

Hilton, Rodney. *Bond Men Made Free: Medieval Peasant Movements and the English Rising of 1381* (London: Temple Smith, 1973).

Kölmel, W. 'Freiheit – Gleichheit – Unfreiheit in der sozialen Theorie des späten Mittelalters', in A. Zimmermann, (ed.), *Miscellanea Medievalia* 12, part ii (Berlin: Walter de Gruyter, 1980), pp. 390–407.

Macfarlane, Alan. *The Origins of English Individualism: The Family, Property and Social Transition* (Oxford: Basil Blackwell, 1978). Provocative and contentious.

Morris, Colin. *The Discovery of the Individual 1050–1200* (London: SPCK, 1972).

Natural law (see pp. 34–40)

d'Entrèves, A. Passerin. *Natural Law: An Introduction to Legal Philosophy* (London: Hutchinson, 1951), ch. 2.

Sigmund, Paul. *Natural Law in Political Thought* (Cambridge, Mass.: Winthrop Press, 1971; repr. Washington, D.C.: University Press of America, 1981).

Tierney, Brian. 'Origins of Natural Rights Language: Texts and Contexts, 1150–1250', *History of Political Thought*, 10 (1989), pp. 615–46.

Villey, Michel. *Le Droit et les droits de l'homme* (Paris, 1983).

The political community (see chapter 1)

Barrow, G. W. S. *Robert Bruce and the Community of the Realm of Scotland* (Edinburgh: Edinburgh University Press, 1976).

Black, Antony. *Guilds and Civil Society in European Political Thought from the Twelfth Century to the Present* (London: Methuen and Ithaca, N.Y.: Cornell University Press, 1984), chs 2–9.

Cohn, Norman. *The Pursuit of the Millenium: Revolutionary Millenarians and Mystical Anarchists of the Middle Ages*, 3rd edn (London: Paladin, 1970).

Duby, Georges. *The Three Orders: Feudal Society Imagined*, trans. A. Goldhammer (Chicago: University of Chicago Press, 1980; French edn, 1970).

Gillet, P. *La Personnalité juridique en droit ecclésiastique, spécialement chez les Décrétistes et les Décrétalistes et dans le Code de Droit Canonique* (Mechlin: W. Godennes, 1927).

Kantorowicz, E. H. *The King's Two Bodies: A Study in Medieval Political Theology* (Princeton, N.J.: Princeton University Press, 1957).

Lewis, Ewart. 'Organic Tendencies in Medieval Political Thought', *American Political Science Review* 32 (1938), pp. 849–76.

Michaud-Quantin, Pierre. Universitas: *Expressions du mouvement communautaire dans le moyen-âge latin* (Paris: J. Vrin, 1970). Perhaps the best book in the field.

Reynolds, Susan. *Kingdoms and Communities in Western Europe, 900–1300* (Oxford: Oxford University Press, 1984).

Struve, Tilman. *Die Entwicklung der organologische Staatsauffassung im Mittelalter* (Stuttgart: Hiersemann, 1978).

The Renaissance (see pp. 10, 117–35)

Bolgar, R. R. *The Classical Heritage and Its Beneficiaries* (Cambridge: Cambridge University Press, 1958).

Curcio, C. *La Politica Italiana del '400: Contributo alla Storia delle Origine de Pensiero Borghese* (Florence: Novissima Editrice, 1932).

Martines, Lauro. *Power and Imagination: City-States in Renaissance Italy* (New York: A. Knopf, 1979 and London: Allen Lane, 1980). A richly documented account of the interaction between culture and socio-political values among different classes from the early communes onwards.

Skinner, Quentin. *The Foundations of Modern Political Thought*, vol. 1: *The Renaissance* (Cambridge: Cambridge University Press, 1978), chs. 1–4. A reinterpretation of political thought in Italy to take full account of the historical context and political 'languages'; emphasises civic independence, republican government and liberty.

The state (see chapter 7)

Canning, Joseph P. 'Ideas of the State in Thirteenth and Fourteenth-Century Commentators on the Roman Law', *Transactions of the Royal Historical Society*, 5th series, 33 (1983), pp. 1–27.

Cheyette, F. L. 'The Invention of the State', in B. Lackner and R. Philp (eds.), *Essays on Medieval Civilisation* (Austin: University of Texas Press, 1978), pp. 143–78.

Coulet, N. and Genet, J. P. (eds.), *L'État moderne: le droit, l'espace et les formes de l'état* (Paris: C.N.R.S., 1991).

Kantorowicz, E. H. *The King's Two Bodies*, pp. 336ff.

Mäger, Wolfgang. *Zur Entstehung des modernen Staatsbegriff* (Mainz: Verlag der Akademie der Wissenschaften, 1968).

Maravall, J. A. 'The Origins of the Modern State', *Cahiers d'Histoire Mondiale* 6 (1951), pp. 789–808.

Mochi Onory, S. *Fonti Canonistiche dell' Idea Moderna dello Stato: Imperium Spirituale, Iurisdictio Divisa, Sovranità* (Milan: Societa Editrice 'Vita e Pensiero': 1951).

Näf, Werner. 'Frühformen des "modernen Staates" im Spätmittelalter', *Historische Zeitschrift* 171 (1951), pp. 225–43; repr. in H. H. Hofmann (ed.), *Die entstehung des modernen souveränen Staates* (Cologne: Kiepenheuer and Witsch, 1967).

Strayer, J. R. *On the Medieval Origins of the Modern State* (Princeton, N.J.: Princeton University Press, 1970). Superficial.

Ullmann, Walter. 'The Development of the Medieval Idea of Sovereignty', *The English Historical Review* 64 (1949), pp. 1–33.

'Juristic Obstacles to the Emergence of the Concept of the State in the Middle Ages', *Annali di Storia del Diritto* 13 (1969), pp. 43–64.

3 WORKS OF REFERENCE

Chevalier, Ulysse. *Répertoire des Sources Historiques du Moyen Âge*. Bio-bibliographique. 2 vols. (Paris: A. Picard & Fils, 1905–7). Information on obscure persons.

Coing, Helmut (ed.). *Handbuch der Quellen und Literatur der neueren europäischen Privatrechtsgeschichte*, vol. 1: *Mittelalter* (1100–1500) (Munich: C. H. Beck, 1973). Jurists and law.

Corpus iuris canonici (*CIC*), ed. A. Friedberg, 2 vols. (Leipzig: Tauchnitz, 1879–81).

Dictionnaire de Droit Canonique, ed. R. Naz, 7 vols. (Paris: Letouzey et Ané, 1935–65).

Geschichtliche Grundbegriffe. Historisches Lexikon zur Politisch-Sozialen Sprache in Deutschland, ed. Otto Brunner, 10 vols. (Stuttgart: Klett-Cotta, 1972–88). See review by Melvin Richter, 'Conceptual History (*Begriffsgeschichte*) and Political Theory', *Political Theory* 14 (1986), pp. 604–37.

Lexikon für Theologie und Kirche (*LTK*), ed. M. Buchberger, 10 vols (Freiburg: Herder, 1957–65). Useful for most medieval authors and concepts.

Savigny, F. K. von. *Geschichte des römischen Rechts im Mittelalter*, 7 vols (Heidelberg: J. C. B. Mohr, 1834–51). Civil jurists (Savigny was one of the great German romantic thinkers).

INDEX

—————— · ——————

The page numbers of sections giving key details on the major authors and topics are in bold face.